Your Telecommuting Agreement

Most telecommuting experts advise you and your boss to sign a telecommuting agreement that specifies details of your telecommuting arrangement and serves as a legally binding document for both parties. Your telecommuting agreement may include some or all the following:

- ✔ How many days a week (or month) you intend to telecommute and which specific days those will be.

- ✔ Your telecommuting start date and a trial time (say three or six months), after which you and your boss will meet to evaluate your telecommuting experience.

- ✔ Your contact information when working at home or at another off-site location. (For more on picking the right location for a home office, see Chapter 5.)

- ✔ Information on how you'll stay in touch (in other words, having your phone calls roll over from the office phone to your home-office phone, daily phone check-ins with your boss, chat, and so on) as well as any specific meetings or in-office events you'll make sure to attend.

- ✔ If applicable, a description of child-care or dependent-care arrangements you'll make while working at home.

- ✔ If applicable, a brief discussion of situations in which you may be called in to the office, what sorts of emergencies make this appropriate, whether you'll make up missed telecommuting days, and so on.

- ✔ A brief description of your office space (and/or a photo, if required).

- ✔ A list of equipment and furniture (if any) the company will be providing.

- ✔ A list of equipment (if any) you agree to provide yourself.

- ✔ Information about other additions you'll be making (such as a cell phone account, extra phone line or lines and/or high-speed Internet access, added homeowner's insurance) along with information as to who is paying for what.

- ✔ Security information, including how any employer-owned equipment will be kept safe, how confidential work-related information will be handled, and how you'll keep your computer and network safe from attack by hackers and viruses.

- ✔ A general description of your job, and how it is evaluated.

- ✔ A brief description of those tasks (if any) that you plan to save for your at-home days.

- ✔ A brief description of your short-term, middle-term and long-term goals for the job, and how telecommuting will help you meet those objectives.

This may seem like a lot of ground to cover, and it may not be necessary for you to address all these issues. Consider your own telecommuting situation to decide which of these areas (or others) that you need to address and which you can safely skip.

Telecommuting For Dummies®

Cheat Sheet

Avoiding the Refrigerator

One big stumbling block for many telecommuters unaccustomed to working at home during the day is the easy accessibility of anything and everything that you may have to eat around the house. The following tips can help you deal with the dreaded fridge.

Locate your office far from the kitchen: When we lived in Massachusetts, our kitchen was on the basement level of our old house, and my office was on the second floor, so I had two long, narrow flights of stairs to contend with anytime I wanted a snack. The stairs were effective deterrents — although once in a while I'd override it by bringing a package of candy or cookies upstairs with me.

Stock up on healthy snacks: The disadvantage of having your kitchen nearby can be changed into an advantage if you stock it with healthier foods than you can easily get at the office. Fresh fruits and vegetables (which you can cut up in the evening for easy grabbing during the day) whole-grain breads, yogurts, healthy soups in easy-heat containers are a few of the things you can have ready for good-for-you snacking. Pick things that are good for you and that you find appealing. That way, you're likely to reach for the right things if you do find yourself in the kitchen.

Give yourself noneating breaks: The point is to find something that you enjoy — and that you can spend 10 to 20 minutes doing — and then head back to work refreshed.

Compensate with exercise: Try jogging, going to the gym, taking a dance class, or bouncing tennis balls off a convenient wall. Cutting commuting out of your schedule — and being able to flex your work hours a little — may give you the opportunity for more regular exercise than you would have had at the office. Even if nibbling isn't a problem, extra exercise is always a good idea.

Equipment You May Need at Home

Your employer can pay for all, some, or none of the following equipment you may need in your home office:

- Desktop computer, including drives, modem, monitor, and keyboard
- Printer
- Scanner
- Fax machine (It should be noted that multifunction printers that handle printing as well as scanning, faxing, and copying chores are available.)
- Laptop computer
- Copier
- Paper shredder
- Extra telephone for business calls
- Extra phone line for the telephone (along with features like voice mail and caller ID)
- Another extra phone line for the fax machine
- Yet another extra phone line for your Internet connection
- Cable modem, DSL (high-speed Internet connection via phone lines), or ISDN (Integrated Services Digital Network)
- Cell phone
- Pager
- Wireless Internet device
- PDA (Personal digital assistant — a handheld device such as a PalmPilot)
- Office furniture
- Rental of office space outside the home

Hungry Minds™

For Dummies: Bestselling Book Series for Beginners

Telecommuting
FOR
DUMMIES®

by Minda Zetlin

Hungry Minds™

Best-Selling Books • Digital Downloads • e-Books • Answer Networks • e-Newsletters • Branded Web Sites • e-Learning

New York, NY ◆ Cleveland, OH ◆ Indianapolis, IN

Telecommuting For Dummies®

Published by:
Hungry Minds, Inc.
909 Third Avenue
New York, NY 10022
www.hungryminds.com
www.dummies.com

Library of Congress Control Number: 2001089308

ISBN: 0-7645-5371-2

Printed in the United States of America

10 9 8 7 6 5 4 3 2 1

1O/RS/QW/QR/IN

Distributed in the United States by Hungry Minds, Inc.

Distributed by CDG Books Canada Inc. for Canada; by Transworld Publishers Limited in the United Kingdom; by IDG Norge Books for Norway; by IDG Sweden Books for Sweden; by IDG Books Australia Publishing Corporation Pty. Ltd. for Australia and New Zealand; by TransQuest Publishers Pte Ltd. for Singapore, Malaysia, Thailand, Indonesia, and Hong Kong; by Gotop Information Inc. for Taiwan; by ICG Muse, Inc. for Japan; by Intersoft for South Africa; by Eyrolles for France; by International Thomson Publishing for Germany, Austria and Switzerland; by Distribuidora Cuspide for Argentina; by LR International for Brazil; by Galileo Libros for Chile; by Ediciones ZETA S.C.R. Ltda. for Peru; by WS Computer Publishing Corporation, Inc., for the Philippines; by Contemporanea de Ediciones for Venezuela; by Express Computer Distributors for the Caribbean and West Indies; by Micronesia Media Distributor, Inc. for Micronesia; by Chips Computadoras S.A. de C.V. for Mexico; by Editorial Norma de Panama S.A. for Panama; by American Bookshops for Finland.

For general information on Hungry Minds' products and services please contact our Customer Care department; within the U.S. at 800-762-2974, outside the U.S. at 317-572-3993 or fax 317-572-4002.

For sales inquiries and resellers information, including discounts, premium and bulk quantity sales and foreign language translations please contact our Customer Care department at 800-434-3422, fax 317-572-4002 or write to Hungry Minds, Inc., Attn: Customer Care department, 10475 Crosspoint Boulevard, Indianapolis, IN 46256.

For information on licensing foreign or domestic rights, please contact our Sub-Rights Customer Care department at 212-884-5000.

For information on using Hungry Minds' products and services in the classroom or for ordering examination copies, please contact our Educational Sales department at 800-434-2086 or fax 317-572-4005.

Please contact our Public Relations department at 212-884-5163 for press review copies or 212-884-5000 for author interviews and other publicity information or fax 212-884-5400.

For authorization to photocopy items for corporate, personal, or educational use, please contact Copyright Clearance Center, 222 Rosewood Drive, Danvers, MA 01923, or fax 978-750-4470.

Hungry Minds™ is a trademark of Hungry Minds, Inc.

About the Author

Minda Zetlin has more than 15 years' experience as an author, speaker and journalist. She specializes in writing about how technology affects our work and our lives.

She's the author of two books that taught business managers how to cope with the year 2000 computer problem and also helped create the near non-event everyone hoped for: *The Computer Time Bomb* (Amacom, 1997) and *Surviving the Computer Time Bomb*. She has written about career, business, and technology for a wide variety of publications, including *Cosmopolitan*, *Success!* and Office.com, among many others.

Minda is a member of the American Society of Journalists and Authors and the National Writers Union. She lives in Woodstock, NY, with her husband Bill Pfleging (who telecommutes to California), a growing collection of computers, and four cats.

Dedication

To Bill, my favorite telecommuter and partner for life. In many different ways, I couldn't have written this book without you.

Author's Acknowledgments

Thanks to everyone at Hungry Minds who worked hard on this book: Karen Doran, Tim Gallan, Neil Johnson, Holly McGuire, and Mark Butler. Thanks also to my agent, Sheree Bykofsky, who brought us together.

There is a small and tight-knit community of researchers, authors and consultants who have been telecommuting's advocates for years, and sometimes decades. Many of them shared their knowledge generously for this book. June Langhoff, and Jack Nilles were especially helpful. So were several of the telecommuting experts at the firm TManage, and Marilyn Zelinsky Syarto of *Home Office Computing* magazine. Gil Gordon not only contributed information from his wide store of knowledge but also served as this book's technical reviewer, and deserves special thanks.

Most of all, thanks to the members of my telecommuting "Brain Trust" — telecommuters spread all over the country, working in many different professions, who took the time to offer detailed answers to many questions about how they manage their telecommuting work and lives. You meet them within this book, but I would like to name them all here: Sue Boettcher, Denise Boggs, Greg Breining, Miriam Carey, Scott Decker, Christine Doane-Benton, Robert Egert, Donna Gettings, Tom Hoffman and Chris Keating.

Publisher's Acknowledgments

We're proud of this book; please send us your comments through our Online Registration Form located at www.dummies.com.

Some of the people who helped bring this book to market include the following:

Acquisitions, Editorial, and Media Development

Project Editor: Tim Gallan

Acquisitions Editors: Karen Doran, Holly McGuire

Copy Editor: E. Neil Johnson

Acquisitions Coordinator: Lauren Cundiff

Technical Editor: Gil Gordon

Editorial Manager: Pam Mourouzis

Editorial Assistant: Carol Strickland

Cover Photos: Stone / Daniel Bosler

Production

Project Coordinator: Ryan Steffen

Layout and Graphics: Joe Bucki, Joyce Haughey, LeAndra Johnson, Jackie Nicholas, Brian Torwelle, Jeremey Unger, Erin Zeltner

Special Art:

Proofreaders: Andy Hollandbeck, Marianne Santy, TECHBOOKS Production Services

Indexer: TECHBOOKS Production Services

General and Administrative

Hungry Minds, Inc.: John Kilcullen, CEO; Bill Barry, President and COO; John Ball, Executive VP, Operations & Administration; John Harris, CFO

Hungry Minds Consumer Reference Group

Business: Kathleen Nebenhaus, Vice President and Publisher; Kevin Thornton, Acquisitions Manager

Cooking/Gardening: Jennifer Feldman, Associate Vice President and Publisher; Anne Ficklen, Executive Editor; Kristi Hart, Managing Editor

Education/Reference: Diane Graves Steele, Vice President and Publisher

Lifestyles: Kathleen Nebenhaus, Vice President and Publisher; Tracy Boggier, Managing Editor

Pets: Dominique De Vito, Associate Vice President and Publisher; Tracy Boggier, Managing Editor

Travel: Michael Spring, Vice President and Publisher; Brice Gosnell, Publishing Director; Suzanne Jannetta, Editorial Director

Hungry Minds Consumer Editorial Services: Kathleen Nebenhaus, Vice President and Publisher; Kristin A. Cocks, Editorial Director; Cindy Kitchel, Editorial Director

Hungry Minds Consumer Production: Debbie Stailey, Production Director

◆

The publisher would like to give special thanks to Patrick J. McGovern, without whom this book would not have been possible.

◆

Contents at a Glance

Cartoons at a Glance

By Rich Tennant

"The new technology has really helped me get organized. I keep my project reports under the PC, budgets under my laptop and memos under my pager."

page 75

"It's the crew Captain Columbus—they want to know what our flat-world contingency plan is."

page 255

Okay, what else? Flex-time, on-site health club, 4-day work week and use of the company drum—I'll see what I can do.

page 5

"Does our insurance cover a visit from Mike Wallace?"

page 151

"A large part of our success is based on our ability to resolve conflicts before we get to work."

page 279

Cartoon Information:
Fax: 978-546-7747
E-Mail: richtennant@the5thwave.com
World Wide Web: www.the5thwave.com

Table of Contents

Introduction

Many people dream of working at home, away from office politics and personalities, able to wear whatever they like, cook lunch in their own kitchens, and follow the hours that suit their own natural rhythms. Working at home while still having the security of a regular paycheck is the ideal combination for many who crave a better work/life balance — or who just don't like working in an office — but aren't interested in striking out with businesses of their own.

More than 16 million telecommuters enjoy this lifestyle every week of their working lives, telecommuting from home (or a convenient location nearby) while holding down jobs with employers that may be all the way across town — or even across the country.

Telecommuting isn't right for everybody, nor does it work well for every job. But if you love what you do, and long to spend more time at home, if you're sick of spending hours every day battling traffic, and you like the thought of working in a home office that you've decorated, then telecommuting may be for you.

About This Book

Telecommuting is a subject that's been surrounded by misunderstanding and myth. *Telecommuting For Dummies* cuts through the hype with real information about what telecommuting is actually like and how real people find success doing it. Many wise and widely experienced consultant experts are in the field of telecommuting (or *telework*), and you'll be hearing from several of them in these pages.

But at the heart of the book are real stories of working telecommuters, who report on the joys and challenges they face every day. I've used real people and given their real names, in most cases, so that you know you're getting an authentic glimpse into the telecommuting world.

If you're wondering whether telecommuting is really right for you, and how to get started as a telecommuter, this book is for you. If you've already started telecommuting, but are now facing obstacles, or simply wondering what the future holds, the answers are here as well.

How This Book Is Organized

This book is divided into five parts. Each part takes a look at a different stage along the path of your telecommuting career.

Part I: Getting Started

If you're curious about telecommuting, or wonder whether it can be right for you, this is the place to start. It's also the right part if you know for sure that you'd love being a telecommuter but aren't quite certain how to get there.

Chapters 1 and 2 give you an overview of telecommuting and guidelines to help you determine whether working remotely is a good fit for your personality and for your job. Chapters 3 and 4 explain how to get a telecommuting job — either by persuading your current boss to let you work at home some of the time, or by finding a new job where this is possible.

Part II: Creating Your Home Office

Setting up an office in your home means answering many questions. What kind of phone and computer do you need? What other equipment do you have to have? How do you keep your computer screen from giving you eyestrain, and your keyboard from giving you carpal tunnel syndrome? What kind of Internet connection and tools do you need to do your job effectively? And where do you put your office in the first place?

Part II takes you step by step through picking the right spot for your home office, installing the equipment you need, getting tech support when you need it, and figuring out how many phone lines you need and what phone services you need on each line. This part also gives a detailed look at how best to connect to the Internet, and how that connection can help you work away from the office without missing a trick.

Part III: Adjusting to Your New Work Life

If you already have a telecommuting job, then this part is for you. It's full of useful information on what to include in your written telecommuting agreement (and why you need one), how to handle relations with your co-workers and boss — and how to handle telecommuting if you are the boss.

This part also helps you get a handle on how telecommuting may affect your home life — and how to keep your home life from interfering with your job during at-home work hours. It takes a look at the special challenges you may face if you're hundreds or thousands of miles away from your employer, and how to make a long-distance telecommuting arrangement a success.

Part IV: The Long-Term View

If you've been telecommuting for a while, and you're wondering what the next few years will be like, then this part is for you. First, I take a look at whether and how telecommuting is likely to impact your career, and how to make sure it stays on track even when you're out of the office. Then I take a look at telecommuting's future overall. I begin with an overview and some predictions for telecommuting's growth. Then I take a look at futuristic telecommuting *on the ground,* checking out a telecommuter whose virtual company has no central office as we know it, and an *extreme telecommuter* who has managed to do his job and travel the world at the same time.

Part V: The Part of Tens

How do you stay enthusiastic and motivated about your job when you're away from the office and the moral support that co-workers provide? Are there devices that can make your telecommuting work life easier? You can find answers to these questions and more in a quick-to-read and easy-to-digest format. This part also offers a list of ten Web sites where you can learn even more about telecommuting — and find that telecommuting job you're dreaming about.

Icons Used In This Book

I use icons throughout this book to help you easily find paragraphs of particular significance. Here's how they work.

I believe the true stories of real telecommuting experiences are the most interesting parts of this book. Wherever possible, I let telecommuters themselves tell their own stories of success, failure, and lessons learned. This icon alerts you when a true story is coming up.

Certain basic principles are true for all telecommuters in all jobs. This icon lets you know that the information here will stand you in good stead throughout your telecommuting career.

Telecommuting has its perils, and you need to know what they are so you know how to avoid them. Ignore paragraphs marked by this icon at your own risk.

This icon identifies practical suggestions, some of them shortcuts, that you can use to make your telecommuting life easier or more successful.

This icon identifies a paragraph where you will find a URL (World Wide Web address) to a Web site where you can learn more on the topic at hand.

Where to Go from Here

Read this book in any order that suits your fancy. You can start with Chapter 1 and go straight through, or start with Chapter 16 (to get a look at the future) and then work your way back. If you're already sure you'd love telecommuting and just want to find out how to get there, Chapter 3, on selling the idea to your boss, and Chapter 4, on finding a telecommuting job, may be good starting points. Or the chapters on creating your home office or setting up your at-home work relationships may be the most interesting for you.

I do have one favor to ask. If you're setting up a home office, and especially if you'll be spending lots of time there, please don't skip Chapter 6, which gives information on creating a safe and healthy work space. Many at-home workers I know, including myself, have had near brushes with serious physical problems from too many hours spent working away in places that weren't set up with our health in mind. Don't let that happen to you.

Other than that, have fun, and feel free to explore. If this will be your first time working on your own, you're likely to find it an immensely liberating — and satisfying — experience. Most telecommuters I know are passionate about telecommuting. Use this book as a tool, and you will be, too.

Part I
Getting Started

In this part . . .

Telecommuting (or telework) is one of the fastest growing trends in workplaces today. It's a win-win proposition, good for both employer and employee.

Chapters 1 and 2 provide an overview of telecommuting
and the advantages it offers. They can help you determine
whether this way of working is right for you. If you decide
telecommuting is something you want to try, Chapters 3
and 4 give guidance on selling the idea to your boss — or
finding a new job where telecommuting is an option.

Chapter 1

Why Telecommute?

*H*ave you ever dreamed of going to work in your pajamas? Gazing at the birdfeeder outside your window rather than the wall of a cubicle? Skipping the morning and evening commutes and using that extra hour to get more work done — or play with your child? At the same time, the dream continues, you'd have a steady job and a regular salary, opportunities for career advancement, co-worker buddies, vacation time, health coverage, and all the other good things that go with working for someone else.

It doesn't have to be a dream. What I've just described is a typical workday for the 16 million Americans who telecommute every week. As telecommuters, they get the job done without having to show up at the office.

Telecommuting definitely is not a free ride. It doesn't mean that you get to collect your salary even if you've spent the day doing your laundry and baking a pie. It certainly isn't a license to hold down two full-time jobs at once. People who do give telecommuting a bad name. They always get caught, too.

It isn't a refuge for the lazy. If you decide to telecommute, you'll actually find yourself working more — not less — than you did when you were at the office. But, on the other hand, it is a way to stop feeling stressed all the time, see more of your family, bring your work and home lives into better balance, and save a bundle on dry cleaning.

If all this sounds like something you want, then telecommuting may be right for you.

What Is Telecommuting?

Telecommuting (also called telework) is an arrangement by which you work remotely from your employer, usually in your own home office, and stay connected to the workplace by phone, fax, and/or the Internet. Whether your job is full-time or part-time, whether your employer is around the corner or halfway around the world, and whether you work at the office three times a week or hardly ever, being a telecommuter presents its own particular set of rewards and challenges.

Only a few years ago, telecommuting was considered slightly . . . odd. So were telecommuters themselves. What kind of person wants to stay away from his or her own office? And what kind of company allows such a thing?

Those attitudes are gradually fading as telecommuting becomes more commonplace, and the number of people doing it grows at an explosive rate. The number of telecommuters in the United States quadrupled during the last decade, from about 4 million in 1990 to about 16 million today, according Cyber Dialogue, an Internet survey company. In other words, about 14 percent of American employees — or one in every seven — telecommutes at least some of the time. Chances are, if you're not a telecommuter, you nevertheless already know someone who is.

Why More and More Americans Are Telecommuting

As I write this, my husband Bill sits at his desk at the company where he works. That company in Emeryville, California, in the heart of Silicon Valley, is thousands of miles from where I'm working. Although it's his office, his desk, and his department to manage, he's only physically there one week out of every month. The rest of the time, he works out of an office that he rents near our rural home in Woodstock, New York. He stays in touch with his team, his boss, and his co-workers by e-mail, online chat, and by phone.

We loved our house and the back-woods-yet-artsy community of Woodstock, but two years ago, we regretfully packed up and moved to Massachusetts. Bill was starting a career in the new field of Internet community, and he'd been offered his dream job at a company there. A year ago, when he was offered what sounded like an even more appealing job at the California company, we hesitated. California was so far from our family and friends, so far from everyone we knew, and finding housing *out there* is notoriously difficult. When his prospective boss suggested that he take the job as a telecommuter, Bill eagerly accepted. Now free to live where we chose, we began making plans for our return to Woodstock.

Two years ago, our friends Robert and Andrea Egert relocated from New York City to the Berkshire Mountains in Western Massachusetts and decided to start a family. Robert changed jobs to make the move. When he decided to leave his new job, his former employer was eager to hire him back — and while he liked the idea of returning to his old company, he and his wife were certain they didn't want to live in the city anymore. Telecommuting turned out to be the answer. Robert now works at home in the Southern Berkshires and goes to his New York office once a week or so for meetings and other functions. He's firmly on the fast track at his management consulting firm. Best of all, working at home, he gets to see a lot of his new son.

The chance to live where they choose has drawn many people to telecommuting. But almost as many reasons exist to love telecommuting as there are telecommuters. A common complaint in the modern world is that people feel rushed, overwhelmed, and overloaded with things to do and places to go. And many American adults say they feel that way every day of their lives. Removing the commute to work and all the frustrations and inconveniences that go into modern office life gives telecommuters the chance to feel in control of their lives. That may be the best perk of all.

Ultimately, the biggest reason more and more Americans are telecommuting is simply that more and more of them can. While telecommuting comes with many challenges — and it definitely isn't right for everyone — I've heard telecommuters say again and again how much they love working from home. And, they add, now that they've tried it, they hate the thought of ever going back to work in an office again.

Why More and More Employers Encourage Telecommuting

Why would employers encourage members of their staffs to stay home instead of coming in to work? You may think they offer telecommuting only out of the goodness of their hearts, but you're wrong. Having employees telecommute is at least as good for the employer as it is for the telecommuting worker. Find that hard to believe? Read on.

Telecommuters save their employers overhead expenses

Who pays for the rent and utilities at your office? Your employer does. Who pays for the rent (or mortgage) and utilities where you live? You do. So having employees use home offices to save employers money at their facilities is a no-brainer. In fact, the Clark County Credit Union in Las Vegas reports that it began allowing employees to telecommute two years ago — because the company's only other choice was building a new office facility at a cost of $4 million.

Advancing technology will only enhance these cost savings. High-bandwidth access is becoming more available and affordable in many places. Internet telephony (or voice over IP) that enables voice conversations over the Web already is cutting the costs of phone calls between headquarters offices and telecommuting workers. And, as employers perfect their Intranets (networks for employee use only), providing access to everything remote employees need is getting easier and more cost-effective.

Telecommuters get more work done

Contrary to that popular image of telecommuters lounging around and watching daytime television, all the telecommuters I've spoken with report that they work harder and get more done in their home offices than they do at a traditional office. Why? For one thing, they don't spend time commuting, which can free up two hours or more a day in urban areas where traffic is heavy. For another, they work without the ongoing interruptions common to an office environment. And, without question, some telecommuters think that because they're out of sight of their employers, they must provide even greater proof of their value, so they make sure to get a lot accomplished. Whatever the reason, statistics confirm that telecommuters are more productive than their office-bound counterparts. (See more about these statistics in Chapter 3.)

Telecommuters ask for less time off

A blizzard or a mild bout with the flu may be enough to prevent you from getting to your company's office, but it may not prevent you from sitting down at your desk and getting at least some work done. Likewise, a trip to the doctor or dentist generally takes up only a part of your day and may be enough to keep you away from the office, but you'd still have enough time to work a partial day at home. For reasons like these, employers report lower absenteeism among telecommuters than among on-site employees.

Miriam Carey: Staying out of *Cubicleville*

After 18 months as a freelance writer, Miriam Carey was tired of the slow payments and other frustrations that can go with being self-employed. She knew she wanted a full-time editorial job. Although happy living in Cleveland, Ohio, "I started looking for work in New York City and elsewhere," she says. "I was terrified I'd be offered a great job in Birmingham, Alabama. I didn't want to move there."

If the thought of moving didn't thrill her, she found the offices she visited even less appealing. "Everywhere I went, I encountered *Cubicleville,*" she says. "That's one of the main reasons I hated working in offices. It is impossible to sit and think while penned up like a farm animal in a cubicle."

Eventually, she called the publisher of *Ohio* magazine, which is located in Columbus, a three-hour drive away. She knew the magazine had an opening for a travel editor, a subject she had lots of experience covering. "I would've considered commuting during the week and maintaining a residence in Cleveland," she says. "I volunteered to do that, but not convincingly. The publisher suggested that I telecommute."

One reason this job is right for her is that her new employer has a positive attitude toward her working from home. "I think it was important to them to have a statewide presence, anyway, so we were both thinking *telecommute,* which is extremely important. If the employer has to be talked into it, then it's the first thing they'll try to take away from you if something goes wrong."

At this writing, Carey has been telecommuting for only a few weeks, but already has some lessons to share. "Negotiating is key," she says. Even though she and the magazine agreed up front that she would work from home, "there are a lot of other factors to consider. One big one for me was the need for a laptop, because as a travel editor, I'd be traveling." The magazine

agreed to the request, and Carey should be receiving her laptop shortly. "There is a whole list of things to consider when you're working out of your home — and you need to make the employer aware of what they are. How will your Internet and e-mail be hosted? Who will pay? Will you get an additional phone line paid for? What about mileage? All these things need to be negotiated first, along with a list of more subtle things: How will the rest of the staff feel about my status as an at-home worker? How will I develop and maintain relationships with the staff from home — and from far away? How often will I visit the office?" (For a guide to working out these issues with your employer, see Chapter 9.)

And, she says, the employer is getting a good deal. "One thing that has struck me about working at home is how much extra time the employer gets out of me. I know that the staff comes in around 9 a.m. They have coffee and go through the papers for story ideas. They work a while — with every kind of office interruption that is natural in that environment — and then take a one-hour lunch, and so forth. At home, I'm already working at 9 a.m. I generally take a 20-minute lunch, and then work through the afternoon, really *focused* on my work. I can ignore the phone, and hardly anyone interrupts me — although a visit from the FedEx delivery person is sometimes the most welcome event of the day. And I get the work done."

Even though she's working much harder, Carey enjoys her job more than she would if she had to work in an office. "Working at home makes complete sense to me and to my employer. We each get so much more out of the bargain. I don't know if I'll ever be able to — or want to — work in an office environment again. I know I'll never accept a position that requires me to sit in a burlap-bound cubicle."

Telecommuters stick with their jobs

Because telecommuting is a satisfying arrangement for many, telecommuters routinely report a higher level of job satisfaction and job loyalty than their on-site colleagues do. In a 1998 Wirthlin Worldwide Survey, 78 percent of telecommuters reported that they were "very committed" to their companies, compared with 53 percent of traditional workers. And most telecommuters are likely to stick with their jobs a lot longer, if only because it may be hard to find another telecommuting slot. Most American companies don't offer telecommuting as an option for employees. Meanwhile, many who've tried telecommuting say they never want to work at traditional office jobs again.

Telecommuters have higher morale

Generally telecommuters are more satisfied with their jobs than traditional employees. In fact, many workers who make the switch from traditional work to telecommuting report increased job satisfaction after the change. And higher morale makes most people more effective at doing their jobs, and they're also more likely to recommend their place of business to other job seekers. With companies competing for limited numbers of qualified workers in these days of low unemployment, anything that serves as a recruiting tool is indeed a big benefit.

Telecommuters transcend geographical boundaries

A company that allows telecommuting is not limited by geography, which means it can literally recruit employees anywhere and everywhere. Consider the company where Bill works: If management there had insisted on hiring someone who would show up at the office every day, they would've faced a difficult choice. They could have tried hiring someone local, which may have been difficult because Internet community still is a narrow specialty. Or they could've offered to pay for our relocation to California. That would've been an expensive proposition. And we may not have agreed to it, in any case.

Why Don't More Employers Allow Telecommuting?

With all these advantages going for telecommuting, why the number of companies that allow or encourage employees to work from home is steadily growing is no mystery. In fact, the only mystery about it is why that number is in the minority, while the majority of employers still insist that staff members show up at an office every day.

The answer lies in a combination of habit and fear. Because telecommuting still is quite new, more corporate managers aren't in the habit of setting up remote work arrangements, but they are in the habit of seeing members of their staffs at the office and talking with them face to face every day. They're understandably hesitant to change a management formula that has worked well for untold years. They also may be bewildered and frightened at the prospects of trying to supervise someone from many miles away — especially when that supervision, in most cases, requires the manager to be comfortable using the Internet.

But times are changing. Old-style managers are being forced to adapt to new work models including telecommuting. Many of America's largest corporations now encourage employees to telecommute — and managers at smaller companies tend to look to these giants and follow their examples.

A low unemployment rate and tight labor market also are a big help. By encouraging telecommuting, companies gain access to a much wider crop of qualified people to hire from, which translates into a competitive advantage for them.

In the end, logic prevails, and most employers must recognize the obvious benefits of allowing their staff members to telecommute. That process is already starting. As the number of employers offering telecommuting grows nearly as quickly as the number of telecommuters, within three or four years, I believe the majority of American companies will offer a telecommuting option, and staying home to work will be almost as commonplace as going off to work. At that point, opportunities for telecommuters will be without limits.

More Good News about Telecommuting

Just in case you're still not convinced that telecommuting can have huge benefits for you and your company, the following sections present more factors to consider.

Telecommuting can save you money

Telecommuting is a classic win-win scenario. At the same time telecommuting produces savings for your employer on overhead and facilities costs, telecommuting saves you on many expenses associated with working in an office.

How much can telecommuting save you? Consider a typical workday. You drive each way to work (spending, let's say, $2 in gas), perhaps paying another $1 for a toll. (Or, you spend about $3 for a bus or train ticket to and from your office.) If you didn't have time for breakfast at home, you probably stopped for a cup of coffee and snack, spending at least another $2. At lunchtime (since you neglected to pack a lunch) you spend $5 for a sandwich or salad and drink at the local deli. On the way home, you stop to pick up the week's dry cleaning (after all, you need to look your best at the office) for another $10. If you're a woman, you may also stop at the drugstore for makeup (again, you want to look your best) and perhaps a pair of pantyhose to replace the ones that got a run during the workday. Even if you didn't buy a takeout dinner on your way home, or pay a babysitter when you got there, you've already spent about $12 today just to be at the office. Working at home thus would amount to a *raise* of $60 a week, or $3,000 a year.

This is, admittedly, a most unscientific guesstimate. But if you're currently working outside your home, I invite you to track just one week's worth of your own *in-office* expenses and add them up on Saturday. The total may surprise you.

Telecommuting gets you out of meetings

Ask any corporate (or government) employee about the least fun aspect of his or her job, and a good chance exists that the word *meeting* is featured in the answer. One telecommuter recently complained to me that he appeared for his day at the office, and immediately was invited to a meeting, the purpose of which was to plan the following week's meeting. In fact, some telecommuters believe that fewer meetings is the real secret behind their increased productivity. They report getting less done when they're at the office than when they're home because of all the time they spend constantly sitting in meetings.

Of course, not all workplace meetings are redundant. Some are essential, and telecommuting certainly won't excuse you from them all. But it does make it easier to avoid many of the nonvital meetings that so many corporate employees say are the biggest time-wasters of their workweeks. Even if you live in the same community in which your employer is located, summoning you to drive in from across town encourages management to make sure your time is well spent once you get there. If you live farther away, chances are that meetings will be arranged around your scheduled visits. Either way, there's an impetus to make sure the meetings that you attend are well planned and efficiently conducted.

Telecommuting keeps you away from office politics

During my own few years of working in an office, I always was hopelessly uninformed about what was going on behind the scenes. I never knew who was sleeping with whom, who was in trouble and about to be fired, or who was about to head a new department. My first boss, wise in the ways of the corporate jungle, assured me that I was better off not knowing. At the time, I disagreed. After all, nobody likes feeling out of the loop. With the benefit of hindsight, however, I think he was right.

Telecommuters report that not being in the office keeps them away from office gossip, and can save them the unpleasant maneuverings of office politics. If you're the kind of person who finds these interactions an unwelcome distraction from the real work at hand, this may be another reason why telecommuting is right for you.

Telecommuting lets you create your own work environment

Five years ago, after many years of working at home, I took a position in a newspaper newsroom. Day after day, I gazed at the linoleum tiles at my feet or out the window to our bleak gray courtyard. On occasional breaks, I would stand looking out of the ladies' room window at the street below, an only slightly more appealing vista. As winter turned to spring, I thought sadly of my garden starting to bloom while I wasn't there to see it. When the job didn't work out, I was almost pleased.

With few exceptions, American workplaces are sterile and unexciting, with most employees stuck inside walled cubicles. In some offices, they're not even allowed to decorate their workspaces with family photos or other favorite items. Working at home gives you a chance to create a work environment that suits your personality and nurtures your spirit. (In my case, a good supply of houseplants and various cats wandering by are part of the scene. For more information on creating an office that fits your own personality, see Chapter 5.)

Telecommuting is good for the planet

As if all the above weren't good enough reasons for telecommuting, believe it or not, you also can consider it the socially responsible thing to do.

Telecommuting is being touted as a solution to two of the bigger problems facing American urban areas: unmanageable traffic and worsening air pollution. Employees who work at home — and thus out of their cars — are helping to cut down on both.

Ironically, if you're trying to sell your boss on the idea of telecommuting, controlling smog may be one of your best allies. Companies in some poor-air-quality areas actually allow employees to work from home on days when the air quality is deemed unacceptable. This is partly in response to campaigns that civic groups are mounting around the country to encourage local employers to let employees telecommute.

Chapter 2

Is Telecommuting Right for You?

In This Chapter

▶ Deciding if telecommuting is right for your personality

▶ Determining whether your job can be done off-site

▶ Assessing your organization's attitude toward telecommuting

▶ Understanding how telecommuting fits your career goals

▶ Creating a career plan

Telecommuting is one of the better new ideas in modern employment. Employees get a more relaxed but productive workday, zero time commuting, and the chance to work in their pajamas. Employers get more motivated, loyal employees, who tend to get more work done than when they're in the office. Given all these advantages, everyone short of neurosurgeons ought to be making plans to telecommute, right?

Well, not exactly. Telecommuting offers impressive benefits, but it has drawbacks too, and it's decidedly not right for every employee, every job, or every workplace. This chapter explores some of the pros and cons of telecommuting, who it works best for, and why it can sometimes be a bad idea.

If you currently work full time in an office, spending all or part of your workweek at home will represent a major transition for you, your employer, and possibly your family. Before starting down this road, it makes sense to give some serious thought, and find unflinching answers, to the questions raised in this chapter.

Working at Home Takes the Right Personality

Not everyone is cut out to telecommute. You, for instance, may not necessarily have the right personality to be a telecommuter. Here are some personality traits that can make working from home easier or harder.

Are you driven and self-motivated?

If you tend to find yourself hanging around the office, determined to finish off your current project before heading out the door, chances are you have the right personality for telecommuting. With no one looking over their shoulders to see whether they're actually working or playing computer video games, successful telecommuters need to be self-starters.

When I asked telecommuters what aspects of their own personalities helped them work effectively from home, their surprisingly similar answers all contained words like "drive" and "determination." "I convinced myself that I had to prove to my bosses that I could do every job I've had successfully from home to defy perceptions about the types of roles that can (and can't) be handled as a telecommuter." That's how one veteran telecommuter put it. "I drove myself to succeed."

Are you organized?

Don't despair if your answer is "No." I've watched some highly disorganized people work successfully as telecommuters. But the bottom line is the better you are at organizing your time, your work materials, and the tasks you have to accomplish, the easier working from home will be. This is doubly true if working from home means your amount of space is limited or you must share it with another activity (for instance, if you work on the dining table). And it's triply true if you spend each week working some days at home and some days in the office. No one — least of all you — will be happy if your boss asks for information you can't provide because you're working in one site and the materials you need are in another. (See Chapters 5 and 6 for advice on setting up an efficient home office.)

Are you a technophobe?

If you're uncomfortable around information technology, if you desperately miss the days before computers took over the world, or if you think the Internet is a big waste of time, you may have trouble telecommuting. Why? Because with most telecommuting jobs, you'll be completely dependent on information technology to remain connected to your office.

E-mails, faxes and conference calls are the more rudimentary of tools that most telecommuters can't work without. Depending on your job and (especially) the technical sophistication in your workplace, you may need to remotely sign on to your office's *intranet* or *virtual private network* (VPN), which simply means that your computer and your office's computer network are actually connected via the Internet (and may even be sharing files). Down the road, you may need to work with videoconferencing, file sharing, and other technologies we may not even be able to imagine yet.

If thinking about working with this kind of stuff makes you break out in a nervous sweat, either learn to be more comfortable with high-tech equipment, or face the fact that it'll limit your telecommuting potential. (For a full discussion of useful technology for telecommuters, see Chapters 7 and 8.)

How articulate are you?

Some people are highly verbal, easily expressing themselves in any situation. Others must struggle to find the right words. This has nothing to do with intelligence, by the way. I once was friends with a brilliant engineer who became a top engine designer at Ford and envisioned solar-powered cars years before even the current experimental models were built. Yet he had enormous difficulty putting together a coherent sentence, and was always happier building things than talking about them.

If your job consists primarily of, say, writing computer programs or executing new product designs, then you may have little need for verbal communications. But for most people, communicating with peers, clients, and co-workers is an integral part of the workday. Being physically away from the office makes those communications more difficult in many subtle and not-so-subtle ways, and if you can compensate for those difficulties by expressing yourself clearly at all times, you'll be one step ahead of the game. It's especially helpful if you're a great communicator on the phone.

By the same token, if you're the kind of person who struggles while writing memos and always agonizes over finding the right words to put in reports or business letters, be aware that telecommuting will probably increase your need to communicate in writing. E-mails, reports, and possibly text chat will necessarily replace some of the formal and informal conversations you'd normally be having if you were in the office. Of course, being able to communicate well in writing is a prerequisite for advancement in many careers, so if this is a serious problem area for you, you may want to consider a business communication course to help you polish this skill.

Do you form strong relationships with co-workers?

The more time you spend working at home, the more dependent you'll be on co-workers to keep you in the loop about what's going on at work, be advocates for your projects and priorities when you're not around, and generally help you stay connected and effective at your workplace.

But just as telecommuting makes these relationships especially vital to your success, it also makes them that much harder to form and maintain. You're not at work every day to talk, joke, and commiserate with them — nor are they there every day to do the same things with you.

This is where I believe I would likely fail as a telecommuter: I'm great at working by myself, but not so great at forming close bonds with co-workers. Fortunately, I've been happily self-employed for the past 15 years. That may be the better choice for people like me who tend to be loners in their work lives.

Where did you meet most of your friends?

In the '50s and '60s, typical Americans found their social circles among other residents of their neighborhoods or small communities. In more recent years, with longer commutes and burgeoning bedroom communities, the workplace has become the source of most friendships and social activities for many Americans.

Think about the last several times you met someone for dinner or a drink. Was it someone from work or someone you met another way? How many of the people you think of as close friends also are co-workers?

If your social life has been centered around your workplace, you may feel particularly isolated when you begin working from home. If your employer is near enough to you, you can try meeting some of these friends after work, or otherwise staying in touch with them. But chances are at least some of these relationships will naturally fade over time, and you should be prepared for this reality if you decide to telecommute.

Are you comfortable spending large blocks of time alone?

Telecommuters and efficiency experts all agree that one of the biggest advantages of not working at the office is that no one ever interrupts what you're doing by stopping by your office to chat. But they also agree that one of the biggest disadvantages of telecommuting is that no one ever stops by your office to chat.

If you live alone, you'll find yourself working in an empty house for most of the day. If you have children or a work-at-home spouse, you'll definitely feel less isolated, but to function effectively, you'll probably still need to go inside your office and shut the door.

Either way, it can be a lonely feeling. This is the single biggest reason why former telecommuters find themselves back at the office, at least part of the time.

Melding Telecommuting with Your Job

Let's say you've done some soul-searching, and you're pretty sure you have the right temperament to work from home. At least, you're sure enough to want to give it a try. The next question you must answer is whether your current job is appropriate for telecommuting, and, if it isn't, is there another type of job you could do and enjoy while working from home?

Just as telecommuting doesn't fit every personality, telecommuting doesn't fit every job or every profession. Here are some questions to help you determine whether any particular job is a good or bad fit for telecommuting.

Do you spend several hours at a time working alone on your own projects?

If you spend a great deal of time working alone, your job may be just right for telecommuting. That's why writers and reporters, computer programmers, graphic artists, and the like are so often successful telecommuters. But other types of jobs fit into this category as well. Typists and transcriptionists, for instance, often can work effectively from home. So can anyone whose job requires a lot of time reading, planning, writing reports, or strategizing.

"Jobs that require long periods of thinking or quiet time are perfect for telecommuting because you actually get that time to think without interruption," Miriam Carey notes. She is a telecommuting travel editor for *Ohio* magazine.

Does your job require lots of interaction with other members of your team at the office?

Jobs that require considerable interaction in the workplace with other members of your team can make telecommuting more difficult. But before you give up, give some careful thought to just how much of that interaction really needs to take place while all of you are physically in one room. Would it be just as easy to work together on an e-mail LISTSERV (in which all messages go out to the entire group), chat, or conference call?

Many would-be telecommuters are forced to remain in the office so as to be available for frequent meetings. If this is you, my next question is how necessary are all those meetings — or at least, how necessary is your presence at all those meetings? Would it be just as easy for you to find out afterward from one of your colleagues what was decided during the meeting?

Remember that the more meetings you skip, the more efficient you're likely to be. Unless you're, say, a consultant who uses presentation meetings to sell your services, chances are, the time you spend in a meeting is time taken away from actually getting your job done. And if you decide your presence is needed at meetings, do you really need to actually be in the room? Or would a conference call or videoconference serve the same purpose just as well?

Do you spend most of your time interacting with people outside your organization?

Unless your job is, say, standing at a customer service desk in a department store, spending a great deal of time on interactions outside your organization may point to a job that is well suited for telecommuting. After all, if you spend the bulk of your workday on the phone with your company's customers or suppliers, what does it matter where you're calling from? The same logic holds true if you're a purchasing agent whose job consists of looking for products on the Internet or poring through printed bids and writing up orders.

This is why jobs in telephone sales and telephone customer service are so frequently held by telecommuters. Employers even use a term — *distributed customer service center* — to denote people answering the same customer service numbers from several different locations. Because most customer service people must be available for customers for a set number of hours, questions of off-site supervision are easily resolved. That makes them an especially appealing telecommuting sell for many employers.

Do you oversee a physical plant — such as a retail store, construction site, or factory?

If you're responsible for a retail store, construction site, factory, or other physical plant, you may need to be at the worksite most of the time, making it difficult to telecommute. Still, at certain times, you need a few hours to concentrate on paperwork, planning, or reviewing new marketing materials. So, while you can't telecommute most of the time, an occasional day at home may still make sense, especially if someone dependable can temporarily take over for you at the worksite.

Does your job require you to spend a lot of time away from the office?

If you find that you're spending a lot of time working away from the office, you may have the perfect job for telecommuting — although you may not get to spend much time in your home office, either. The extreme example of this type of work is a sales representative who often spends so much time on the road that he or she visits the office only occasionally to attend a meeting and pick up mail. In the current trend, fewer and fewer of these folks actually have offices, working instead from laptop computers that can readily connect to the company's network. On the few days when they do show up at head-quarters, they're assigned temporary desks and phones.

The work life of a traveling sales rep is not what we typically think of as telecommuting. But it can provide some good examples of how to work effectively from outside the office while still remaining a member of a team. If you have a job that requires being out of the office a lot of the time anyway, then you're probably already set up to do some of your work on a remote basis. Your colleagues are already accustomed to communicating with you when you're not around. Telecommuting is just one step further in the same direction.

Are you expected to be available at a moment's notice?

If you have to be available at a moment's notice, you may find it difficult to get the freedom to telecommute. In some cases, your physical presence in the workplace may be a real necessity — for example, if you're the front-line troubleshooter when people in your organization have trouble with their personal computers.

Telecommuting, in other cases, may be more a matter of workplace expectations. For example, secretaries and executive assistants spend much of their time typing, answering correspondence, making travel arrangements, and fulfilling other functions that can easily be done at home. But, in a traditional workplace, an assistant is expected to be available at all times to answer his or her boss's phone, screen calls, take lunch orders, and even, in some organizations, fetch coffee. Furthermore, because the assistant is expected to know the boss's business better than anyone else in the organization does, it is difficult to hand these tasks off to anyone else. If yours is a job where your boss or co-workers expect you to be available to solve their problems at a moment's notice, telecommuting may *not* be a realistic plan.

What does your union think of telecommuting?

Had someone asked you a few years ago, "What does your union think of telecommuting," the simple answer would have been: "Not much." In the past, most labor unions opposed telecommuting by their members. The two basic reasons for this opposition were

✔ Union leaders envisioned their members doing piecework (such as sewing) in an inadequate space with unsafe equipment, thus turning each home worksite into a one- or two-person sweatshop.

✔ Telecommuting seemed to work against the unions' own best interests. Organizing workers who are all in the same place is easier.

In more recent years, however, most labor unions have had little to say on the subject of telecommuting, and many have claimed to have no experience with it. But those that do are coming around. In a study conducted in 1998 by Dr. Margaret Klayton, associate professor of business administration at Mary Washington College in Richmond, Virginia, some 92 labor unions were asked about their policies on telecommuting. Only 14 of them said they'd had much exposure to telecommuting, but those 14 were all in favor of telecommuting programs.

Why the change? Because many union members, like other people, really want to try telecommuting. "The membership is pushing union management to try to get telecommuting as a benefit in a lot of contract negotiations," notes June Langhoff, author of *The Telecommuter's Advisor* (Aegis, 1996) and senior editor of *Telecommute Magazine*.

Langhoff also notes that many professions in which telecommuting may be appropriate are represented by labor unions. Among them are newspaper reporters and other contract writers, government employees (state and federal), and even police in some localities. Meanwhile, many unions are adapting to reality by learning to contact a dispersed workforce via e-mail, Web sites, and newsletters.

If you're interested in telecommuting, and you have a union representing you, raise the issue with your union contact early on. You may discover that your union has negotiated telecommuting provisions into its current contract, or is planning to in the next contract. And if your union management doesn't know much about the subject, perhaps your inquiry will help encourage them to learn.

Exploring an Employer's-Eye-View of Telecommuting

The more I looked into telecommuting, the more I learned about people successfully telecommuting to jobs where I never would have thought working at home could be an option. Conversely, I encountered more and more people who were dutifully traveling to jobs that had all the elements that a good telecommuting position needs.

Eventually, I came to a simple conclusion: It isn't the job, it's the organization. In an organization open to the concept of telecommuting, any employee can benefit from working at home, at least occasionally. In an organization that's hostile to telecommuting, no job is the right job for telecommuting.

In an online workshop for the International Telework Association and Council (ITAC), Bob Fortier, president of InnoVisions Canada, described a forward-thinking company that employs large numbers of dockworkers. When management first set out to design the company's telecommuting program, they planned to select prospective telecommuters by job title — a method that would have left out the dockworkers.

"Luckily, that organization found a better way to select teleworkers, because as it turns out, some of the dockworkers actually telework from time to time," he writes. "How? Well, for example, at performance appraisal time, some of the supervisors (also dockworkers) want to telework in the quiet and privacy of their homes." Or, he added, injured dockworkers stuck at home can do light clerical jobs rather than remaining idle.

Obviously, this is the exception, not the rule, and the word *dockworker* tells us exactly where these employees must spend the bulk of their time. But it's a good illustration of how useful telecommuting can be if an organization is open-minded enough to put trust in its own employees.

Contrast the dockworkers with my own (mercifully brief) experience as a business reporter for a small regional newspaper a few years ago. I'd been working as a freelance writer for slightly more than ten years at the time, and life as a newspaper reporter sounded like a fun change of pace. So I accepted the job, even though I'd have to commute 40 miles each way to get there. The only problem: I live in Upstate New York, and I started the job during what turned out to be one of the snowiest winters on record.

Now, newspaper reporting is a profession with a longer history of telecommuting than any other. Remote newspaper reporters were traditionally called *correspondents* rather than telecommuters, but if you think about it, it amounts to the same thing. In fact, more than 70 years ago, Ernest Hemingway was a successful telecommuter, working as a reporter for *The Toronto Star* while living in Paris, France.

So there was no reason I couldn't have telecommuted too — at least part of the time or at least on snowy days. Nothing about my job required me to actually be at the newspaper office. I'd usually start each day by getting assignments from my editor, usually in a conversation that lasted two minutes or less, which could just as easily have taken place over the phone. Most of the research for my articles was done over the phone, and on those occasions when I actually went out on a story, I would usually find myself traveling back toward home. Yet I commuted the 80 miles each day, trusting my four-wheel drive to get me safely through the worst of the snowstorms.

Then came a particularly bad snowfall. With my home county under some three feet of snow, the local government declared a state of emergency. Anyone found out on the roads for non-emergency reasons would be given a ticket. At that point, I decided to stay home.

After years of freelancing, I knew exactly what to do. I called the paper and requested some article assignments, which I researched by telephone, wrote on my home computer, and filed via modem in plenty of time for our afternoon deadline. The stories appeared in the next day's paper, and no reader could have guessed where I was when I wrote them. When the state of emergency continued the following day, I followed the same procedure.

I finally made it back to the newsroom on the third day to find my department editor quite pleased. It turned out that none of the members of our small department had made it in during the state of emergency, but all of us had managed to do our jobs anyway. This, she said, would finally prove to upper management that telecommuting could work.

But, unfortunately, she was wrong. No word on the effectiveness of our remote work was forthcoming from the upper reaches. Instead, a different announcement came down the pike: The few people who actually came in to the office during the state of emergency were given two days off as a reward.

Did I feel gypped? You bet I did. I may as well have spent those two days lounging by the fire and watching movies on TV, rather than getting my stories in. It was as if work done from home really didn't count as work.

That was a company with an extremely antiquated attitude toward telecommuting. Having the ideal telecommuting job did me no good at all there. The fact that several of us had proved by our actions that it truly was possible to get the job done from home didn't matter.

The moral of this story is this: When evaluating your job to see how it might work for telecommuting, take time to carefully consider how telecommuting is viewed within your organization. Ultimately, this helps you determine whether you can successfully telecommute much more than your actual duties will.

Matching Your Goals with Telecommuting

We all have dreams of what we'd like to do and where we'd like to be years into the future, as well as changes we'd like to make right now. Will telecommuting help you reach these goals?

The answer is: It depends. Telecommuting for the right reasons can help you balance your work and home lives, improve relations with your family, and take your career to new heights. Telecommuting for the wrong reasons can lead to frustration and may even drive you back to the office with your tail between your legs. Nearly as many bad reasons for telecommuting exist as there are good ones. Here's a look at some of each.

GOOD: *Spending more time with the kids*

When I was a child, I hardly ever saw my father during the week. A psychiatrist who had to work into the evening, he would never arrive home before my bedtime, though he would sometimes sneak into my room to give me a goodnight kiss.

Children grow up quickly, and working parents sometimes miss important moments in their development — moments that can never be recaptured later. Working at home means being there when your child gets home from school, or wakes from his or her nap. Rather than spend your coffee break gossiping with co-workers, you can spend it singing *Itsy-Bitsy Spider* to your 2-year-old. If your boss — and your spouse — are willing, you may even be able to trade a few hours of your *normal* workday to spend with your children against a few evening hours spent working after they're in bed.

BAD: *Solving the child-care dilemma*

The shortage of affordable, dependable childcare is a national disgrace. It's a big problem for every working parent, but telecommuting usually is a poor solution to the problem. It's okay for occasional backup, such as a school snow day, or when the baby sitter calls in sick. But, if you're working full time and want to telecommute, plan on making child-care arrangements for at least four hours a day, and preferably more. Many home-working parents, especially those with large houses, find having a baby sitter in the home is a good compromise. It enables them to work undistracted when they have to, and visit with the kids during break times.

Not only will having childcare available help you get your job done without losing your sanity, it may also help you gain approval for telecommuting in the first place. Most employers frown on arrangements that combine telecommuting with taking care of the kids. If you make a telecommuting proposal without including a plan for adequate childcare, you may be turned down on that basis. (For more on telecommuting proposals, see Chapter 3.)

GOOD: Less stress

It isn't your imagination — commuting is stressful. And, for many people (including me), working in a traditional office is stressful as well. Furthermore, most Americans find they're constantly *rushed* and feeling like there isn't enough time for all the things they need, and want, to do. Having your office in the home can save you the hour (or two!) you'd normally spend commuting each day.

Beyond that, being able to work at home simplifies life in countless other ways. For instance, while finishing this chapter, I've been able to take an occasional break to check on a pot of turkey vegetable soup I'm making for dinner.

What's more, the freedom of working at home may allow you to exercise more regularly than you could when you worked in the office. If so, that's an even greater benefit. In addition to reducing stress, you may actually be adding years to your life.

BAD: Less responsibility

It's a mistake to assume that telecommuting means doing less work. In fact, telecommuters usually report that they do more, not less, than when they're in the office.

And, if you're telecommuting to the same job you'd otherwise be commuting to, you'll find yourself saddled with more responsibility, not less. Why? In addition to the actual responsibilities of your position, you're also now responsible for clear communications between you and the office. If you missed being there for an important meeting, it's your job to find out what was said. If people at the office report to you, it's your responsibility to make sure they have all the information they need to get their work done when you're not around. And making sure your boss knows what you're working on, and where you are on all your current projects, also is up to you.

GOOD: Starting your own business

Some employers and other experts doubtless disagree with my premise that starting a business can be a good reason to telecommute. But being away from the office, especially if you have flexible work hours, may make it possible to take those first steps toward entrepreneurial independence. In addition, if you've spent your entire career up to now in a traditional workplace, telecommuting gives you a sense of what it's like to work on your own.

Some obvious pitfalls come to mind when combining a telecommuting job with starting a new venture. The first is that you still need to make sure you're doing your job, and doing it well. This will sometimes leave you feeling like you're neglecting your new business during its crucial startup phase. Be prepared for a fair amount of frustration and some long, long workdays.

BAD: Escape from a rotten boss or work situation

If you hate your boss or your job and dread getting to work in the morning, telecommuting may look like a workable solution. In fact, it would be a big leap from the frying pan into the fire. When you telecommute, your boss becomes a much more important link between you and the home office than he or she ever would be if you still were in the office. Creating the kind of interoffice relationships that can help you move to a different area within your company also become more difficult.

Even more important, telecommuters must be self-motivated. With no one around to see whether you're sitting down at your desk or turning on the morning talk shows, the temptation to goof off can be overwhelming. Your best line of defense against this temptation is to love your job so much that you're almost eager to get to work. Developing strong self-motivation when you hate your job is almost impossible.

GOOD: Career advancement

Most telecommuters fear that they'll be "out of sight, out of mind" when management goes looking for someone to promote, and thus telecommuting will put the brakes on their careers.

But evidence shows that, in fact, the opposite is true. According to telecommuting expert Gil Gordon, "If anything, most managers of telecommuters report that their telecommuters are often more promotable rather than less because the experience of working at a distance helps demonstrate their capacity for more responsibility." At the same time, most telecommuters report that they work more efficiently and get much more accomplished when working from home, which also increases their chances for promotion.

Making a Telecommuting Career Plan

Most people allow their careers to just happen, taking whatever opportunities come their way. While this can be an effective way to advance, it doesn't take larger, far-reaching goals into account. I believe it's truly worthwhile to stop now and then and think about what you really want out of your job and your future.

If you've made the decision that you want to telecommute, take a little time to think about exactly what it is that draws you to telecommuting, what you hope to get out of it, and how that fits in to your larger priorities and wishes. Don't be afraid to dream a little. If you like, get out a notebook or a journal if you use one, and use your writing to explore the following questions:

- ✔ What will telecommuting enable me to do that I can't do now?

- ✔ What will a typical day of working at home be like? What aspects of it will I like and dislike?

- ✔ What do I want to be doing five years from now? Two years from now? Next year?

- ✔ How will telecommuting fit in with those plans?

- ✔ How long do I intend to keep telecommuting? Six months? A year? Until my youngest is in kindergarten? Forever?

You don't have to have answers to all of these questions. In fact, I'd be surprised if you did. But taking the time to think seriously about them helps put telecommuting in the right perspective for you and helps you determine if telecommuting is truly the right arrangement for you.

As for me, I'm completely sold on the benefits of working from home. And the turkey soup was delicious, too.

Chapter 3

Teaching Your Boss to Love Telecommuting

In This Chapter

▶ Your employer's viewpoint

▶ How research helps you sell the idea of telecommuting

▶ How to pitch telecommuting to your boss

▶ What to do if the answer is no

*Y*ou've carefully considered the pros and cons, and decided that telecommuting is for you. Or at least you're intrigued enough to know you want to give it a try.

That was the easy part.

Now that you know you want to telecommute, getting permission to stay home is the next step — and likely to be the most difficult step in your telecommuting career. I must tell you up front that no magic formulas are available to help you do it. Well, actually, a few magic formulas (a cost-benefit analysis, for example) are out there, but there's no guarantee that they'll work. You may have the perfect job for telecommuting. You may have the perfect home-office setup. The benefits to your company may be impossible to deny. And you might still wind up with a non-negotiable *no* for an answer.

You can, however, stack the deck in your favor. One of the better ways to do this is by understanding what your telecommuting means to your boss, your boss's boss, and your organization at large. Telecommuting, without at doubt, is a win-win arrangement, in which employer and employee benefit. Use the information in this chapter to help your boss see why.

How Employers See Telecommuting

 If you currently have a job, your best chance at telecommuting is probably with your present organization. If you don't have a job right now, or you're sure you don't want to stay at your current job, Chapter 4 offers information about finding a new telecommuting position. Either way, you'll be several steps ahead of the game if you can look at telecommuting through an employer's eyes.

Attitudes toward telecommuting vary greatly from organization to organization. But here are some views commonly expressed by managers when faced with the concept.

Telecommuting is a management challenge

Many executives believe it's harder to manage remote employees than on-site ones. They're absolutely right. No matter how you look at it, communicating with someone who's in a cubicle right down the hall, who's available for quick meetings and informal chats, and whom you can actually see working at his or her desk is definitely easier. However managers may try to *manage by objective,* having a sense of how much time you spend at your desk certainly helps them.

Your best response is to frankly acknowledge that, yes, managing a telecommuter is harder than managing someone in the office — but don't forget to mention that it's a worthwhile challenge. Many managers report that by learning to deal with telecommuters, they've gained management skills that help them work better with all their staff members, even the ones on-site, because it forces them to think objectively about the tasks and goals that are appropriate to each job.

Your next step is to point out the things that you can do to make your boss's job easier. For instance, many telecommuters have set arrangements where they call or e-mail their bosses at the end of each workday to report what they accomplished that day, any issues or problems, and what they plan to do the following day. An arrangement like this makes it much easier for your boss to keep track of what you're doing while working away from the office. It also helps you ensure that you're managing your time properly, and setting the right goals for your job.

Telecommuting jobs should be measurable

If what you do can be objectively measured in some way, then managing by objective becomes easier and less of a challenge to your boss in a telecommuting arrangement. This is why typists and telephone customer service representatives, to name just two jobs, are often offered telecommuting jobs: Measuring what they do is a simple matter.

Managers sometimes argue that a job is wrong for telecommuting unless it is as easy to measure as one of these examples. To put it bluntly, that's ridiculous. If it were true that the only measure of your job performance is whether you're sitting at your desk, then you can just as easily be replaced by a department store mannequin.

The truth is that every job can be measured. Figuring out exactly how to assess your productivity and your performance is one of the important first steps for you and your boss in a telecommuting arrangement. So, as you prepare your telecommuting proposal, give careful thought to the question of exactly how your off-site performance will be measured, and be ready with some specific suggestions that will make sense to your boss. Now may be a useful time to take a second look at your last performance review. The aspects of your performance that were evaluated in it may give you a clue as to how to measure your off-site work.

Telecommuting is new management

Throughout corporate America, a struggle is going on between old and new styles of management. Old-style management, sometimes called *top-down management,* is reflected by the more traditional, structured workplace, where every employee has a set time for arriving for and leaving work, and managers pay close attention to what employees are doing at every moment. In the newer management styles, work is less structured and more goal-oriented, and such new-fangled ideas as flex time (in which employees arrange work times outside the usual work schedule), job sharing, and telecommuting are common.

Newer-style managers talk about "empowering" employees and having them "own" their jobs — almost as if the employee is an entrepreneur. Older-style managers behave more as if employer-employee relationships are more like parent-child relationships. (While it's easy — and fashionable — to put down old-style management, remember that among its good aspects are such things as job security, loyalty between company and employee, full benefits, and salaries adequate to feeding an entire family.)

Good or bad, the older style is fading away as the newer style slowly takes over, which is welcome news for anyone who wants to telecommute — or *telework,* which is described in a sidebar later in this chapter. You can use this fact to your advantage, if yours is a company that likes to think of itself as cutting-edge. If yours is a more traditional-style workplace, the idea of telecommuting may be harder to sell.

Telecommuting is experimental

While telecommuting may have been in its experimental stages five years ago, nowadays it's a recognized and respected business practice with a solid track record of benefiting employers. Although it may represent a newer management style, it's no longer a newfangled idea.

You can use some of the statistics in this chapter to demonstrate that telecommuting has been around for a while, a significant portion of the workforce is doing it, and that it is a proven idea that works well. However, the truth is that if your organization doesn't have much experience with telecommuting, then it *is* experimental within your company. Keep that in mind as you plan your telecommuting proposal.

Telecommuting is a perk for employees

Telecommuting is such a boon to employees, it therefore must represent a loss for the employer — because all perks cost the company in some way. This is *zero-sum* thinking. Zero-sum logic says that anything that increases the value to you in a transaction must decrease the value to me by the same amount, so that the sum of the exchange is always zero.

However, in fact, telecommuting adds value for employer and employee, making it truly a win-win proposition. Using the phrase *win-win* helps you get this idea across.

You can explain two other factors to help get the point across to your manager that telecommuting will be good for both of you. The first is showing the financial benefits your organization will derive from your telecommuting by presenting a cost-benefit analysis. (More about that later in this chapter.) The second is to talk to your boss about the time you spend on the road commuting. Remind him or her that this represents a loss for both of you. For instance, instead of spending an hour commuting each way to and from work, you can spend one extra hour working each day, and still have another extra hour to devote to your family.

Like I said, win-win.

Telecommuting destroys team feeling

A common and sometimes legitimate management concern about telecommuting is that it destroys teamwork — particularly given that newer-style managers tend to want employees to work in teams. Much of what we who work at home think of as "wasting time around the water cooler" is the kind of social interaction that helps co-workers understand each other as human beings and creates personal bonds that help them work well together at crunch times. It's true that if you're completely removed from that social interaction, it may make you less part of the team.

But you won't be. First of all, you're seeking to telecommute from your current position, which means that you already have relationships in place with other members of your work team — it's no longer a matter of getting to know new co-workers. Similarly, almost all telecommuting arrangements involve *some* time in the office — at least one day a week or, for long-distance telecommuters, a trip to headquarters every month or two.

Because you recognize the importance of these at-work relationships, you can schedule your tasks to take better advantage of your own telecommuting routine. If you have a report to write, for example, you can use your time away from the office to get it done quickly, without any distractions. If, on the other hand, you need to develop new ideas for a marketing campaign, you may use your day at the office to gather your teammates together for a brainstorming session.

When you and your boss first sit down to work out your telecommuting schedule, you can make your plan to include any regularly scheduled meetings. For instance, if your team has an update meeting every Wednesday morning, you can plan to be in the office Wednesdays, ensuring that you don't become completely isolated from your team's group dynamics or group decisions. You can help stay even more connected by planning lunches with co-workers on one of your days at the office.

The bottom line: Impress upon your boss that you understand the importance of your at-work relationships and that you're ready to do what it takes to make sure you stay connected to your team.

If we let you do it, we have to let everyone do it

Letting one person telecommute means giving permission to everyone on staff to do it. This concern, more than any other, keeps perfectly qualified telecommuters stuck at their office desks. "I hear this from our supervisors all the time," notes Kathleen (KC) Parrish, a transient analysis section leader for the Arizona Public Service Company. "They have one or two people they need to constantly stay on top of, so they'll tell the other 15 or 20, 'No.'"

To get around this obstacle, begin by acknowledging to your boss that telecommuting is neither right for everyone, nor does everyone want to do it. Managers who offer telecommuting as an option often find that only about half the eligible telecommuters ever take them up on it.

Furthermore, a written telecommuting policy that is easy to understand and consistently applied may be the best way you can appease a boss who worries about and wants to avoid exhibiting the appearance of favoritism. By *consistently applied,* I don't mean to say that every employee with the same job title must have the same telecommuting privileges. In most organizations, only employees with solid track records of doing excellent work, meeting deadlines, and getting their jobs done efficiently without supervision are considered for telecommuting.

The problem, however, is that supervisors don't like doling out bad news any more than anybody else. Consequently, they may not tell underperforming employees about any problems with their performance. If a colleague of yours thinks he or she is doing fine but is refused permission to telecommute, that employee will have some tough questions for your supervisor to answer.

If your supervisor faces this kind of situation, telecommuting for your department will likely be a tough sell. But if you want to try, keep the following in mind:

- By refusing to let you and other qualified co-workers telecommute, everyone loses the opportunity to bring their work lives and home lives into better balance, something which can make all of you more loyal to your employer.

- Because statistics show that telecommuters get more work done, your organization loses the benefit of increased productivity in your department.

- Because they don't know that their work isn't up to snuff, your underperforming colleagues lose the opportunity to improve their performance — and the department loses the benefit of their having done so. If they want to telecommute, so much the better: The prospect of telecommuting in the future may be just the incentive they need.

Consider the flip side to the performance question: What if your own performance is considered too poor for telecommuting? If this is the case, your chances of working remotely in your present job may be limited, because generally only top performers are chosen as telecommuters.

Begin with an analysis of why your performance is found wanting. "My boss is a jerk!" may be your first reaction, but try to be as objective as you can. If your boss really *is* a jerk, you may not want to telecommute in this job because it'll make you more dependent on the jerk's support.

Another possible explanation is that your job is not right for you. If you dislike your job and you're not doing it well, chances are that you and it are a bad fit. If so, telecommuting isn't likely a solution to your problem. Consider a change of workplace or career, instead.

Telecommuting versus telework

Is working at home *telecommuting* or *telework?* And is there really a difference?

Throughout this book, I use the term "telecommuting" because I believe it's the more widely recognized and easily understood of the two. But not everyone agrees with me.

Some experts specify that *telework* refers to all work done away from the office, while *telecommuting* refers specifically to working remotely to avoid commuting.

Others basically say, "Who cares?" They believe the difference is minor enough to be considered insignificant.

I generally agree with the latter group, except for one thing: When trying to sell the idea of telecommuting within your company, you must use the term that best helps you make your case. And "telework" may be it. "Telework" is a newer, more modern, and more serious-sounding term for working at home, which may be why industry groups tend to prefer it. (ITAC, for instance, stands for International Telework Association & Council.) So you may want to call your telecommuting proposal a "telework proposal" instead.

But let's say that after careful analysis you decide you want to stay in your present job — and you still want to telecommute. Your best strategy at this point is to sit down with your boss and try to set measurable goals for improvement — with telecommuting as your reward if those goals are met.

Research, Research, Research

The more you know, the better off you are. This is true in almost every situation, but never more so than when you're planning to make a telecommuting pitch. You may depend on your boss to know more than you do about many aspects of your job, but unless he or she has a lot of experience managing telecommuters, it's up to you to become the expert on this subject.

To your manager, telecommuting may mean trying something new, and that can be somewhat uncomfortable. It's also likely that he or she must first get approval from upper management. Either way, your best shot at success is to come into the process armed with as much solid information as you can to back you up.

Where do you get this information? Some of it is available within your own company. Some of it can come from associations within your industry or profession. (If you're not already taking advantage of these groups for networking support and information, now is a good time to start.) Some of it may come from professional publications, or from books about telecommuting (such as this one).

And don't forget the Internet, the most powerful research tool ever invented. Chapter 20 provides a list of Web sites that are especially useful for telecommuters. Several of them offer information specifically geared to helping you sell the idea of telecommuting within your organization.

Wherever you go to gather information, the purpose of your research is finding answers to two fundamental questions:

- ✔ How will telecommuting benefit my organization?
- ✔ How can I demonstrate that telecommuting will work for my job?

If you can't successfully answer these two questions, it's unlikely that you'll be allowed to telecommute. Here's a closer look at each of them.

How will telecommuting benefit my organization?

A corporation has human characteristics. Before it makes a major change, it wants to know, "What's in it for me?" Don't expect to get anywhere if your only answer is, "A happier employee."

Fortunately, that doesn't have to be your only answer. One reason telecommuting is growing at such an impressive rate is that solid statistics demonstrate how telecommuting benefits corporations. And those benefits can be quite significant.

Telecommuting and the bottom line

One recent survey, sponsored by AT&T and conducted by the International Telework Association & Council (ITAC), found that telecommuting employees each saved their respective employers an average of more than $10,000 a year.

How?

- ✔ **Absenteeism:** Because they're still able to work when circumstances force them to stay home, telecommuters were able to save their employers 63 percent of absenteeism costs — an average annual savings of more than $2,000 per telecommuter.

- ✔ **Recruitment and retention:** Most companies spend about one third of an employee's salary in recruitment and replacement. More than half the telecommuters in the survey said the ability to telecommute was an important motivator for staying with their current employer — adding up to an average savings of just under $8,000.

This last number is likely to increase in the future, for two reasons:

- Most researchers predict a shortage of qualified labor, making it more difficult and more expensive to recruit new employees and forcing starting salaries higher.

- Telecommuting is gaining wider acceptance in large and small companies, as well as in government offices, across America. Because many employees like the idea of telecommuting, they tend to gravitate toward employers that offer the option. If your company steadfastly refuses to allow telecommuting, it will cost your company more and more to recruit new staff — and keep its existing staff from jumping ship.

✔ **Productivity:** When surveyed, employees who telecommute reported that they're 15 percent to 20 percent more productive in their jobs because they can work at home. According to ITAC, this translates into annual savings of more than $9,000 per teleworker. Unfortunately, the ITAC survey team wasn't able to check these numbers with the survey respondent's managers. This, along with the general difficulty of accurately reporting one's own productivity, has led even some well-known telecommuting proponents to question this statistic.

It's worth noting that when KC Parrish put together the pilot telecommuting program at Arizona Public Service Company, she also put in place software for measuring how telecommuters' work was affected. Because she is an engineer and was studying the work of engineers whom she supervised, it was possible for her to measure the changes quite accurately. She even adjusted the statistics not to count work performed during staff meetings that the engineers would have been required to attend had they been in the office. When she put all the numbers in a spreadsheet and looked at the results, she found productivity gains of 15 percent to 20 percent.

Telecommuting and your organization

All the above statistics are a big help when you set out to sell your boss on the benefits of telecommuting. Ultimately, though, you'll need to show how telecommuting can benefit your particular company, your particular department, and your particular job.

Begin by examining how your telecommuting can help your organization to reach its specific goals. What are those goals? If you're unsure, there's an easy way to find out: Look at a copy of your company's mission statement.

A mission statement usually is a one-page statement that describes what a company thinks its most important functions are. Many companies have them. If yours does, read it carefully. You may well find some elements that can benefit from telecommuting.

For example, if part of your company's mission is to provide excellence in serving its customers (a popular goal these days), working at home may enable you to deal with customer queries and complaints at unusual hours. This can be especially useful if your firm has overseas clients whose workday differs from yours.

If it focuses on the excellence of product design, and you're involved in this work, it's possible you can do your job better and more efficiently working from home with fewer threats of distraction. These are just two of the countless possibilities — the point is to use whatever you can find.

Your boss may also be a good source of clues on how to sell your company on telecommuting. Listen to problems he or she may be having, and think how telecommuting may contribute to the solution. But be careful to avoid using lack of telecommuting privileges as a reason you can't meet your job's current expectations. Instead of saying, "I could meet more of my deadlines if only I could telecommute," try, "I bet I can get that report in early if I spend a day working on it at home."

The cost/benefit analysis

The most powerful tool at your disposal for selling your organization on the benefits of telecommuting is a well-crafted cost/benefit analysis. As the ITAC statistics show, most telecommuters save their employers money in higher productivity, lower absenteeism, and reduced facilities costs. Unfortunately, these savings are *soft;* that is, they're real, but difficult to quantify. It's hard to point to them in a departmental budget.

On the other hand, if you begin telecommuting, your company may have to pay for a computer, fax machine, or other office equipment for your home, as well as at least one extra phone line and possibly a high-speed Internet access via cable modem or DSL. It may also pay for *help desk* services to provide you with technical support. And it will probably pay messenger or overnight delivery costs to get essential work materials back and forth between you and the office. These expenses are *hard; that is,* easy to quantify as components of a budget. This is why managers sometimes veto telecommuting on the grounds that it costs too much.

The cost/benefit analysis compares what your organization will spend with what it will save by allowing you to telecommute. The idea is to quantify some of those soft numbers, and demonstrate to your boss (and possibly upper management) exactly why telecommuting is good for business.

One way of going about this is to assume, based on the ITAC research, that as a telecommuter you'll be 15 percent more productive (which should be worth 15 percent of your annual salary for the days you telecommute) and that your absenteeism will go down 10 percent.

It may also make sense for you to include office space costs, but that can be a little tricky. If, for instance, you'll be telecommuting two days a week, and your desk will be unoccupied while you're home, it may be difficult to sell your boss on the idea that you're saving money in office space. On the other hand, you may be able to share your office with another telecommuter — 17 percent of respondents in the most recent ITAC telecommuting survey reported that they did this. Or, your office can be used by new employees, temporary workers, or visitors to the firm while you're away.

Based on these numbers, June Langhoff has put together the following sample cost/benefit analysis. You can find more details at her Web site, www.langhoff.com.

Benefits	
Productivity increased	$7,500
Absenteeism reduced	453
Office space saved	1,440
Parking space saved	40
Potential annual savings per employee	$9,433

Assumptions: Figures are based on telecommuting two days per week, an annual salary of $50,000, productivity increase of 15%, absenteeism reduced by 10%, parking at $600/year reduced by 40%, and use of central office facilities of 120 square feet @ $30 per square foot rent per year reduced by 40%.

Costs	
Training	$200
Second phone line with voice mail and Caller ID	320
Software license fees	450
Help desk fees (outsourced)	125
Notebook computer & modem	2,000
Total first-year costs per employee	$3,095
Annual savings per employee (benefits minus costs)	$6,338

This is a good model to use when constructing your own cost/benefit analysis. But you can make it more powerful by finding more ways to relate it specifically to your company and your particular job. How? Here are just a few ideas:

- ✔ **Include expenses you know you can save by taking on more work.** Let's go back to my old newspaper-reporting job for a moment (see Chapter 2). My commuting time to and from work was one hour each way, or two hours each day. Imagine, for a moment, that I had telecommuted four days a week, gaining me eight hours of extra time — and more productive time — that I could have spent at home. With those extra hours, I could easily have added one extra news story to my weekly workload. Assuming the newspaper would have paid a stringer $100 for that extra story, I could truthfully claim to be saving the paper $100 a week.

  Don't make a claim like this unless you're truly ready to back it up by taking on the extra work in question!

- ✔ **Compare actual missed workdays with days you could have worked at home.** Begin by totaling up the workdays you missed during the past year. (Your company's human resource department may have this information if you don't remember for sure.) Now, consider whether you could've spent some of that time working if you had been set up to work at home. If, for instance, you had to take your child to a doctor's appointment in the morning, but could've worked a half-day in the afternoon, credit yourself back one half-day. If you could've gotten an entire day's work done, but had to stay home because of a school snow day, credit yourself a whole day.

  Now total up the number of workdays you could've gained for the year by telecommuting. You can put a rough dollar value on your workday by dividing your annual salary by 240 — an approximation of days worked in a typical work year. The dollar value of your workday, multiplied by total days you could've worked at home, is how much you could've saved your company in absenteeism by telecommuting.

- ✔ **Include what your company spends on you when you're at work.** Do you take advantage of snacks or beverages provided free while you're on the job? Do you use a company-subsidized cafeteria? Does your company provide van service to get you to work, or taxi service if you have to go home late? All of these represent money you could save if you weren't at the office.

How can I demonstrate that telecommuting will work for my job?

Once you can demonstrate that telecommuting will benefit your organization, your next task is to prove that it can be done by someone in your job — in other words, you. Generally speaking, in the corporate world, safety lies in following, not leading. So the best way to prove that something can be done is to show that it has been done already.

Begin by researching your own company's history with telecommuting. Maybe people in other departments, unbeknown to you, are happily telecommuting already. In that case, you can refer your manager to the manager of those telecommuters for information and advice. It may even be that your company already has a telecommuting policy in place, in which case you'll simply have to demonstrate that you fit within its parameters.

On the other hand, your company may have already had a negative experience with telecommuting. For example, maybe a participant in an existing pilot telecommuting program took a second job at the same time. (Don't ask me why people do this, but sometimes they do.) In that case, you need to know that by proposing a telecommuting arrangement, you're treading on dangerous ground. Plan to demonstrate to your company leaders how they'll know that you're working when you're at home, and that you'll always be easy to reach.

Once you find out about your company's telecommuting history, look outside your company to your main competitors and other companies in your field. Do they allow telecommuting among their employees? If so, a manager at the competing company may be willing to talk to your manager about telecommuting. Some industry studies also point to how many people are telecommuting and what the positive and negative effects have been for participating companies. All this is useful information in putting together your telecommuting pitch.

Your third step is to find out whether others in your particular profession are telecommuting. It may be that, while the nature of your company requires most employees to be in the office, your particular job is well suited to telecommuting.

In fact, that is what happened to my husband Bill. Although the company where he works focuses on providing useful medical information on the Internet, Bill's specialty in Internet community sets his work apart from most of what the company does. Internet community is all the areas where users of a Web site interact directly with each other, with the organization itself. Typical venues are message boards, chat, and moderated live events with experts or celebrities, but may also include interactive live webcasts, voice chat, 3-D chat, and other more exotic activities. Although he has one staff member reporting to him in the office, the rest of the people who work for him are also remote. Because his profession is all about communicating on the Internet, he's especially adept at working with people who may be thousands of miles away. In short, his job is tailor-made for telecommuting.

Fortunately, his boss recognized this when she hired him. A few months later, his friend and former colleague, Donna Gettings, was offered an Internet community job for an Internet site directed at children of the immigrant community. She wanted the job but didn't want to relocate to the West Coast, where the company was located.

She managed to sell the company on the idea of hiring her as a telecommuter. It helped that she offered to take a lower salary than she would've needed in Silicon Valley (where housing costs are extremely high) and that she had the expertise to demonstrate exactly how she could work with computer files and other information that she needed without actually being in the office. But one of the biggest factors in her favor was the fact that she could point to Bill, who already was successfully doing a parallel job on a telecommuting basis. "I talked to Bill about some of the strategies he used," she says.

Making the Telecommuting Pitch

Once you've completed all your research, it's time to make a telecommuting pitch to your boss. You'll probably be better off planning to start with a verbal pitch and following up with a written proposal. Each of these is part of the same strategy, with the same ultimate goal — to give your boss (and possibly your boss's boss) the information that leads to a decision in favor of you telecommuting. But there are two different parts of the process.

The verbal proposal

What's the right approach? Should you wander into your boss's office and casually raise the subject of telecommuting? Or should you ask for a formal meeting and arrive with a carefully crafted graphic presentation?

I can't tell you because I don't know your organization's social norms and customs. These norms, which are also called corporate culture, dictate how you open communications on this subject. Remember that you're trying to sell the idea of telecommuting, so this is a good time to use any sales skills you have.

What follows are some things to keep in mind during your conversation.

Learning as much as you can

Whether you get the go-ahead to try telecommuting, you can learn a great deal from conversations on the subject with your manager. You'll find out what your boss likes and doesn't like about telecommuting. You may get a sense of some of your boss's hot buttons — issues you can stress that'll raise your boss's interest in telecommuting. You should wind up with plenty of ideas about what points to stress when you make your written proposal, what points to play down, and how to attack the issue next time if you get turned down this time.

Asking lots of questions

Two good reasons for asking questions are that the answers tell you what you need to know to make a better telecommuting proposal, and that asking questions is one of the more powerful sales techniques. Asking questions tells customers (in this case your boss) that their concerns and reservations are being taken seriously. It can draw them into a collaborative effort to help you overcome obstacles to the desired result. Asking insightful questions can help you change your boss's attitude toward telecommuting as well.

For a masterful discussion of asking questions during a telecommuting pitch, as well as plenty of actual examples of questions you can ask, go to www.gilgordon.com and look in the "Telecommuting Tools" section for "Objection Handling."

Having telecommuting facts at your fingertips

This is one place where all your careful telecommuting research pays off. If your boss says, "Sounds like a great idea, but I doubt it will work in our industry," you can rattle off the names of three competitors that are already doing it. If your boss finds the productivity gains hard to believe, you can quote statistics from studies that show that they're real.

You have to walk a fine line, however, because you don't want to come across as a know-it-all, even if, indeed, you do know it all. One good way to do this is to offer facts and figures in response to specific questions, instead of volunteering them. Managers are likelier to pay attention to and remember information they've specifically asked for.

Becoming your organization's telecommuting expert

You may only care about one telecommuting job — your own. But it may still be in your best interest to position yourself as the local expert on the whole question of telecommuting. Besides, you're about to produce a well-crafted telecommuting proposal that'll tend to put you in that role, regardless of whether you want it. You can fulfill that role best by gathering information that bolsters the idea of telecommuting in other job functions and areas besides your own.

The written proposal

Assuming you haven't gotten an absolute, unchangeable "no" to your verbal pitch, your next move is to follow up with a detailed, written telecommuting proposal. If the answer is "yes," congratulations! You'll still want to put the basic elements of your telecommuting arrangement on paper, but now you're writing a telecommuting agreement, rather than a proposal.

As with your verbal proposal, begin by considering what your organization's norms are for written communications (Formal or colloquial? Full of detailed footnotes, or more general?). If you've already written a proposal that was successful, you can work from the format you used before. If not, try asking co-workers or your boss for examples of written proposals that were well received.

Once you've decided on format and style, your proposal needs to include all or most of the following:

- ✔ **A general introduction:** You say what you're about to say, then you say it, then you say that you said it, is how an English teacher of mine once described writing school papers. It holds true for this kind of writing, as well.

- ✔ **An overview of telecommuting:** This is a good place for statistics on how telecommuting increases productivity and reduces absenteeism. You can also include some of the numbers in Chapter 1 on the rapid growth of telecommuting. In the monkey-see-monkey-do corporate world we live in, the fact that there are already 20 million telecommuters out there should be a powerful inducement for your boss to give it a try.

- ✔ **Benchmarking:** *Benchmarking* refers to comparing what your company is doing with what other comparable companies are doing. If there are other companies in your industry with telecommuting programs in place, describe what they're doing, what their telecommuting practices and trends are, and why it's working for them. You can also offer information on other people from other industries who are telecommuting in jobs similar to yours.

- ✔ **A cost-benefit analysis:** This is the place to include details of the calculations you've made to determine how your telecommuting would save your company money. Once you've run the numbers, you should also describe some benefits that do not immediately translate into more dollars — such as having you available for after-hours customer calls, and resource recovery. (Resource recovery refers to an organization's ability to recapture important files, documents, programs, and work products in case of a fire, flood, or other disaster at its offices. As a telecommuter, you'll have duplicates of important documents on your home computer. This can help your company recreate its records if they are unexpectedly lost or destroyed.)

✔ **A proposed telecommuting policy:** Who should telecommute and who shouldn't? What criteria does a prospective telecommuter need to meet? If you're writing a telecommuting proposal strictly on your own behalf, you may not need to bother with questions of telecommuting policy. But if you're positioning yourself as your organization's telecommuting advocate, then it may make a lot of sense to give an example of what a logical policy might look like. It will help your case as well if it provides an answer to the *if-I-let-you-do-it-I-have-to-let-everyone-do-it* argument.

✔ **A proposed telecommuting agreement:** Telecommuting arrangements work best if both parties have agreed in writing and know what to expect. This is why you and your boss should both sign a telecommuting agreement before you start. At this point you can either write up a proposed agreement or simply describe the telecommuting arrangement you're proposing. Remember to address the following:

- How many days a week or month do you want to telecommute? Which particular days (if any)? Are there specific staff meetings or other in-office events that you'll make sure not to miss?

- Who will pay for any new computers or other office equipment you'll need as a telecommuter? You will almost certainly need at least one other phone line. Will your employer pay for it? What steps will you take to make sure sensitive or confidential information on your computer remains secure?

- How long do you want to try telecommuting? (Your boss probably won't agree to an open-ended telecommuting arrangement, and neither should you, in case you discover you don't like it as much as you thought you would.) Three months or six months is usually a good test period for a trial telecommuting arrangement. If all goes well, you can continue it on a more permanent basis.

✔ **A conclusion:** This should be a sort of executive summary that stresses the highlights of your telecommuting proposal, and reminds the reader once again why telecommuting makes so much sense for your company.

If the Answer Is No

I'm hoping that you're just reading this section out of idle curiosity. But what do you do if your telecommuting proposal really did get refused?

Begin by taking a few days to process the feelings of frustration and disappointment that are a natural reaction when you don't get something you really want. You may want to go on to the next step — and you will, soon — but you'll be in much better shape to do so if you've given these feelings some breathing room first.

Next, make sure you fully understand why you were turned down. If you like, make a second appointment to sit down with your boss and discuss the matter. (Make it clear that you're not going to beg or insist; you simply want to make sure you understand why the answer was no.) Try to find out whether there's any chance that you may be allowed to telecommute sometime in the future.

If you were turned down because of performance

Make sure you understand which aspects of your performance made you a wrong choice for telecommuting, in your boss's judgment. Once you know where the problem area lies, you may be able to improve your performance in that area. Or, it may be a matter of changing your boss's perception — perhaps you've been doing a lot better than he or she realized.

In either case, see if you can get your boss to agree to give you a second evaluation in six months or so. Find out if he or she will reconsider your telecommuting proposal at that time, assuming your evaluation has improved.

If you were turned down because of the nature of your job

Management may believe that your job is impossible to do effectively from a remote location. This attitude may be difficult for you to change, but one way to try is to make sure your boss knows about all the technological tools that will help you stay in touch while you're not at the office — for instance, having calls to your office forwarded to your home.

You may also be able to demonstrate that certain aspects of your job can be done from home by occasionally working a home day on an ad hoc basis — while writing evaluations, for example.

If you haven't already researched telecommuting options elsewhere in your company, now is a good time to start. Your particular boss in your particular department may feel strongly that you need to be at the office every day. But in other departments with other bosses, telecommuting may be an accepted practice. If so, a lateral move to another area may be the solution.

The fact that you're researching telecommuting for your proposal gives you a perfect excuse to ask colleagues and managers in other departments about their thoughts on telecommuting. You can use those same contacts for networking purposes when looking for a different in-house job.

If you were turned down because of company policy

If upper management is dead set against the whole idea of telecommuting, you may not have much that you can do to change their minds. Especially if you've already given them statistics that show how telecommuting can benefit your company.

Your best strategy at this point may be to wait. Fortunately, current trends are on your side. Soaring real-estate prices have already driven many companies to start telecommuting programs when they wouldn't have otherwise. And if the labor shortage continues, as many experts believe it will, skilled workers may be able to write their own tickets. And some of them will insist on telecommuting.

In the meantime, there's *guerilla telecommuting.* Guerilla telecommuting is telecommuting done on the sly, without formal approval or formal supervision from upper management. Guerilla telecommuters aren't called telecommuters, but they work from home on certain days as part of an informal arrangement with their immediate supervisors. Guerilla telecommuting may sound stealthy, but it's extremely common — and it's one reason no one knows for sure exactly how many telecommuters there really are. If your boss is willing to have you telecommute, but upper management said no, guerilla telecommuting may be the solution.

One final question

How attached are you to your current job? And how badly do you want to telecommute? It isn't necessarily easy, but if you really want to work at home part of the time — and your current employer really isn't going to let you — the ultimate solution may be to look for a different job. One where you know telecommuting is an option, right from the start.

Kathleen Parrish: Becoming the in-house telecommuting expert

Six years ago, engineers at Arizona Public Service Company faced a dilemma. The utility operates the Palo Verde Nuclear Power Generation Station, which puts out more electricity than any other nuclear power plant in the country. Through years of careful training, the company built up enough in-house engineering expertise to bring the technology for fuel design in-house at an annual savings of $3 million.

But just as the company was about to sign a contract confirming this arrangement, business changes intervened. The utility had gone through reengineering and had made cuts in its staff. The remaining staff would be moved to the plant, some 60 miles from their former offices in Phoenix. Clearly, many of the company's engineers would resign and seek work elsewhere, rather than commute an extra 120 miles each day. Without enough experienced engineers on staff to handle the fuel technology, the contract — and the savings — would have to be abandoned.

This is the powerful business case Kathleen (KC) Parrish, the engineer who had negotiated the contract, was able to put before senior management as part of her proposal to begin a telecommuting program. Even so, upper management was deeply resistant. For one thing, utilities in general are old-style companies that are not often willing to try new work arrangements. For another, Parrish explains, many of the company's leaders come from Navy backgrounds. "And where does the captain of a submarine want his critical staff to be?" she asks.

Despite the resistance, Parrish was able to create a successful telecommuting program by following three basic principles: Focus on how telecommuting will benefit the company, not the employee; put a dollar amount on those benefits; and once people are telecommuting, measure the benefits so as to prove that what you promised is coming true.

The new telecommuters were engineers who could do their design work much more efficiently at home, away from office interruptions. Many gained two hours of extra time — or 10 hours a week — that they would have spent traveling to work and back. Because they could network into the utility's system from home, they were also able to run simulations and calculations at odd hours, without worrying about server overload.

For all these reasons, the benefits turned out to be enormous. Using a simple point-and-click method of measuring activity, Parrish found that telecommuters worked 15 percent longer, and were 20 percent more productive than when they worked in the office. In addition to saving the fuel contract, advanced fuel designs run through the computer during off-hours saved the company some $5 million in maintenance.

When she presented those numbers to senior management, resistance melted away, she says. "No one was going to argue with $5 million in savings." She has now become Arizona Public Service's in-house telecommuting expert, running regular training workshops for new telecommuters, their immediate supervisors, and upper management.

Ironically, the leadership that brought telecommuting to the company means that Parrish herself cannot telecommute. The week before she was to start staying home as part of the pilot program, she was offered a promotion to her current position of section leader — a managerial role that she couldn't fill as a telecommuter. But she's happy with the tradeoff. "I never thought I'd have a management position," she says.

Chapter 4

Finding a New Telecommuting Job

. . . .

In This Chapter

▶ Deciding whether finding a telecommuting job is feasible

▶ Determining your needs

▶ Choosing a job type

▶ Hunting for a job

▶ Doing well when you land a job

. . . .

You've tried and tried, but you just can't sell your current employer on telecommuting. Or you hate your current job, want to move on, and think being able to work at home would be great. Or you've been out of the workforce for a while, want to go back to work, but can't stand the idea of sitting in an office all week. Whatever the reason, you know you want to find a new job, one that you can work at away from the office.

The Telecommuting Outlook

What kind of job can you expect to get? The answer to that question depends on a variety of factors. Obviously, the skills and experience you bring with you determine what jobs are available. But, because you're looking specifically for a telecommuting job, the kind of job you'll find also depends on how flexible you can and are willing to be about working from home.

Regardless of how skilled you are, if being able to telecommute is a requirement before you'll accept a job, your options are more limited than if it weren't. Many employers are steadfast in their determination not to let employees telecommute. Those who do allow telecommuting usually want it to be the company's choice, not yours. They may also want to be able to end the telecommuting arrangement at their discretion.

Likewise, not all jobs can be done on a telecommuting basis. Support jobs, service jobs, some sales jobs, and many management-level jobs require you to be in the office, able to talk face to face with other members of your team or your customers every day. All these factors mean you'll have to be less choosy when taking a telecommuting job than if you were willing to come into the office.

But you have one enormous element in your favor: timing. Literally, no time has been better than the present to search for a remote job. Consider the sections that follow.

Labor shortages

During the past few years, unemployment has reached historical lows. Finding people to do the job — any job — is increasingly difficult for most employers. Finding employees with a specific skill (such as knowledge of the latest programming language) can be particularly hard. Prospective employees increasingly can name their own terms, including the ability to telecommute.

Burgeoning technology

These day, it's a rare company that doesn't use computers for almost everything it does. (Even the guy who comes in his truck to snowplow my driveway in winter sends me his invoices by e-mail!) If you currently have a job, how many hours of it do you spend sitting in front of a computer? With the proper technology, those are hours you could spend at home.

Growing bandwidth

Many technology experts believe that the growth of broad bandwidth Internet access will spur the growth of telecommuting more than any other factor. In the past, the only way to connect to the Internet was by using slow modems and inadequate phone lines that limited how much information remote workers could send back and forth to their workplaces.

But things are changing. With cable modem, satellite, and Digital Subscriber Line (DSL) services available in even the remotest of locations (at least, within the United States), workers can sign on from anywhere and do what they need to do. At my house, a place so rural I've had bear walk by my front door, cable modem service is unavailable at this writing but will be in place by the time this book is published. And, if I needed high-speed Internet access today, I could have it by attaching a small satellite dish to my roof.

Geographic disparity

Even though unemployment is near its all-time low, it's also more uneven than at any time in the past. In some northeastern post-industrial cities, unemployment still is in the double digits, while some jobs remain unfilled in Silicon Valley. Faced with this reality, employers in tight labor markets often find themselves paying moving and house-hunting costs and sometimes financing to bring prospective employees from one location to another.

However, this practice has several drawbacks from the employer's point of view. First of all, it's expensive. Second, there's the risk that after paying all those expenses, the new employee won't work out or won't like the job. Third, even if the new person works out, that person has relocated to an area with a tight labor market, making his or her skills a tempting target for competitors looking to hire employees away. Allowing employees to telecommute from other locations instead avoids all these problems.

Urban sprawl

Hiring employees to come to the office in today's larger urban areas can be economic and logistical nightmares. Employers in Manhattan, San Francisco, or Boston simply can't afford to pay most of their workers a wage big enough to enable them to live nearby (at least not in a neighborhood the employee would consider safe). In any case, quality of life issues make many people reluctant to locate in densely populated urban areas.

The only alternative for many people is to commute to work, traveling an hour, or sometimes even two, each way. But this isn't anyone's idea of a happy solution. Travel time is time lost to employer and employee. Unpredictability of traffic and public transportation make it difficult for employees to consistently arrive on time — or willingly stay late. And anything from a meeting with a teacher to an appliance delivery can cause them to miss an entire day.

A recent *New York Times* article credited urban sprawl and rising real-estate prices with bringing about a rebirth of corporate interest in telecommuting. I'm not sure I'd agree those were the only reasons for rising interest — or that telecommuting was dead and needed to be reborn in the first place. But they're certainly powerful motivators for employers who've been dead set against telecommuting to rethink their positions.

Corporate acceptance

In the past, most telecommuters worked for small companies, which usually are readier than large ones to try new ways of doing business. In 1999, ITAC found, for the first time, that telecommuters responding to its survey were as likely to work for large companies as for small ones.

Nothing signals Corporate America's acceptance of new ideas as clearly as when the nation's large corporations begin to participate. And this trend is likely to snowball: The more companies that allow telecommuting, the more other companies are willing to give it a try.

All of this is good news if you're looking for a telecommuting job. It means you'll have a wider variety of companies available to you than ever before.

Your Telecommuting Needs

Before you start your job search, you must decide exactly what kind of telecommuting arrangement works for you. Many different configurations exist, so knowing what you want up front saves time and effort for you and prospective employers. The following questions can help you create a clear picture of what you want from a telecommuting job.

Why do you want to telecommute?

Telecommuting may be your answer if you have a small child, or a sick family member, and you feel you need to be at home. Or it may be that you've spent the past 20 years in the corporate grind and you need some time away from it. Or it may be that you have medical problems that make frequent travel between home and the workplace difficult for you. Your reasons for telecommuting will dictate exactly what sort of terms you're willing and able to accept.

Wanting to be home so as to be nearby or available for a small child or sick family member is a commendable reason for telecommuting. But if you plan to be the primary caretaker in this situation, be aware that you cannot combine those kinds of duties with a full-time job, even a telecommuting one. You'll be expected to be at work at least eight hours a day, and to be available for at least occasional days at the office. You may be able to *flex* your time to accommodate something other than the usual 9-to-5 work schedule, but you need to plan to be available during most of your working hours.

If you try to combine dependent care with full-time telecommuting, you're likely to turn in an unsatisfactory performance, affecting your chances for advancement and for obtaining future telecommuting work. Worse, the pressure from a full-time workload means that you generally won't be able to do a great job as a parent or caretaker either. For reasons like these, many corporate employment policies specifically state that telecommuting cannot be used as a means to replace in-home care.

Does this mean you can't work if you're home with a child or other family member? No. You have two viable choices. You can either make another arrangement — day care, baby sitting, or a home-health aide — to care for your dependent or dependents during at least part of the work day, or you can opt for part-time or contract work so that you can tailor your work hours to your caretaking schedule.

Are you willing to spend some time working on-site first?

Kathleen Parrish of the Arizona Public Service Company is so committed to the idea of telecommuting that she created a pilot program for her company and trains managers and telecommuters throughout her organization. When she hires engineers, she seeks out independent, self-directed individuals who she believes will make successful telecommuters.

But when I asked her if she'd ever hire someone to be a telecommuter from the start, her answer was simple: "Heck, no! I'd want to get to know them first. They need to work full time in the office for at least a year to build up good working relationships. Otherwise, there are bonding issues."

Most executives agree with her. In fact, management consultants who special-ize in creating corporate telecommuting programs routinely advise their clients to allow only employees who already have a solid track record at the office to telecommute. That is why it often is easier to gain telecommuting privileges at your current job than to find a new job where you're allowed to telecommute.

One way around this is to start out working in the office and plan to begin telecommuting within, say, six months to a year — if you're willing and able to postpone telecommuting for that long. If you do decide that you're inter-ested in such an arrangement, here are a few things to keep in mind:

 ✔ You're better off working out a specific plan before you start the job. You and your boss need to agree, for example, that if all goes well, six months after starting, you can begin working from home one day a week, then two days, then three days. This is much better than just a general statement, "In six months, we can discuss telecommuting." You may spend six months in the office only to find that the promised discussion leads to an unyielding "no."

✔ Put the agreement in writing, if possible. Even an informal memo to your boss that confirms the arrangement you've agreed on is better than nothing. Several telecommuters have told me that they were hired with a specific plan to telecommute later on, but when later on came around, the boss tried to refuse.

This is understandable enough. Most managers find it easier to deal with someone who's on-site. And, if you've been doing your job successfully, and seemingly happily, for the past several months, your boss may be reluctant to make changes, on the popular *if-it-ain't-broke-don't-fix-it* principle. This can be a sticky situation with no easy solution. But at least when you have something in writing, no one can question what the agreement was supposed to be.

✔ Your performance counts for you — or against you. If your new employer comes up with a written agreement promising to allow you to telecommute in the future, chances are that the agreement will say on it somewhere that telecommuting is contingent on your performance. Generally, only employees who've demonstrated they can do their jobs well and with minimal supervision are considered for telecommuting. You'll need to keep this in mind during your first months on the job.

How many days a week are you willing to spend in the office?

You need to spend only one day a week working at home to be considered a telecommuter for the purposes of surveys and telecommuting programs. Is that enough to satisfy you? It may be, if your reasons for wanting to telecommute are to spend a little extra time with your spouse or take one small step out of the rat race. On the other hand, you may want more.

Most full-time jobs require you to spend at least one day a week in the office, or perhaps a few days a month, if your duties or workload vary from week to week. This is especially true if your job is at a managerial level.

How much time you're willing to spend in the office is a decision you'll have to make based on your own telecommuting needs. The important thing is to discuss the issue with your prospective employer before you accept a new job. Otherwise, you may discover that what you and your new boss think of as telecommuting are two different things.

Can you handle long-distance telecommuting?

You won't have to worry about showing up at the office on a weekly basis if your office is thousands of miles away. On the other hand, you sometimes must be away from home for several days or even a week at a time. You'll have to face the aggravation of frequent airline travel and possible time zone changes.

Because it is difficult to retrieve items left at home when you're at work, and vice versa, you also must be well organized. Perhaps even more frustrating, you won't be able to simply run into the office to deal with an unexpected problem or opportunity.

Long-distance telecommuting isn't for everyone. But it does offer one tremendous advantage: You can leverage the differences in the amount of work available in different geographical regions. For instance, although my husband Bill and I enjoy the rural New York state area where we live, each of us would face limited prospects if we had to be employed in this region.

It's an unspeakable drag to drop him at the airport once a month, conduct our marriage by phone and online chat, and then pick up a tired Bill a week later. But his long-distance telecommuting gives him a chance at interesting Internet jobs that simply don't exist around here. And his Silicon Valley paycheck goes a lot farther here than it would there.

Would a part-time job work for you?

If you aren't free to work a 40-hour week, or if you've been away from the workforce for a while, a part-time telecommuting job may be a good choice. Part-time work also can be a good way to supplement your income if your day job isn't enough to make ends meet or if you want to try your hand at a new career. Most of the people who work part time for Bill over the Internet have other full-time jobs. Some are doing it for fun or extra cash, and some see it as getting a foot in the door in an Internet-related field.

It is obvious that a part-time job by itself may not be enough to pay you a living wage. And many part-time jobs don't come with health benefits, which can be a big problem. But if you're trying to combine, say, raising a small child with doing some kind of work, a part-time job may be one solution.

Should you be an independent contractor?

Yet another solution for those who want to work at home is to become an independent contractor. In this scenario, you're self-employed, free to schedule your work hours in accordance with your own needs and your customer's deadlines. Being an independent contractor means taking on work one task at a time, picking and choosing those tasks that appeal to you and for which you have time. The task can be anything from typing a report to planning a conference to writing a *For Dummies* guide.

As an independent contractor, you'll be self-employed and, for tax purposes, will usually operate your own one-person business. You'll also be responsible for obtaining your own health insurance, either via a spouse or other family member, a professional association, or simply a local insurance provider. (This may sound like a minor matter, but health insurance premiums can be almost as expensive as your monthly rent.)

Being an independent contractor can be exhilarating, frustrating, scary (when there's no work around), and deeply satisfying. For a detailed look at this way of life, see *Freelancing For Dummies* and *Home-Based Business For Dummies*.

Planning Your Telecommuting Career

What kinds of jobs are available for telecommuters? The variety is huge and growing all the time. The following list provides a few of the jobs in which telecommuters are working on a remote basis today.

Advertising Copywriter	Programmer
Animal Foster Home Coordinator	Public Relations Representative
Business Consultant	Reporter
Business-to-Business Materials Broker	Researcher
Customer Service Representative	Sales Representative
	Stockbroker
Fact Checker	Technical Support Person
Federal Government Worker	Telephone Operator
Graphic Artist	Transcriptionist/Typist
Meeting Planner	Translator
Mutual Fund Manager	Travel Agent

Internet jobs

The growth of the Internet during the last few years has made telecommuting possible in many jobs where it would not have been before. It allows remote workers to effortlessly send information and documents back and forth, chat face to face via videoconferencing, log on to their at-work computers, and receive and send messages to and from anywhere in the world.

But besides all that, the Internet itself is a great source of telecommuting jobs. All across the country and around the world, dot-com companies are springing up, providing Web surfers with information and opportunities on everything from cars to financial advice to live video of their toddlers in day care. In addition, this new section has brought to life countless Web design firms, e-business consultants, software companies, online media firms, and any number of other companies that exist to support other businesses in the Internet economy.

By their nature, Internet-based companies provide a fertile ground for finding telecommuting jobs. After all, the Internet was designed for the specific purpose of transferring information from one physical location to another. That means that most work that is done on the Internet can be done from anywhere that you can plug in a modem.

The corporate culture of Internet companies is another plus. Many of them are founded by younger people who do not come from management backgrounds with long traditions of doing business the old-fashioned way. The fact that they're comfortable working on the Internet means they're comfortable communicating with people from sites remote from the workplace and with the technology that makes it possible to do so.

Not all jobs for Internet companies work as telecommuting jobs. If you're a receptionist, or an internal computer systems expert, for example, you physically need to be at the office every day. And not all Internet companies welcome telecommuting — some even have firm policies forbidding it. Still, this is the more promising industry for a telecommuting job search.

Don't think that you need to be a technology whiz to get an Internet job. Dot-coms do have an ongoing need for programmers, Web developers, information systems support staff, and an assortment of other technology specialists, but they also have a need for people with some low-tech skills.

Here's a look at a random assortment of Internet jobs:

Abuse Manager

The Internet is a wild and woolly place, full of people who enjoy making trouble for its own sake. So Webmasters at most Web sites, especially larger portal sites, find themselves plagued with users who try to hack into the site, post inappropriate material, steal other users' passwords or accounts, stalk other users, disrupt conversations in chat rooms, and otherwise wreak whatever havoc they can.

Dealing with problems like these demands an odd mixture of people skills, detective skills, enjoyment of the chase, persistence, and a thick skin. Some technological acumen is helpful, but a background in law-enforcement, security, or detective work is even better.

Community Manager

Internet Community is any place on a Web site where human beings interact with other human beings — chat rooms, special event chats and webcasting, message boards, and customer service areas, to name a few. Such areas can be tricky for reasons that have little to do with technology.

This is my husband Bill's profession. It just so happens that he knows quite a lot about computers, but he says the work experience that prepared him best was the time he spent as a counselor working with the mentally ill. Highly developed people skills are the key to this job.

Customer Service Representative

Similar to the job of a telephone customer support person, the job of e-commerce customer service representative comes with more options and therefore requires more skills. Instead of simply speaking on the phone, Web-based customer service reps may also find themselves answering e-mail and using online text chat to communicate with customers. They may use a technology called *collaborative browsing,* leading customers around the site to help them find what they're looking for. They may even use videoconferencing in some companies. A background in customer service is the most helpful preparation for these jobs.

Graphic Designer

Again, graphic design work is similar to the kind of job it would be in a more traditional setting; however, knowledge of currently available design software is a big help. People with backgrounds in more traditional visual arts often are well suited to be graphic designers for Web pages.

Information Architect/User Interface Architect

Information architect, or user interface architect, is a fairly new profession that involves designing the experience that greets a user when he or she visits a Web site, and organizing the information and offerings to make the site as easy to navigate as possible. Information architects come from diverse backgrounds — some have technology experience, others start out as editors, graphic designers, or in some cases actual structural architects.

Producer

In a way similar to how a Broadway producer mounts a musical, a producer of a Web site brings together and coordinates the various designers, programmers, content providers, and other professionals to create one area of a Web site. More than technological skills, this job demands a great degree of organizatio, and the ability to juggle several different priorities and agendas at once. People with project management experience often make good producers.

Taxonomist

What the heck is taxonomy? This exotic-sounding specialty refers to how information within a Web site is categorized and searched, and taxonomists often work in teams to develop lists of keywords that users can enter to find what they're looking for.

Anyone with a thorough background working with words is probably well suited for this job. Once again, a library science background can help. Writers can also wind up as taxonomists.

Writer/Editor

Writer and editor positions are pretty much the same jobs that they'd be with newspapers or magazines, except that instead of appearing on paper, the articles and other content you write or edit is posted on the Web site. Coming up with story ideas, researching and writing articles, and all the usual editorial matters fall into this category. Writers and editors used to working in print media usually have little trouble making the transition to the Web.

Volunteer Coordinator

Many Web sites use volunteers, especially as experts in subject areas that the site covers. Volunteer managers or coordinators recruit, train, and work with these volunteers, a function that falls under the Internet Community umbrella. Once again, people skills are paramount, and a background working with local volunteer organizations is a big plus.

This list of Internet jobs is by no means complete. It isn't even close. It is, however, intended to demonstrate two facts: First, a wider variety of jobs relates to the Internet than one might imagine, and second, many of those jobs don't require a background in technology. Best of all, any of them can be done on a telecommuting basis, at least part of the time.

Choosing a job that's right for you

What do you personally look for in a telecommuting job? "Anything that'll let me stay home!" is not the right approach. Instead, consider the jobs you've enjoyed and have been successful at in the past, and how those same skills can serve you as a telecommuter.

For example, if you enjoyed working as a substitute teacher, you may be able to use your skills and knowledge in the growing field of *distance learning* — education via the Internet. Or you may find that you work well as a volunteer coordinator, because anyone who can handle unruly school children can probably work quite effectively with adult volunteers.

If you've worked in a doctor's office, you may be able to become a medical transcriptionist, work for a health Web site, or provide medical information over the phone for an insurance company. Taking your own skills and preferences as a departure point gives you the best chance of finding a telecommuting job that's right for you.

Investing in training?

Depending on your current skill set and the type of telecommuting job you want, investing in a training program may be exactly what you need to do to prepare for a new telecommuting career. Many types of training programs are out there — some good, some not so good. Before you sign up for any of them, it's a great idea to find out exactly how employers in your target profession view the type of training and the school itself.

How can you find out about an employer's thoughts on training? Ask them! Many executives are pleased and flattered to be asked for career advice from an aspiring employee, and they may be willing to spend several minutes on the phone advising you on which training programs are worthwhile, which are not, and how to break into the field you want. At the end of the conversation, you'll have accomplished not one, but two useful tasks. First, you'll have gathered information that will help you decide whether to take the training course you were considering. Second, you'll have made a valuable contact who may offer you a job later on.

Many people specifically seek training in computer programming as a way to get into a higher paying profession that allows them to work from home. This may be a good idea if you have an affinity for programming, and if the thought of writing code all day appeals to you. **Hint:** If you enjoy math and logic puzzles, then you may like computer programming.

Keep in mind that programming languages can come and go quickly, and the language employers are falling over themselves to hire someone to write this year may be dead as a dodo next year. So if you choose this career path, you'll constantly need to be changing and upgrading your skills. Once again, consult with prospective employers and experienced programmers before committing to a particular language or training program.

Donna Gettings: Live here, work there

Donna Gettings is an expert on persuading new employers to agree to a telecommuting arrangement. She has managed to do it twice in one year.

Last year, Gettings was offered a job as community manager for Netsperanto.com, a Web site geared to American children of immigrants. The only problem was that the company was on the West Coast. She was on the East Coast and not interested in relocating. She knew she could do the job effectively as a telecommuter. The hard part would be convincing Netsperanto.

How did she do it? "I did a lot of explaining," she says. "For example, I offered to make duplicate copies of documents — one on my hard drive and one on their network with the proper FTP access." *FTP*, or *File Transfer Protocol*, enables off-site access to computer systems and files.

"I explained to them that a community manager doesn't need to be on site full time. My staff would be totally remote, ergo I'd be using e-mail, messaging, and chat for communication, anyway."

She also was able to point to previous telecommuting experiences. Back in what she calls the "pre-Internet days," Gettings ran her own medical transcription business. "I worked from home, and so did my employees. We used the telephone for communication."

Finally, she appealed to their purse strings. "I reminded them of the lower overhead. And for the cost of a flight out there and housing, I also took a small cut in pay to make it seem more equal." That was okay, she says, because of the cost-of-living difference between Silicon Valley and her Virginia town.

Gettings started with a two-month orientation at Netsperanto's office and then returned home to begin telecommuting to her job. All was going well, until a few months later, when, like many dot-com startups, Netsperanto folded.

As of this writing, Gettings recently had started another telecommuting job as Online Community Director for Sewing.com, a sewing and needlecrafts site. This time, her employer is even further away — in New Zealand.

Job-Hunting for Telecommuters

Where do you search for your new telecommuting job? These days, many people conduct their job searches on the World Wide Web. The Web is a great place to find a job, and it can be a particularly good source for telecommuting positions. But remember, it's far from the only source. Don't forget more traditional sources of jobs — and less traditional ones, too.

Searching the Web

Where can you find telecommuting jobs on the Internet? With so many places to look on the Web, checking them all can actually become a job in itself. Conversely, a growing number of employers these days use Web sites to find new employees.

Most of these job search sites offer a place to post your resume or other description of your work experience. Some sites claim that prospective employers frequently search these databases. Perhaps some employers do check them, but I'm willing to bet that most do not. If you were a harried human resource person looking to fill a slot, would you spend time browsing listings of job hunters and then contact them one by one, only to find that most already have found jobs elsewhere? Or, would you simply post a job listing and let applicants come to you?

Posting your qualifications online is useful, however, at other sites that enable you to forward your information to an employer by clicking a button in response to a job listing. This saves you the trouble of typing (or cutting-and-pasting) the information into e-mail after e-mail. Yet thinking of these sites as job-hunting conveniences rather than relying on them as a sole means of finding a job may be better.

Some of the many sites where you might find an off-site job focus only on telecommuting jobs. Others offer all sorts of job listings. You can tease out the telecommuting jobs by doing searches on the words "telecommute," "telecommuting," "telework," and "remote." You can also pick out jobs that you're well qualified for and ask if the employer in question would consider a telecommuting arrangement.

Finding the listings for telecommuting jobs on a general job site may take more work than it would at a specific telecommuting job site. On the other hand, you'll probably find a wider assortment of jobs at a general site. Here are a few of each to choose from.

Telecommute-only sites:

- ✔ www.tjobs.com (Telecommuting Jobs)
- ✔ www.telework-connection.com
- ✔ www.2020tech.com/ww4f (Will Work for Food)

General sites:

- ✔ www.monster.com
- ✔ www.Workaholics4Hire.com

✔ www.hotjobs.com

✔ www.careers.wsj.com (*The Wall Street Journal*)

In addition to the general-interest job sites, Web sites that are particularly useful to you are certain to be available. For example, if I were searching for writing work right now, I would probably visit the *Inscriptions* Magazine site (www.inscriptionsmagazine.com), the American Society of Journalists and Authors' writer referral site (available to members via www.asja.org), and probably several others.

How do you find Web sites listing your specific type of job? Try any or all of the following:

✔ Ask acquaintances in your field if they know of good Web sites (or good publications) for job-hunting.

✔ Join the professional association(s) in your field and/or visit their Web sites.

✔ Use an Internet search engine (such as Yahoo!, Google or Alta Vista) to search on the word "jobs" and the name of your profession.

✔ Read trade or professional publications in your field, and visit their Web sites.

✔ Ask executives and human resource professionals in your field where they post job listings.

✔ Post the question on online message boards or forums for people in your profession, or in a LISTSERV, which circulates e-mail from each member of the list to all members of the list. This can be especially useful because users of online message boards and LISTSERVs are usually comfortable on the Web and have probably done a lot of exploring.

Besides specific Web sites listing jobs in your profession, local or regional Web sites are likely to list jobs in your geographical area. A good way to find these listings is to visit the Web sites of local newspapers and radio stations, and your town's informational Web site.

When you meet anyone for the first time over the Internet — whether it's a prospective date, a prospective friend, or a prospective employer — a certain amount of healthy suspicion is in order. Until you meet face to face, all you know about this person or this company is the information you can find in their messages and/or Web site, which can easily be faked.

If a company considers hiring you, it's completely appropriate to ask for independent information about that company, assuming it isn't a name readily recognizable. Your interest in learning more about a possible employer only makes you look more professional and less desperate for a job. Articles in reputable publications, annual reports and other financial filings (if it's a public company), and samples of the company's work or products all can help you determine whether a company is legitimate.

Checking out other places for work

In addition to looking through job listings on the Internet, you can also try the strategies described in the following sections for landing a telecommuting job:

Read the classified ads in your local paper

The classified ads of your daily newspaper must never be your *only* strategy when looking for work, but you never know when you might find a telecommuting job listed there.

Read trade or industry publications

Not only will the help-wanted ads sometimes have listings for jobs, you may be able to find clues about who may be hiring telecommuters in your field. If you read an article about a fast expanding company in a densely populated urban area with low unemployment, that's a company with a powerful motivation to begin working with telecommuters. If a company is relocating from one part of the country to another, it is probably losing a lot of staff and may be open to the idea of working with people remotely.

These are just two examples of the sorts of news items that mean a company may be ready to consider hiring telecommuters. If you think you've found a company in this situation, it's worth a call to the human resources department to find out.

Use your personal network

Don't forget to let your friends and acquaintances, especially your business acquaintances, know that you're in the market for a job that allows you to telecommute. As noted in Chapter 1, there's a very good chance you already know someone who's telecommuting. Even if you don't, getting the word out that you're interested in remote work may well lead to some acquaintances who telecommute. Ask the telecommuters you meet for advice about finding remote jobs — and whether their own companies are hiring. Personal contacts often are a more effective way to find a new job.

Look for telecommuter-friendly companies

Where does one find telecommuter-friendly companies? Two places to look are June Langhoff's Web page (www.langhoff.com) and ITAC's home page (www.telecommute.org), which profiles "Stars of Telecommuting." Once you know an employer is open to the idea of telecommuting, you can get in touch to ask about available jobs.

Consider working for the government

Many ask why even consider working for the government. Well, because Federal Government mandates encourage telecommuting work arrangements, and many state and local governments are following the trend. Governments have a vested interested in combating air pollution, traffic congestion, and urban overcrowding. Telecommuting addresses all three problems.

Try job-hunting where you surf

Are there e-zines you like to read, Web pages you like to visit, chat rooms or message boards you especially favor? These Web sites are designed, built, written, monitored, maintained, sold (as advertising space), updated, and hosted by real live people who are getting paid for their work. Depending on your experience and skills, a job may be there in cyberspace for you. And most Web sites have an assortment of work that can be done on a telecommuting basis.

Some Web sites helpfully remind you that they're looking for employees by putting a link to "Jobs" right on the front page. Others have information about jobs in the "Contact Us" or "About Us" sections of the site. If not, you need to go ahead and contact them, asking about available telecommuting jobs. The fact that you're already a loyal user of the site makes you more attractive as potential employee. It also means you'll probably have fun working there.

Turn a traditional job into a telecommuting job

Do you have a former employer who's eager to hire you back? A local company that can really use your services? A job you know is a perfect fit, and that you're sure you can do successfully as a telecommuter?

Don't turn your back on a good job prospect just because your prospective boss assumes you'd be working on site. You won't know for sure that telecommuting is out of the question for this job until you actually ask.

Chapter 3 discusses several strategies for convincing a skeptical boss that telecommuting really works. You can use some of the ideas and information there to sell the idea of telecommuting to a new employer as well. Keep in mind that you have a big advantage over someone trying to change an existing work situation. Because you haven't yet accepted the job, telecommuting, like salary and benefits, can become part of your negotiation.

Turn contract work into a telecommuting job

Many telecommuters I know started out doing contract or freelance work for the organizations that eventually hired them to fill staff positions. This often is an easier transition to make than the one from on-site employee to telecommuter. Why? Consider these factors:

- ✔ You're already working away from the office, so there's no need for a supervisor to learn to trust you to work without supervision.

✔ You're not leaving a conspicuously empty desk behind.

✔ Because you didn't start out as an employee, your telecommuting is less likely to raise the *if-we-let-you-do-it-we-have-to-let-everyone-do-it* objection. Indeed, unless a formal announcement is made, other people in your company may not even be aware of your transition from contract worker to employee.

✔ You've already demonstrated the value of your work so that no one is likely to feel they're wasting money by paying you to stay home.

This isn't the right solution for everyone: Being a contract worker can be difficult, and not all jobs lend themselves to working this way. But it can be an excellent way to get your foot in the door on your way to a telecommuting position.

Using Geography to Land a Telecommuting Job

Earlier in this chapter, I mentioned that geographic disparity within the labor market is one reason for telecommuting's continued growth. You can use this disparity to help find a telecommuting job if you're willing to work for an employer in another location or region.

Accepting such work means you'll have to travel on a regular basis because you'll need to visit your employer's office at least occasionally. So it may not be appropriate for telecommuters who are raising small children or are wanting to stay near home for other reasons. On the other hand, if the job is located in a higher-cost area than where you live, you may be able to negotiate for a higher salary than you can expect locally.

How do you go about finding a job in a different region? The Internet is always a good place to start. Some particularly dense regions have their own job-hunting Web sites, such as San Francisco's Bay Area Jobs (www.bayareajobs.com). You can also visit the Web sites of local newspapers in the area, because many of them put their classified listings up on the Web. Or you can go to your local library and peruse an actual copy of the local paper.

Note that heavily populated urban areas that you're near are probably a good place to look for telecommuting jobs, because you can travel back and forth with relative ease for at least occasional visits that most telecommuting jobs require. For instance, where I live is about 100 miles from New York City and 200 miles from Boston. So those are good places for me to look for a telecommuting job.

Applying from afar

What's the procedure for applying for a distant job? Chances are, your first step will be to send an e-mail along with your résumé. The text of the e-mail serves as your cover letter, and it must be prepared in as professional and well-thought-out manner as a paper cover letter.

Attaching your resume to the cover e-mail as a *rich text file* (.rtf) enables the recipient to open it in virtually any word-processing program. Yet doing so still allows you to use bolds, italics, and other stylistic tools to create an attractive document. However, please note that you must also cut and paste the text of your resume at the end of your e-mail, along with a line or two explaining that the attached version is printer-ready.

Why include the resume in the text of your e-mail? Because the person at the other end may be too busy or too lazy to download an attached file. Furthermore, many cases of viruses being carried in attached files make some people reluctant to download attachments from people they don't know. (Yes, I know a virus can't be carried on a text file. But there are plenty of people out there who believe that the only way to be safe from viruses is never to download anything under any circumstances.)

The long-distance phone interview

If you're being considered for a job in another area, at least some of your interviews will take place over the phone. Of course, this is an opportunity to explain why you're the best person for the position, but just as important, it's a chance to let your prospective employers know just how good you are at communicating when you're not face to face. How can you ace your phone interview? Here are some useful tips:

✔ **Learn good phone skills:** Ideally, people need to be as comfortable speaking to you by telephone as they are when you're in the same room with them. Because your usual body language signals don't transfer by phone, you must use your words and tone of voice to establish a bond, make the other person (or persons) feel comfortable, and communicate the importance of your message.

  Not everyone has good phone skills. How can you tell if you do? If you're comfortable with long, intimate, or complex phone conversations, then chances are you're good at communicating using this medium. If you're not, consider practicing or even getting a coach because phone skills are essential in most telecommuting positions.

✔ **Listen:** Many people in phone conversations don't listen carefully to what the other person is saying. It's particularly easy to make this mistake during a phone interview, especially when you may be too busy planning your next response or statement to pay proper attention to what's being said to you. But listening, and letting the person you're speaking with know you've truly heard what he or she said, is an incredibly good way to create a bond while talking on the phone.

✓ **Radiate competence:** Without your power suit, winning smile, firm handshake, or any of the other things that help show a prospective employer how professional and self-assured you are, you must be doubly sure to convey this message over the phone. That means answering questions with confidence and without hesitation. If you don't know the answer to a question and you don't want to guess, then say you don't know — but don't turn it into something you're ashamed of or must apologize for. Be confident that it's okay, in some instances, not to have all the answers.

✓ **Prepare some questions of your own:** Most interviewers enjoy having job candidates ask a few questions of their own. Some will even ask if you have any. A couple of thoughtful questions can let the interviewer know that you understand the job and have given it serious thought. When in doubt, however, one good fallback is to ask if you'll be working directly with the interviewer (assuming he or she isn't from human resources). Similar titles have different meanings in different companies, so it's always useful to find out exactly what those interactions will be. The answers may surprise you.

The chat interview

In certain cases, you may also be interviewed by online chat. For example, you can expect a chat interview if you've applied for chat hosting, message board monitoring, or other online jobs that require you to communicate well on the Internet.

If you're uncomfortable chatting, spending some time in chat rooms and familiarizing yourself with this medium, before the interview, is worth the effort. Here are some further tips.

You need to type fast

Okay, you're not going to run out to secretarial school to bone up on your typing for your interview, but it is a good idea to spend enough time typing, and especially chatting back and forth in a chat room. That way you'll know you can find the letters on the keyboard quickly enough to maintain a reasonable conversational speed.

Get comfortable with online conventions

A host of special symbols and abbreviations is used in chat rooms (and to a lesser degree, in e-mail). A few may come up in an interview, so you're better off knowing how to recognize the more common ones. Many do's and don'ts also apply to chatting. For example, it's bad form to CAPITALIZE EVERY LETTER. The person you're chatting with will thinking you're SHOUTING! Using all lower-case letters is equally as bad because they're tough to read, especially if you skip the punctuation. For a good guide to *netiquette,* online abbreviations, and *emoticons,* check out www.darkmountain.com/netiquette.

Give short answers

In fact, when training people to be effective online chatters, Bill likes to say, "a short answer is better than a complete one." If you have a lot to say, write a line or two, and end it with a comma, an ellipsis (. . .), or some other indication that more is coming. But if your interviewer has to wait five minutes while you type out a long paragraph — and then pause a few minutes more while reading it, you'll likely cripple the flow of the conversation.

Selling a prospective employer on telecommuting

Applying for a job in another area means addressing the issue of telecommuting early in the process. In many ways, getting a prospective employer to agree to a telecommuting arrangement is similar to getting a current employer to do so. See Chapter 3 for some useful information and statistics that can help you make your case.

Keep in mind that with long-distance telecommuting, you have to travel back and forth to the job. Your new company will have to pay for your transportation expenses and for a place for you to stay while you're in town. That will have an impact on the numbers in your cost-benefit analysis.

Your best strategy is to convince your prospective employer that you're more competent and/or less expensive than anyone they'd be able to hire locally. You may also be willing to agree to a slightly lower salary to make up for some of the travel expenses — especially if the cost of living is lower in your hometown than where the company is located.

Landing the Job

Okay — you've found the perfect telecommuting position for you. Or you've found a job you know you'll enjoy and can do brilliantly as a telecommuter. Now, how can you make sure they hire you and agree to the telecommuting arrangement you have in mind?

Presenting yourself properly is key to job-hunting success, no matter what job you're seeking. Many good books are on the market, covering every aspect of job-hunting from how to write a résumé to what to wear to a job interview, so I won't address all those questions here.

In some ways, however, landing a telecommuting job differs from landing a traditional job, and you need to be aware of the differences, because you can use them to your advantage. The following sections address some areas you need to stress when applying for a telecommuting job.

Show you're a self-starter

Every manager who knows anything at all about telecommuting knows that only self-motivated people will succeed at it. So it's up to you to let a prospective employer know that you'll be the kind of self-motivated, initiative–taking person who can handle working without supervision.

How can you demonstrate this? Begin by taking a careful look at your résumé. Does it describe instances where you took on projects, *owned* them, and carried them to completion? New projects that you initiated or created? Supervisory roles where you were responsible for keeping a team of other people on track? Ideas you came up with for ways to work more effectively?

Of course, your résumé needs to describe these kinds of experiences, no matter what kind of job you're applying for. But it's doubly important when it comes to showing your potential as a telecommuter.

During the interview process as well, make sure that you come across as someone with independence and initiative. Show that you know exactly what you want and where you want to go in this company. Following up a job interview with a short note or e-mail message, thanking the interviewer for the opportunity to meet, and emphasizing your excellent qualifications for the job, always is a good idea. It's an especially good idea if you're looking to telecommute because responding that way also shows initiative.

Demonstrate that you've done this before

When applying for any type of job, nothing impresses a prospective employer as much as previous experience. So it makes sense that telecommuters report that showing that they've worked independently in the past is a big help when trying to land a telecommuting job.

About a year before he started his current job, my husband Bill was given a promotion that presented us with a quandary. The new job was located at the parent company's office about 150 miles from Williamstown, Massachusetts, where he'd been living and working. Williamstown is the kind of rural community we enjoy; Waltham, where the new job was located, is a suburb of Boston. On top of that, we'd purchased a house only two months before.

The house is what turned the tide. Bill's new managers took pity on us, and they worked out an arrangement that enabled Bill to work from home on Mondays and Fridays, making the three-hour drive across Massachusetts early Tuesday morning and returning late Thursday night.

Neither one of us was thrilled with this arrangement. But it saved us from having to pull up stakes from where we'd just settled in. Then, when the opportunity for the California job arose, Bill pointed to those Mondays and Fridays (not to mention lots of weekends!) to demonstrate that he knew how to work effectively in a home office. Now, he plans never to take a non-telecommuting job again. "I shouldn't have to; I've proved I can do it," he says.

You don't have to have a telecommuting job under your belt to prove you can do another one. But you do need to think about what accomplishments in your past demonstrate your ability to work remotely. Were you occasionally allowed to work from home on specific projects on your last job? Did you learn to coordinate your work effectively with people in other locations? What about volunteer or other outside activities? Find ways to stress work that you did on a remote basis.

A Warning about Scams

Just yesterday, I opened my e-mail and read the following:

> "How would you like to create a six-figure income every four months? Create and amass PERSONAL WEALTH, multiply it and protect it? Realize a three to six times greater return on YOUR MONEY?"

Does that kind of thing sound familiar? It does if you surf the Web, receive e-mail, or even read notices tacked to telephone poles.

The widespread interest in telecommuting is proof that large numbers of people genuinely are interested in working at home. Some are housebound by illness or family responsibilities, and desperate for ways to make money. Others just like the idea of earning without leaving the house. Either way, it's a ripe market for the dishonest.

What do scam artists want? Usually — but not always — your money. Somewhere along the line you'll be asked to fork over some dough for a training book or video, business secret, secret recipe, sales leads that will help you attain great wealth, or products that you can turn around and sell at amazing profits.

Besides money, these firms may also be collecting useful information about you. If you call a phone number, for instance, the machine at the other end may keep a record of your phone number. Eventually they can compile a list of callers' numbers that are legitimate and in use, belonging to people who may be interested in loans, financial services, or other such products. Companies that want to telemarket to you will pay considerable amounts money for these lists, so the original advertiser makes money regardless of whether you send any in.

Worse yet, I've seen one site that tells visitors (anyone who browses to the page) that they have already been hired and requests that they send in W-2 forms immediately. What could that *employer* possibly want with your W-2s? I don't know, but I can hazard a guess: Anyone who fills out a W-2 form has to include his or her social security number. Social security numbers are useful to criminals who commit identity theft by using legitimate social security numbers to gain access to others' accounts, create their own accounts or debts, and otherwise hide what they're doing while pretending to be you.

Here are some things to remember when reviewing job or business opportunity offers:

- Paying up front for business secrets, books, videos, job application fees, or anything else that will supposedly help you make money is never a good idea. If you want a book about, say, how to cash in on the real estate market, you can find one from a legitimate publisher at regular or online bookstores. And it probably will cost you less.

- Multilevel marketing plans, in which you buy products and educational materials from one person to turn around and sell to someone else, have disappointing results for most participants. Very few succeed in making money — usually by working extremely hard — and most don't make enough to earn a living at it.

- Beware of any proposal that promises you can make money with little or no effort. Making money is never effortless. So they have lied to you once already.

Part II
Creating Your Home Office

The 5th Wave — By Rich Tennant

"The new technology has really helped me get organized. I keep my project reports under the PC, budgets under my laptop and memos under my pager."

In this part . . .

You've landed a new telecommuting job, or convinced your boss to give telecommuting a try. You're ready to enter the new world of working from home. But getting started can be confusing. Should you give up your guestroom? Work on your dining table? What about insurance? Taxes? OSHA regulations?

Use this part to help you handle some of the logistics, and choose the right equipment, for your new away-from-the-office office.

Chapter 5

Home, Sweet Office

***

In This Chapter

▶ Defining a good home office space

▶ Choosing the right spot for you

▶ Putting your home office outside the home

▶ Pros and cons of telework (or *hoteling*) centers

▶ Taking the home office tax deduction

***

Working at home, even if it is only one day a week, represents a major change from working in an office. Now you, and you alone, are responsible for creating a work environment that helps you work productively, comfortably, safely, and happily.

Before you start working at home, take some time to think about exactly where and how your home office needs to be set up, and what will make it truly the best workspace for you. Having the right office space can make working at home a pleasure.

What Makes a Good Home Office Space?

In the modern world, you can work pretty much anywhere. One manager I know reports finding a colleague of hers telecommuting from a local water park: While the kids ride the rides, Dad is on the sidelines in the shade, hard at work. The brilliantly successful Harry Potter books were written, in part, at an inexpensive café where the author nursed a single cup of coffee for hours. As for me, I'm sitting in a diner right now, writing these words over a dinner of roast lamb and cauliflower.

Just because office work is more easily transportable than it has been at any time in history doesn't mean that you don't need a place of your own when you're at work. You do. But that need has as much to do with mood and motivation, psychic comfort and feelings of self-worth, and privacy and motivation, as it does with the actual necessities of working at home.

The Door/No Door Controversy

Conventional wisdom on setting up a home office is simple: If at all possible, you must have a room with a door that you can close. Lights will be brighter, the sky will be bluer, and everything will be just a little bit better if you have an office that you can actually go inside and shut the door.

I was all set to pass along this bit of wisdom because I've found it to be especially true for me. But then I put the question of the ideal home office to my crew of telecommuter advisors, and their answers surprised me. It turns out that an office with a door you can close is just right for some people but all wrong for others. Here are some of their comments:

"I set up my office in the corner of the living room with a view of the front yard so that I could keep tabs on what was happening outside as well as know when the kids were home," reports Donna Gettings, community manager for OneMADE.com. (See Chapter 4 for more on Gettings.)

"We have a long driveway, so I am always able to tell when people are coming and can prepare to greet them at the door. That way, I'm there for the kids and for any visitors or delivery people who may need a response from me. It also allows me to screen visitors the way one screens calls with an answering machine.

"My workspace is three-sided so that I am working in sort of a wedge environment. My printers are to the right of me and my reference books to the left of me in the triangle. In front of me are the desk and the materials I need on an immediate basis. I have a chair that swivels, so I can reach all items in short order. I end up not taking up a lot of space in the room.

"For my family, that leaves a long side of the *triangle* where I am open to their involvement if they so desire. There is room behind me for people to mingle, congregate, or just plain play on the floor, as when my children were young."

I asked Gettings if she thought it would be better to have an office in a separate room with a closing door. "I don't think it's better to be in a separate room at all," she answered. "I worked at home with small children and I much prefer being available to them whenever possible. I've never needed isolation to get work done."

Meanwhile, a similar arrangement turned into a big problem for Denise Boggs, who telecommutes as foster home coordinator for Citizens for Animal Protection in Houston. Her job is to find temporary homes for homeless animals.

Because Boggs' husband also telecommutes and was working upstairs in their home, she set up her office downstairs in the main living room/kitchen area. "It didn't work for a number of reasons, mostly relating to kids and traffic," she says. "I'd find myself picking up while on the phone or worrying about when I'd get to the dishes."

As a result, she's now moving her office to a small upstairs bedroom. "For me, it's important mentally," she explains. "If your work station is in the main area of your house, you can't shut the door and leave it behind. I've heard people say they need to keep their work life and home life separated. I now agree. There is something about turning off the light and shutting the door that says, 'I'm finished for today.'"

Several other telecommuters I consulted stressed how important it is to have offices separate from the rest of their homes to avoid disruptive noise and keep their work clutter out of their living space, as well as to help them concentrate.

I myself have lived in four different places during the past several years, and have had a total of six home offices. One was in a corner of my living room, and even though I lived alone at the time, I hated having it there. One was a balcony loft overlooking a bedroom in a New York City apartment. Although that office was open on one side, I made it feel more private by hanging up Japanese bamboo rolling shades that I lowered when I wanted to be left alone.

My favorite of them all was on the top floor of a narrow 200-year-old house we lived in in Massachusetts. It was small, but had windows on three sides, including one that looked out over the street so I could see if anyone was coming to the door. Not only did it have a door that I could close, it was so distant from the rest of the house that if my husband Bill needed to talk to me, he'd usually have to use the telephone.

Unfortunately, that office was in the wrong house in the wrong town for us. The office that I'm writing this in right now is also on the second floor and has a door that I can close, but only half of the room is my office. The other half is our guestroom. Not that we have guests all that often. In fact, it's relatively rare. But there's something I really miss about knowing that my office is completely mine, my own domain, where no one can intrude without my express permission.

The irony in all this is that I did have an office that was mine alone, and I gave it away several years ago. When Bill and I first moved in together, he used half the upstairs guestroom as his home office, and I used a small room off the living room as my office.

The problem was that I'd often be working in there while Bill (and occasionally his friends) used the living room for, well, living. The sound of the TV and their conversations filtering through my door annoyed me and disturbed my concentration. The fact that he could talk to me whenever he liked by raising his voice only slightly made me crazy. Eventually, I insisted on a trade.

It turns out that quiet and being at once removed from the other goings-on in my household are the more important elements of a home office for me. On the other hand, Bill really likes having my old office. He enjoys being able to call out to me easily if I'm in the living room while he's at his desk. And, far from disturbing him, he likes being able to hear the TV, and often leaves it turned on while he's working. If I want to work too, I go upstairs . . . and close the door.

Picking the Right Place for Your Home Office

Where is the best place for your own home office? According to ITAC's Telework America survey, an extra bedroom (such as my office) is by far the more popular choice, with a living room office coming in second.

But these are only two of the many possibilities. For instance, many of today's more successful high-tech companies were started in garages (although I have to say that sounds more feasible in California than here in the frozen Northeast). Some telecommuters I know work successfully on a dining or kitchen table — though I don't think even they'd recommend it as a long-term solution.

The best way to choose a home office is to be as open-minded as you can, consider all the available choices, and figure out what works best for you.

What space do you have available?

You can't put your office in a spare bedroom if you don't have a spare bedroom to begin with. If your home is a studio apartment, your choices of where to put an office in it are obviously limited.

Available space is the single biggest factor in deciding where to put your home office. But remember that you may have more of it than you think. Sometimes, we let our own assumptions about how we *must* use our living space limit our options — especially if we've lived in the same place for a while and we're accustomed to things being where they are.

For example, you may assume that the reason I once had my home office in the living room is because no other room was available. At the time, I certainly felt I had no other choice. But looking back, I remember an interesting fact: That house, too, had a guestroom that I easily could've used as an office.

At the time, I had just relocated from the city where I grew up, to a small country town, 100 miles away. I was feeling insecure in my new surroundings and determined to hang onto my city friendships whatever way I could. In my mind, that meant providing a perfectly inviting, warm, and cozy guestroom, free from the clutter my work invariably produces. All I can say in my own defense is that I didn't realize until I tried it how much I disliked having a living room office.

Are any assumptions preventing you from considering perfectly usable workspace? Does your home have a formal dining room? If so, how often do you use it? Would you consider buying a folding dining table (believe it or not, such things exist and some are actually nice) to use in your living room or other public space for those occasions when you entertain? Maybe your occasionally-used dining room could turn into a perfect home office.

Here are some other ideas for expanding available space:

- ✔ **Reclaim *public* space.** An unused corner of a hallway, stairway landing, or utility room may contain enough space to be transformed into a small office. Screens or shades can give you the privacy you need to work.

- ✔ **Consider storage areas.** Granted, a storage area is no one's idea of the pleasantest possible place to spend one's working hours. But if you're someone like me who strongly prefers a separate, private area in which to do your job, a storage area may be the best available solution. Some walk-in closets, for instance, are large enough to house a chair, desk, and file cabinet — or you can keep the file cabinet right outside your office door. (I used a walk-in closet as a workspace while I was in college. I painted it sky blue and quite enjoyed working in it, but then I like working in small spaces.) A garage, if properly weatherproofed, or a utility room can also house an office, if necessary.

- ✔ **Rebuild or reshape your home.** Obviously, you don't want to consider this option until you've been telecommuting for several months — long enough to be sure that telecommuting fits your personality and your job requirements. But once you're sure that telecommuting really is for you, why not invest in creating a home office that you'll actually enjoy working in? An attic, for instance, can be converted into an office by insulating it and finishing the walls. A porch can be converted into a sunny office with plenty of windows. I've recently started thinking that a short wall could easily divide my office and the guestroom, making two smaller rooms that would be more useful than the one large one is now.

- ✔ **Move.** Moving is, of course, a drastic solution and, like remodeling, not one to consider until you're sure you'll be telecommuting in the long term. With today's soaring real-estate prices, depending where you live, relocating to larger quarters may not be feasible.

But keep this in mind: The ITAC survey shows people who work at home have homes that are an average 500 square feet bigger than those who don't. What that means to me is that people with home offices need larger homes to fit them in. So, if working at home is definitely part of your future, and your home isn't the right size to accommodate that comfortably, finding one that is may be a good idea.

What will you put in your office?

Just about every office needs a desk, chair, computer (with monitor and printer), phone, file cabinet, lamp (or proper ceiling light), and shelves or drawers for holding office supplies. Depending what you do, you may need extra items. For example, I also have a scanner and copier, paper cutter, reference books, a small chest of drawers (for storing issues of magazines where my work has appeared and research materials for upcoming books), several sealed cardboard boxes (more old issues), and several bookshelves.

My husband Bill, who works on the Internet all day, has to have several computers set up in his office, and usually has two or three running at once. He also keeps a variety of tools and computer components around because he frequently disassembles the computers to repair, upgrade, or reconfigure them. Another friend of ours, who is a photographer and graphic artist, has to have a drawing table and a light box in her office. One aunt of mine, who practiced law out of a home office, needed an entire wall of books to do her job.

Ask yourself: What will you need in your own home office? The answers help dictate exactly how much and what kind of space is appropriate for your workplace. Keep in mind, though, that not everything you need for your office necessarily has to be in your office. If you need paper only once in a while to refill a printer tray, you probably can store it on a shelf in a bedroom across the hall. The same goes for books and reference materials that you only need once in a while.

Do you spread out materials when you're working?

Bill, who maintains my computer as well as his own, sometimes complains that my desk is an avalanche waiting to happen. He's right, but then I've never seen a writer's office that wasn't overflowing with papers. Because my projects frequently take several weeks, or even months, to complete, I sometimes have to have the same papers spread out for long periods of time. By its nature, writing is a paper-intensive job, even in this computerized age. I once saw a picture of Salman Rushdie in his office, and it was just as piled up with papers as mine is, which made me feel much better about the whole thing.

If you too find you can't get your work done without a pile of papers all around, the placement of your home office needs to take this into account. You may not want a desk covered with papers for all to see in your living room, or you may want to be sure no one socializing in your work area sets a wet glass on top of an important document.

Does your job raise security or privacy concerns?

If the kind of work you do raises concerns about security or privacy, putting your home workspace in a separate room may not merely be just a good idea, but it may be a legal imperative. Sensitive materials can include medical or personnel information, unpublished software, details of new products or marketing campaigns, and many other items. If you're in doubt, ask your boss.

How accessible do you need to be while working?

If you like watching your children play while you're working and you don't mind the occasional interruption, then a workspace in a living room, den, or bedroom may be just right. On the other hand, if you need privacy and isolation to concentrate on what you're doing, such arrangements can be a big problem.

You also need to decide how accessible you need to be for delivery people and others who come to your front door. If you'll be receiving overnight deliveries or messenger packages, and especially if you're the only one home, you must make sure you can hear the doorbell and get to the door in time to accept important deliveries. An office with a view of the front door area is especially handy because you can see who's coming before they arrive.

Likewise, keep in mind that having your office in an accessible, family location also increases the chance that papers and other material in and around your desk will be disturbed.

How much quiet do you need while working?

An office in a shared space may mean noise during your workday. Depending on who you are and what you do, this lack of quiet time may be a major annoyance, perfectly acceptable, or your actual preference. My husband Bill, for instance, grew up in a large, boisterous Irish-American family, and seems to genuinely appreciate background noise while he's working.

If you need quiet to concentrate on your work, take that need into account when selecting your office space. A room above a noisy street may not be the best idea. The middle of the living room may not be, either.

Even if noise doesn't bother you, it can be a big problem if you spend a lot of your work time on the phone. Crying or screaming children, lawnmowers buzzing, or trucks roaring by can distract you and the person at the other end of the line.

Worse, if you're dealing with customers or others outside your company who may not know they're talking to someone at home, you can sound unprofessional. Problems with background noise in home offices can be tricky, and you need to give it some thought before choosing your office location.

What about pets?

If you have a pet, and you don't close the door to your office, he or she is likely going to follow you in there. There's something about a human sitting still at a desk for several hours that cats and dogs seem to find appealing. My little orange cat, Teenie, is perched on my knee as I write this.

"I love having my cats and dog with me while I'm working," Denise Boggs notes. "When I'm really stressed about something, I can pet them and look at things from their perspective, and it helps me get a grip on reality. I also talk to them about situations (yes, I'm crazy), which helps me work things out orally." Boggs says talking things over with her listening pets helps solidify her ideas before she tries them out on humans. "I used to knock things around with co-workers, if I was trying to work out a problem," she notes. "I still go to co-workers after consulting with the animals, only now I have cleared a bunch of the junk out of the way before pitching my idea."

If you love your pets, having them around while you're working can be one of the great pleasures of working at home. But for those of us who don't have animal-related jobs, they can be a real problem when you're talking on the phone. You may find yourself stretching your phone cord to its maximum length with one hand while awkwardly flinging a cat out of the office door with your other hand. If it sounds like I'm speaking from experience here, you're right.

I find that being able to shut our cats out when necessary is one advantage of having an office with a door. If you locate your office in the living room, you may have to consider locking the pets up someplace else or face the fact that the person on the other end of the phone line may hear an occasional bark or meow while you're talking.

Will your schedule mesh with the rest of your household?

Remember the smaller office I traded for half of the guestroom? I might have been able to stay there if I hadn't so frequently found myself working in the evenings while my husband was relaxing. So while planning your home office location, be sure to think about how your schedule is likely to coordinate with others' in your household.

Telecommuters tend to work on flextime, putting in more hours than they would at the office but on a much less orthodox schedule. They may start work at 6 a.m. or 10 a.m., take a break in the afternoon to run errands or work out before the stores or gym get crowded, and then work a few hours in the evening or even late at night.

Considering how your work times will mix with your family's activities is important when picking the place for your home office. Don't put your office in the den, for instance, if it means you'll be trying to work in the evenings while your family plays games or watches TV. Likewise, if you're likely to work into the night, putting your office in the bedroom may be a bad idea. You could wind up keeping your spouse awake.

What other needs and preferences should you consider?

You're going to spend many long hours in your home office. So it needs to be a place that not only fits your professional requirements but also your personal ones. If you're someone who needs plenty of daylight to feel energized, try to find an office space with plenty of windows. If you tend to be claustrophobic, don't pick a space that's too confined. If you find the refrigerator an irresistible temptation, don't locate your office next door to the kitchen. If you loathe the thought of climbing stairs, don't put your office on the third floor.

Furthermore, if you (like me) tend to suffer from insomnia, it's a bad idea to put your office in your bedroom. Sleep experts say the bedroom must be used only as a bedroom. In particular, bringing the stressors of your job into your sleeping area can make your insomnia worse. If you absolutely cannot reasonably locate your home office anywhere else, you can at least use a screen, curtain, room divider, or other device to create the effect of two separate rooms.

When the Best Place for a Home Office Isn't Home

You've looked all around, considered every corner of your home, and you just can't find a place that works as a home office. Or else you just don't have enough room. Yet, you still really want to try telecommuting. What should you do?

Don't make the mistake of trying to squeeze yourself into an inadequate or inappropriate workspace. I explained earlier in this chapter that with modern equipment, it's possible to work anywhere. It's a little like camping: Modern camping equipment makes it possible to sleep outdoors, safe from the elements in almost any weather. But that doesn't mean you must do it every night.

Before approving your telecommuting plans, a responsible employer will probably want some assurance that you have an adequate and safe workspace when you're away from the office. If you can't find it inside your home, your best move may be to look outside of it.

In our case, the reason was bandwidth. Because Bill works for an Internet company, he needs to be connected to the Internet all day long. He uses it not only for e-mail and Web browsing but also for applications like chat, moderated chat, and file transfer protocol (FTP). He often has to upload and download large files.

Being able to do these things effectively requires a high-speed Internet connection. (To find out more about the various types of Internet connections available, see Chapter 7.) At least for the moment, our little town just doesn't have it. For weeks, we worried about what to do. Finally, Bill rented a small office in nearby Kingston, New York, where high-speed access already is available.

Renting an office space at first may seem like an expensive solution, but because you don't really need much space in the first place and it doesn't have to be a public place of business, it may be more affordable than you think. In addition, you can try the following:

- **Ask your friends and neighbors if they have any spare spaces.** You probably can rent a friend's spare bedroom for little or nothing. Or you may be able to barter for the space, offering home-cooked meals, space in your garage, or anything else you may have to offer.

- **Look for "room (or space) for rent" ads.** After all, you don't really need an office — a room is probably enough. The cost of renting one room within someone's house is usually quite minimal. When negotiating such a deal, make sure you know ahead of time whether you're also expected to help pay utility expenses.

✔ **Split the cost with another telecommuter.** The number of people who work from home is growing exponentially. Real-estate prices are growing just as quickly. Put these two facts together, and it seems likely that other people in your community will need a place to work and can't fit one into their homes. By networking among your friends and colleagues, or even putting an ad in the local paper (or posting one in a neighborhood business), you have a better chance of finding someone else who's willing to share the cost of renting a small office space. Some telecommuters find this a particularly good arrangement because having someone else working nearby relieves some of the isolation of working away from the office without creating a nonstop distraction.

✔ **Find a local business with too much space.** A local office with empty desks may be happy to rent one of them to you to help cover expenses. This can save you from having to worry about proper office furniture and lighting. You may even be able to use their voicemail system. However, if you try this, be ready to address security and confidentiality concerns with the host business as well as your own employer.

Telework Centers

Employees have, at most, two choices. Either they work at their company's office, or at an office of their own, usually at home. But some employees have a third alternative: telework or hoteling centers.

Telework centers are offices away from the main office that offer visiting employees a desk, computer, Internet connection, and phone for one or several days at a time. At the end of the visit, employees leave, taking all their materials with them. If they return, they'll likely be given a different spot next time. Because it's the workplace equivalent of checking in and out of a hotel, these facilities are sometimes called *hoteling centers.*

Many large companies, including Charles Schwab & Co., IBM, and Lockheed Martin, operate their own telework centers. But so do community colleges, consultancies, and many others, including the federal government. Many of these centers are available for rent by local employers for use by their telecommuting employees.

Why would an employer rent remote offices for its employees when it already has perfectly good offices available? In some cases, it makes sense for specific employees' jobs. Some sales representatives, for example, spend so much time on the road that there's little point in giving them a permanent office that they'd visit only once or twice a month, anyway. For large companies with many employees, it's much more logical to offer telework centers in a variety of locations, where traveling workers can hang their hats for as long as they're in the area.

Two other big motivators for using telework centers are urban sprawl and overcrowding. Most employers have enough common sense to know that an employee who has just spent two hours in traffic on his or her way to work — and has the same trip to look forward to on the way home — is probably not at peak efficiency while in the office. A telework center that's only 15 minutes away may be a better alternative for both parties, at least for part of the work week.

If your company offers telework centers, don't assume that working there is your only telecommuting choice. You may still be able to use a home office, if you prefer, on days when you don't go to your regular office. In fact, you may be able to use all three.

Is working in a telework center better than working at home? It offers some advantages and disadvantages. Here are a few of each:

Advantages:

- Contact with colleagues.

- Support staff, such as a receptionist, is usually available.

- Your boss and co-workers are less likely to think you're goofing off.

- Escape from home-based distractions like dirty dishes and visiting neighbors.

Disadvantages:

- No working in your pajamas.

- You still have a commute, although it's a shorter one.

- If circumstances (such as a sick child or a snowstorm) keep you home, it will be harder to do your work there without a home office.

- Security (of your laptop and other belongings) can be a concern in telework centers.

The Home Office Tax Deduction

Will having a home office help you save on taxes? Possibly. But you have to clear a number of legal hurdles before you can take the deduction, and many telecommuter home offices don't qualify. Still, it's worth noting that tax laws change every year, and recent changes (in 1999) made the home office deduction a little easier for more people to use.

You will, of course, have to itemize your deductions if you want to take the home office deduction. I must add here that because I find taxes to be an incredibly complicated and confusing matter, I would never consider filing mine without the help of a qualified accountant, and I urge you to do the same. Or at least consult an accountant if you're interested in finding out how the home office deduction can work for you.

Having given this disclaimer, here are some basic guidelines that can help you determine whether the home office can make a difference to you. This information comes courtesy of Fred Grant, a CPA working on Intuit Inc.'s *TurboTax* program.

Do you qualify?

Even with recent changes, qualifying for the home office tax deduction isn't easy. Most people bring work home from time to time. So, from the IRS's point of view, it's important to avoid opening floodgates that would enable every taxpayer who ever reads a report on the living room sofa to deduct large portions of his or her household expenses.

For that reason, the IRS has set the bar quite high for home offices. Unfortunately, most telecommuters' home offices don't qualify. To find out if yours is the exception, consider how you'd answer the following questions.

Is your home office ever used as anything else?

Your home office does not necessarily have to be in a room of its own to qualify. But it must have space of its own, clearly separate from the rest of your home. And it must never be used for anything except your work. This means that if your kids do their homework on your computer, or your spouse uses it to e-mail photos to your cousins, or you like to spread out sewing patterns on your desk after hours, your home office doesn't qualify — at least not if the IRS finds out. And the IRS takes this rule seriously. They once disallowed a home office because they spotted a dog's bowl in a photograph the taxpayers had brought in.

If you rent a space outside your home as an office (and your employer doesn't pay for it), it probably will be easier to simply deduct that expense. But the same warning applies: The rented space must be used only as a workplace.

How much time do you spend there?

Your home office must be your *principal place of business*. This is the requirement that presents problems for most telecommuters. Defining a principle place is subject to some interpretation, but I'd say right off the bat that if you're telecommuting less than half time (that is, less than three days a week, or two weeks a month if you're a long-distance telecommuter), you're probably out of luck.

One exception is if you also have a home-based business that you perform exclusively out of your home office. For example, even though she goes to Columbus once a week at most, Miriam Carey may not be able to deduct her home office in Cleveland three hours away. Except that, in addition to being *Ohio* magazine's travel editor, she's also a freelance writer with independent income from work she does solely in her office, and — this is important — the money she makes more than covers the expenses she deducts.

Why are you telecommuting?

The IRS requires that you telecommute "for the convenience" of your employer, and not your own. That is, telecommuting must actually be a requirement of your job, or something your employer imposed on you.

Fortunately, this convenience issue doesn't usually come up, except during an audit. If you're audited, you'll want a statement from your employer confirming that you're working at home at their convenience. Even so, it's the IRS agent's call, and he or she can judge, based on the nature of your job and your circumstances in general, whether your office passes the convenience test.

Is it worth it?

By now, you may be too discouraged to even consider trying the home office deduction. But if you believe your office qualifies, you now must determine whether the home office tax deduction saves you enough on taxes to make it worthwhile. It's quite possible that although you can qualify for the home office deduction, taking it is a bad deal.

Are you planning to sell?

The downside to the home office tax deduction is depreciation. If you use the home office deduction, you'll have to take depreciation on the value of your home and that depreciation will be recaptured, or taxed, when you sell.

This very thing happened to me. For years, I operated as a freelance writer out of an apartment that I owned in New York City, taking the home office deduction every year. When I moved to the country, I didn't immediately sell the apartment, renting it out to cover the mortgage instead. I thought I might someday want to come back, and I knew a nice apartment in Manhattan would be difficult to find.

Two years ago, I finally did decide to sell, having come to the conclusion that my husband and I would never want to live in New York City, and that I needed to take advantage of the real estate boom. Because I'd rented the apartment out in the interim, I had to pay capital gains taxes on my profits. And my profits were bigger than I might've expected: Depreciation shaved more than $30,000 off the purchase value of my home — giving me $30,000 more to pay taxes on.

Depending on your plans, taking the home office deduction and having to take depreciation may not be worthwhile.

Furthermore, keep in mind that if you define part of your home as a business area to take the home office deduction, you may lose the personal residence exclusion for capital gains tax purposes when you sell. Normally speaking, if you sell a piece of real estate (or pretty much anything else) for more than you paid for it, that profit is considered a capital gain, and you have to pay income tax on it. The personal residence exclusion, however, says you don't have to pay this tax when selling a home where you've lived for at least two years. However, if you take a home office tax deduction, you're claiming that percentage of your home is not where you live, but where you work. Consequently, it's an exclusion to the exclusion, and you do have to pay capital gains tax on that percentage of your home.

Do you have a mortgage?

Of course, all these capital gains issues don't come into play if you rent rather than own your home. However, if you do own your home and have a mortgage, the home office deduction may not be worthwhile for yet another reason. Your largest living expense is almost certainly mortgage payments that are made up mostly of mortgage interest, which is deductible, anyway.

How much of your home is your office?

If you take the home office deduction, you can deduct all the expenses that relate directly to your work (such as computer equipment you buy). You can deduct the cost of a phone line if it's used only for work, and you can deduct work-related long-distance expenses. You can also deduct costs for repairs or improvements made specifically to your office.

Many of your other household expenses are also deductible, but only in proportion to your actual office space. That is, if your office occupies 10 percent of the space in your home, 10 percent of the following costs are deductible:

- ✔ Rent or mortgage payments
- ✔ Common charges, maintenance, or homeowner's association fees
- ✔ Utilities (but probably not cable)
- ✔ Snow removal
- ✔ Cleaning and repair
- ✔ Insurance

Several others probably are deductible, depending on where you live. Basically, anything you need to keep your home habitable probably qualifies.

Okay, so how do you figure the proportion of your office to your home? Keep in mind that your office space must be used only as your workplace, otherwise this whole thing is a no-go. Measure the room or space, and then compare its square footage to the total square footage of living space in your home. The resulting number tells you what percentage of your home is office space, and what percentage of household expenses you can deduct.

Too little is too little

Just in case I haven't yet discouraged enough on this subject, I have one more bit of bad news. If your home office tax deduction is too small, you may not be allowed to take it at all.

If you have a business of your own that you conduct out of your home office, then your home office expenses can be deducted from your earnings to reduce the net profit on which you need to pay taxes. Although that may sound good, as a telecommuting employee, your home office expenses usually are claimed as *miscellaneous itemized deductions* — and an amount equal to 2 percent of your adjusted gross income for the year is not deductible. In other words, if your home office deduction seems too small of an amount to bother with, chances are the IRS will think it is, too.

Chapter 6

Feeling at Home in Your Home Office

. . . .

In This Chapter

▶ Creating a home office where you can feel at home

▶ Using feng shui to help create a better home office

▶ Staying healthy in your home office

▶ Keeping your home office secure

. . . .

You've considered all your options, decided a home office is the right place for you, and you've already found a good spot for it. Now, take some time to make it your own, a place where you feel comfortable and happy — a place that feels like it's *yours*. You'll be spending a great deal of your time there, so you'll want to make that time as pleasant as possible.

Creating an Office that Feels Like You

Here are some things you'd find if you visited my home office:

✔ A dried bouquet from my wedding

✔ An incense burner

✔ All my books

✔ Several plants, including a philodendron my mother gave me to celebrate a new job in 1984, which is now named "killer" because it has now grown to enormous proportions

✔ A penny whistle (I occasionally play a tune at my desk when there's no one around to overhear.)

Other home offices I've seen have contained a wood stove, a large poster of Oscar Wilde, chocolates, a doll collection, and a toy basketball set. You get the idea.

Several telecommuters have told me that having a good stereo system in their offices makes the workday much more enjoyable. I agree that music can definitely make work more fun. Instrumental African, Celtic, or New Age music appeals to me more while I'm writing.

I used to keep a boombox in my office, but these days I tend to use the computer itself as a music system. When I'm online, I can listen to various online radio stations. (I like NetRadio, which has choices of about every kind of music you can imagine, but there are many others.) Offline, I can listen to my CD collection, most of which I've stored digitally on my computer's hard drive, using free software called *RealJukebox*. Many other music-recording software choices are available.

Adding the music that you like is just one way to make your office more enjoyable. "I'd suggest painting the room a cheerful color," says Denise Boggs of Citizens for Animal Protection. "I painted mine a bright yellow. It looks like a happy place to be working. Those library-type muted earth tones, typical of home offices, made me depressed and groggy. I chose light colored furniture, too."

The point is that this is *your* office. It should *feel* like you. And anything that makes you feel happy to be there is probably a good idea.

Feng Shui

Ever notice how some places just have a better feel than others? It may not be anything you can put your finger on, like décor or lighting — they're just more welcoming somehow. The reason may have something to do with feng shui.

Feng shui is the ancient Chinese art of arranging things — from villages to office furniture to small objects — for the best energy flow. Feng shui works on a principle of directing one's *chi* (sometimes spelled "qi"), which means energy or life force. If this sounds like superstition, keep in mind that acupuncture, another Chinese practice that has proved its effectiveness to Western medicine, also is based on redirecting chi.

Several of the telecommuters I know have had feng shui consultants come to their home offices to advise them on where to place their furniture and how to decorate.

"I used to pack my bookshelves tight, sometimes with two rows, one in back and one in front," reports Christine Doane-Benton, a public relations specialist who telecommuted successfully as a magazine software reviewer. At the time, she had a feng shui consultant review her entire home, including her home office.

"She removed those book, and filled only two-thirds or less of every shelf, either leaving the leftover space open or placing a decorative object in that space," Doane-Benton recalls. "As she did this, my entire office area started to feel lighter and less oppressive." (For more on her office, see the sidebar titled, "Christine Doane-Benton: An office with a view," later in this chapter.)

"When you're in a place that you absolutely love, that's positive chi, and when you're in a place that makes you feel awful, that's negative chi. Most people can recognize the difference," explains Carol Olmstead, FSIA, a certified feng shui practitioner in Bethesda, Maryland.

"Feng shui literally means 'wind and water,'" she continues. "I tell people to try to imagine a beautiful spring day when you're out by a lake, and a breeze is blowing. That usually gives them a good feeling."

To try and create that feeling in your home office, she recommends following some simple principles.

- **Don't sit with your back to the door.** "That is the most vulnerable position," she says. "The feeling is that people could sneak up on you. You should be facing the door so that you can see people coming and feel their energy."

  Ideally, she adds, the desk should be in the far left-hand corner of the office, in relation to the door, and the office should be in the far left-hand corner of the house in relation to the front door. Why? "Feng shui uses an octagon-shaped chart to map the areas of a home, room, or office. And typically the far left corner is the wealth and power area."

- **Control the clutter.** "Clutter represents imbalanced energy, which is blocked energy," she says. "So what I recommend is to find the right kind of storage options for whatever you've got, whether it's wicker, wood, or metal."

  If you have papers spread out all over your office for a project you're currently engaged in, that's energy, she adds, and it can be good. But the moment you're finished working on the project, it becomes clutter. "It slows you down," she says.

- **Fix or replace broken items.** "They represent disregard for your work," she says. It's tempting, she adds, to use old hand-me-down furniture and otherwise skimp on decorating, because no one but you is likely to see your office. But that's a big mistake. "If you have something broken in your office, remove, repair, or replace it — and do it immediately."

- **Bring in the natural world.** "Feng shui is all about connecting you to the outside world and balancing your inner and outer worlds," Olmstead says. "You want to bring that in any way you can. One way is full-spectrum light bulbs (which simulate natural light). Or, if you lack windows, you can have pictures of the outside world on your wall. Pictures of water are especially good because water represents flow and abundance into your work."

She also recommends putting plants in your office — either real ones, or, if you're brown-thumbed, silk ones. "I don't recommend dried ones because they're dead energy," she adds. "But if you absolutely have to have dried ones, then keep them clean (a blow dryer is useful for this) and try to change them with the seasons."

✔ **Have a little bit of red somewhere.** Feng shui is based on five elements. The color *red* and the triangle shape represent the element fire. "Fire adds some passion and power to your life," she says. That's important for your business."

You can find out a lot more about feng shui by reading *Feng Shui For Dummies,* by feng shui expert David Daniel Kennedy.

Telecommuting and Safety

Your home may seem like the safest place you can possibly be. And it probably is. But it may not be as safe a place for you to work as it is for you to live.

One big reason labor unions have traditionally been opposed to members working at home is the historical problem of poorly maintained home-based workplaces with unsafe working conditions. This was more of a problem with the sort of piecework that typically was done at home in those days.

Today's home workers face a different set of challenges. All the same workplace safety issues that would exist if you were in a traditional workplace still are present when you're working at home. The difference is that in your employer's office, it's management's responsibility to make sure the workplace is safe. When you work at home, management may still get involved, but the responsibility for workplace safety falls much more on you.

Telecommuter safety and the law

In 2000, a furor erupted in the telecommuting world when the Occupational Safety and Health Administration (OSHA) responded to a letter from a Texas company that had asked how responsible the company was for the safety of telecommuters while they were working at home. OSHA responded that the employer was just as responsible as if the employees were working at the company's facilities.

Immediately, angry protests poured in from business representatives, notably the U.S. Chamber of Commerce. Companies across the country put their telecommuting programs on hold. Telecommuters and would-be telecommuters complained. Within days, OSHA withdrew its answers to the Texas company's questions. A month later — after a Congressional investigation — OSHA issued a statement largely reversing its answer. Among other things, it said, "OSHA will not conduct inspections of employees' home offices. OSHA will not hold employers liable for employees' home offices, and does not expect employers to inspect home offices of their employees. If OSHA receives a complaint about a home office, the complainant will be advised of OSHA's policy."

Although employers breathed a collective sigh of relief, they aren't completely off the hook because OSHA is not the only agency involved. A work-related injury sustained while working at home probably is still covered by worker compensation law, which varies from state to state. In general, worker compensation holds employers accountable for workplace injuries and does not distinguish between home offices and outside-the-home offices. So, if you hurt yourself while working at your job in your home office, your employer may be at risk.

The point is *not* that you should disregard your own safety while working at home, but rather it is to prepare you for the real possibility that your employer may take an interest in your working arrangement. That interest is a legitimate one. Your employer may do one or more of the following:

- ✔ **Conduct an inspection of your home office.** This is the most drastic approach to guaranteeing home-office safety, and only a few employers do it. Managers are understandably reluctant to intrude on an employee at home, and employees are understandably resistant to the intrusion.

  Nevertheless, if you're paid a salary while doing some of your work at home, then in some legal sense, your home becomes an extension of your company's work facilities. It isn't out of line for company officials to take a look at it.

  If your employer inspects your home office, you should be given at least 24 hours advance notice. Everyone involved also needs to be clear that the purpose of the inspection is merely to ensure that your workplace doesn't pose any physical threat to you, that company-owned equipment is properly secure, and that sensitive company information is properly protected. It shouldn't matter to anyone whether you have dust bunnies in the corners, piles of dirty laundry on the floor, or stacks of dirty dishes in the sink.

- ✔ **Ask for photographs of your home office.** This unusual step is an attempt to protect the employer's interests and the employee's privacy at the same time. In this case, you'll probably be asked to provide shots of specific areas at specific angles so as to give a complete view of your workplace. Once again, safety and security — not neatness or décor — are the issues.

✔ **Provide instructions on setting up your home office.** In this approach, the idea isn't to investigate what kind of workplace you create, but to make sure that you know what your workplace needs to be like. Companies with telecommuting programs in place often have instruction sheets or manuals explaining exactly how to set up your home office to minimize chances of work-related injuries and avoid other problems. Your promise to follow these instructions may be part of the telecommuting agreement you sign with your employer. You may also have to fill out a checklist of home office safety precautions.

✔ **Nothing at all.** Telecommuting still is a new idea for most companies. Companies that have been doing it for a while tend to be smaller companies. And telecommuting arrangements often are informal and sometimes geared specifically to individual employees whose jobs or life circumstances create a need for them to work from home.

For all these reasons, telecommuting often is managed by loose, ad hoc arrangements rather than formal corporate policy. And, in many cases, no one has stopped to think about potential liabilities that home offices can represent. In some other cases, corporate attorneys have considered the issue and decided that the less employers know about employees' home offices, the more legally protected they are. These companies have deliberately decided not to interfere.

Can you really get hurt working at home?

"It's so funny you asked this, because I did mine w-r-o-n-g!" reports Miriam Carey, who is profiled in Chapter 1. "I tried to economize — and keep my place fashionable — by using an existing armchair. What a mistake that was. I've thrown my back out. I'm going tomorrow to buy a more ergonomically correct chair and floor pad." (If you don't recognize the term "ergonomic," read on!)

Carey isn't alone. A recent audit of one large company's telecommuters showed home-working employees can be surprisingly unconcerned about their own health and safety. One had saved money on a desk by stretching a wooden plank across two file cabinets and placing his desktop computer on the plank — even though the file cabinets were not the same height. Others had so many papers stacked up they couldn't leave quickly in case of an emergency. Still others were overloading outdated wiring or working in enclosed, poorly ventilated spaces, creating fire hazards.

I'm also guilty of doing what Carey did in an earlier home office of my own. When I moved from city to country, the only desk I brought with me was a lovely antique, a family hand-me-down, that was much too high for typing on a keyboard. Instead of getting myself another desk, I placed my computer on a low coffee table, then dragged an old armchair in front of it. And there I would sit, working, more or less doubled over with my laptop about level with my knees. I suspect the only reason I didn't earn myself a backache with this arrangement is that I was somewhat short of work in those days, and didn't spend that many hours a day at the computer.

Fortunately for my spine, my future husband Bill came into my life about this time, took one look at my work arrangement, and flipped. The next thing I knew, he'd dragged me to a used office supply store and insisted that I buy myself a proper desk and chair.

People are human, and we have a tendency to think of ourselves as indestructible — right up until we find out the hard way that we aren't. So, unfortunately, it's easy to make the kind of mistakes that can lead to a serious problem from working in a home office.

Your best protection is to learn as much as you can about office safety and *ergonomics,* the science of creating working environments that are as healthy as possible for the human body.

To get you started, the following sections describe a few home-office elements to consider.

Desk

Your desk, chair, and computer, in combination, must allow you to sit up straight while working, with your hips, knees, and elbows all bent at 90 degree angles. This 90-degree setup is considered the best work position for avoiding *repetitive-stress injuries,* including the infamous *carpal tunnel syndrome.*

Your desk needs to be solid and stable, for your own safety and for the safety of anything that you place on top of it. Some desks come with adjustable feet, allowing you to raise or lower your desk by an inch or two. These can come in handy, in case you find yourself wanting to change your desk height over time, either to accommodate a more comfortable position, or because the equipment on your desk changes.

Computer desks with special keyboard shelves that flip up and down may not be as good of an idea as they appear to be. If the shelf is between you and your desk, it can push you further away from the desk itself, forcing you to reach forward repeatedly for things that are actually on your desk. This repeated reaching can strain your shoulders, neck, and back. Using a mouse on the desk, while the keyboard is on a shelf, is an especially bad idea.

I prefer a desk with drawers in it for storing things that I need to reach quickly. Drawers can also help keep clutter off the desk, which besides being good feng shui, is good ergonomics. Too many things on your desk can leave you unthinkingly twisting yourself into awkward positions to avoid knocking anything off.

Chair

A good work chair is your first line of defense against stress injuries. Unfortunately, good ones don't come cheap, and finding the right one can take a lot of trial and error. Here are some things to look for:

- **Armrests:** Experts say chairs with armrests are better because you can support your elbows and take some of the strain off your shoulders and neck.

- **Adjustability:** The more adjustable your chair is, the better it can be customized to fit your particular body. Some chairs can be adjusted as many as seven different ways. The more important are height, adjustable pressure on the back (so you can get the correct amount of lumbar support), and armrests that can be adjusted in close to your body, which should put you in the best-supported position. The height adjustment makes it possible to rest your feet on the floor, with your knees and your hips at 90-degree angles. Slightly greater than 90 degrees is okay in each case, but slightly less is not, because you may wind up reducing your circulation.

- **Five wheels:** Five wheels provide greater stability than do four.

- **A seat *pan* that fits:** If the edge of the seat digs into the backs of your legs, it eventually will reduce the circulation in your lower legs.

- **It feels good:** The best test of any chair is how you feel when you sit in it. That's why the best way to find the right one is to try a variety of office-supply stores, including a few that specialize in ergonomic designs. Take the time to actually sit in a large assortment of chairs. Chairs that look similar can feel surprisingly different when you sit on them, and the higher-priced ones are not necessarily the more comfortable ones. Trial and error is the only way to find out.

Work habits

How you work is just as important as the quality of your furniture in protecting you from work-related injury. Most telecommuters love working away from the office because it offers an escape from the frequent interruptions that keep them from working productively.

But while those frequent interruptions may be bad for your concentration, they can be good for your body. Most interruptions force you to take your eyes off the screen, your hands off the keyboard, and usually require you to turn or twist in your seat, pulling you out of your rigid typing position.

While working uninterrupted in a remote office, you can easily go for hours without taking your eyes off of the monitor or moving from your desk. This is not good for your health, and probably not too good for your sanity, either. Instead, create your own interruptions. For instance, set a kitchen timer on the other side of the room that forces you to get up and move around at least once an hour.

A friend once told me about visiting a university where the computer rooms operated on motion-sensor lights. This meant you'd occasionally see engineers in that department stand up from their workstations and wave their arms around in the air. At first, that struck me as a silly oversight. With a moment's reflection, I realized ergonomic planning was smart.

When you get up, do a few simple stretches to help get your blood circulating, and relax your cramped muscles. Focus on any area that regularly gives you trouble. For example, I often have trouble with my neck, so I do neck rolls, bend my neck back, and even give myself a neck rub for a few seconds every now and then. (If you decide to try a neck roll, start by dropping your head forward. Then slowly roll it around over one shoulder, then your back, and then the other shoulder, in a circle. Be sure to do this s-l-o-w-l-y, and be careful not to bend your neck farther than is comfortable.)

And, for as long as you are sitting at your desk, don't play statue. Staying rigidly in one position — even if it's the recommended 90-degree-angle position — is bad for you in the long run. Instead, slump back, sit forward, move from side to side a little, and generally mix things up. Give your muscles a little variety.

Keyboard

If you're like many people, you spend a good part of your workday working on a computer of one sort or another. That means the monitor and the keyboard are essential to your workplace health.

The greatest workplace threat by far to computer users is *carpal tunnel syndrome.* This injury comes from restricting the carpal tunnel, which can damage the nerves running between your wrist and your hand. Early symptoms include tingling and numbness in the fingers and shooting pains in the forearms. Left untreated, carpal tunnel syndrome can cause permanent nerve damage and require surgery. It can leave you with weak and clumsy hands forever. Whatever you do, don't take this problem lightly.

Using your keyboard correctly is the best way to prevent carpal tunnel syndrome. Ideally, you should keep your hands suspended above the keyboard, rather than resting them on the desk in front of the keyboard, but this can be a difficult position to maintain over hours and hours of work.

Using a wrist rest (a pad placed in front of your keyboard for your wrists to rest on) is another good solution. Experts say gel wrist rests are a better choice than foam ones. In either case, however, the goal is to have your wrist at as straight an angle as possible. If you're bending your wrist up to reach the keys while you type, you're asking for trouble.

During my brief newspaper career, I found myself typing nonstop for many hours a day, and I began going home with significant pain in my wrists. Alarmed, I went to see my doctor, who told me I had *tendonitis,* which could be a precursor of carpal tunnel syndrome. When I left the newspaper shortly thereafter, Bill, who was building me a new computer, insisted on outfitting it with an ergonomic keyboard. Although I thought it looked strange at first, I soon came to love it because it made typing seem more effortless than had the traditional keyboard. The ergonomic keyboard also is designed with something of a ramp that, at least for me, almost acts as a built-in wrist rest. I still have that keyboard, and I'd hate going back to the other kind now.

Although it worked for me, some workplace health experts caution that ergonomic keyboards don't solve the carpal tunnel problem for everyone. Instead, they suggest *tactile* or *click* models that provide some kind of response when you've typed a key. Otherwise, they say, users have a tendency to press each key as far as it can go, stressing their hands and fingers more than they should.

Mouse

I have a confession to make: I hate mice. I personally find them the most annoying possible way to navigate around a computer screen. I also believe they're the least ergonomically sound way to do so. At least one carpal-tunnel sufferer I know believes overuse of a mouse is partly responsible for his problem.

My husband Bill (who spends more time in front of his computer than most people could possibly imagine) spent years using a mouse and found himself with a sore wrist. He graduated to a *trackball* and found that it was better but not good enough. He finally settled on a touch pad (a gray square that enables you to navigate the screen by stroking your finger or thumb across it) and says it solved his problem. He and I have been using touch pads ever since. A light pen, which enables you to move around the screen by shining a small beam on the desired spot, also may serve as another good solution.

Monitor

Your monitor is just as important as your keyboard in keeping you healthy while working in your home office. I personally find I do better with a high-quality monitor with high resolution. This tires my eyes out less when reading text on the screen for hours. I also find it helpful to use Microsoft Word's zoom feature to slightly enlarge the type I'm looking at — for example I'm working at 106 percent zoom right now. I'm always careful to set the zoom back to 100 percent before passing a document on to anyone else.

But the location of the monitor may be even more important than the quality. Here's how to position yours:

> ✔ It needs to be at arm's length to reduce glare and thus eyestrain.
>
> ✔ It needs to be at eye level. I can attest to the difference this makes: When I switched from a monitor with a tall base to one with a short base a few months ago, neck aches were the immediate result. I solved the problem by setting the monitor on a monitor stand that brought it up to eye level again — and incidentally made it possible to store things under the monitor.
>
> ✔ It needs to be straight in front of you. I would've thought this was too obvious to mention, except that I've seen too many people working in offices with monitors set at odd, possibly artistic angles. This forces the user to turn his or her head to see the screen. That's inviting neck strain.

The one exception is for transcriptionists who touch-type and spend more time looking at the documents they're transcribing than at the screen itself. If this is you, you must be sure to use a document holder for the material you're typing. You can experiment, working with the monitor directly in front of you for a while, then with the documents right in front of you, to see which is more comfortable and keeps your neck the straightest most of the time.

Lighting

Proper lighting is vital for avoiding eyestrain. This is a bit tricky, though, because good lighting can be a different matter in different situations. When you're working on paper, or reading, you want strong light. Ideally, it needs to be pointed directly at what you're doing, which is why crane-style architect's lamps are so popular in many offices.

When you're working with your computer, however, you don't want a bright light directly on your monitor screen because it will add to the glare and increase your chances of eyestrain. This applies to natural sunlight, as well as artificial light.

On the other hand, if you're anything like me, you hate the idea of being in an office without lots of windows and lots of natural daylight. Fortunately, it's possible to have both. Begin by making sure you position the monitor so that daylight doesn't hit it directly. This probably means you don't want to have a window directly behind you. But one directly in front of you also can be a bad idea, because looking at a backlit monitor is hard on your eyes as well. In most cases, the best solution is to position the monitor sideways to the window, so that diffused light comes in over your shoulder.

You also need to have blinds on your window so you can control the effect on your monitor screen. For example, my desk is right next to a window facing west. In the morning, early afternoon, and evening, I keep the Venetian blinds up. But in the late afternoon, as the sun angles lower, sunlight comes straight in the window, straining my eyes and hitting the monitor full on. At that point, I usually lower the blinds.

As far as lighting the monitor itself is concerned, special monitor lights are available. Some are specifically designed for ergonomic purposes, putting the correct amount of light on the screen and minimizing the glare that hits your eyes. Monitor screens also can help reduce glare, and some people believe they reduce harmful radiation as well.

Phone

How much time do you expect to spend on the phone while working at home? If you expect to do more than the occasional 10-minute check-in call, consider getting a headset phone, especially if you often find yourself talking on the phone and using your computer at the same time.

Cradling a phone on your shoulder while you use your keyboard and mouse is putting an undue strain on your neck muscles and forcing yourself to hold your head at a crooked angle. Don't do it! And do choose a headset phone over a speakerphone: The sound quality is always noticeably better.

Voice recognition and microphones

The best way to avoid wrist strain and carpal tunnel syndrome is to avoid typing altogether. Modern voice recognition software can be trained to understand what you say to a good degree of accuracy, and if you can learn to work this way, you can vastly reduce the strain on your hands, wrists, arms, shoulders, and neck. (I, personally, find I can only compose on the keyboard, but I suspect this has something to do with many years of writing this way. It may be easier for someone who does something else for a living.)

If you decide to try voice recognition, keep two things in mind. First, be patient: It takes time and a fair amount of reading out loud to properly train software to recognize your speech patterns. Second, the software works much better if you have a high-quality microphone to use with your computer. Better yet, get earphones with a microphone, and you'll also be all set to use your computer to make long-distance calls.

Temperature

You won't be able to work effectively in your home office if you aren't comfortable there. If you're too cold, the discomfort saps your attention and the chill can weaken your resistance, making you more vulnerable to colds and flu. Too hot is no good either: Sweltering can make you sleepy and cut into your concentration. To be at your best, you need to be at a comfortable temperature, whatever that means for you. Ideally, your home office should be its own heating and cooling zone, so that you can set a temperature that feels good without having to readjust the temperature throughout your home.

Many people, including me, tend to get cold if we sit still for too long, and working at my desk is no exception. I combat this by keeping a special electric footrest under my desk. If I step on a button, it actually blows hot air at me and warms me up pretty quickly. If you, too, tend to get chilled from sitting at your desk, I highly recommend getting one.

Aches and pains

Your best guide to ergonomics in your office is your own feeling about whether something is comfortable. If you're too hot or too cold, then you need to make an adjustment. The same goes for your back, neck, shoulder, arm, and wrist muscles. You can have the most ergonomically advanced, most expensive desk chair in the world, for example, but if you're getting a backache, it isn't right for you.

Whatever you do, never ignore pain. Pain is your body's way of telling you that you're stressing a particular muscle or other area and that you have to adjust how you work. If something doesn't feel good, it probably isn't good for you.

Ventilation

Proper ventilation is important not only to avoid the risk of fire but also to ensure that you're comfortable while working in your home office, especially if you happen to be a smoker. Windows you can open, air vents, and fans can all contribute to good ventilation for your workspace. Pay special attention to ventilation issues if you've chosen a windowless room, closet, or basement as home-office space.

Wiring

Computer, printer, scanner, copier, external modem . . . it seems like everything you put in your home office has its own power cord and needs its own power supply. No wonder home office workers tend to overload their household wiring.

This represents a fire hazard, however, as well as a hazard to the equipment itself. It's hard to reduce the number of electrical devices in your office, but a few things can be done to minimize the risk.

Most modern wiring runs on circuit breakers — switches that control power to various parts of your home. Find out which circuit breaker or breakers control the power in your office. One easy way to do this is to have someone stand in your office while you throw the circuit breakers one at a time and yell to you when the lights go out. Mark that switch so that you can easily find it when you need to.

Use a surge suppressor to even out spikes of power coming through your wires. One of the better ways to do this is by attaching a six-outlet surge suppressor directly to the outlet in your wall. If you do use an extension cord, make sure it's an appropriately heavy gauge.

Even with a surge suppressor, your equipment may not be safe from lightning. Surge *protectors,* which cost a bit more, offer better protection against lightning than surge suppressors. Uninterruptible power supplies (UPSes) also offer a high degree of protection and also contain a battery that provides a few minutes of power in case of an outage. This feature is great because you get the chance to save and properly shut down whatever you're working on.

However, none of these devices offers absolute protection against sudden increases in power, and all of them may lose effectiveness after being hit by several surges. So when storms or power outages threaten, here are some precautions that will keep your computer and your work safe:

- ✔ Disconnect from the Internet and turn off your computer.

- ✔ Turn off your surge suppressor or protector. Most come with an on/off switch.

- ✔ Unplug the phone line from your modem. Phone lines conduct electricity, and if lightning strikes one of them it can flow through the line and burn out your modem. I know because it has happened to me. Twice.

- ✔ In the event of a power outage, you should also turn off your surge protector, suppressor, or (after saving) your UPS. Why? Because, after a power outage, power usually comes back on with a surge, which will contribute to wearing out your device.

- ✔ Replace your surge suppressor, surge protector, or UPS every year or so. A year's worth of power spikes is probably enough to weaken your device's effectiveness.

The outlets in your home office, and ideally throughout your home, need to be grounded. How can you tell if they are? Three-pronged outlets are often grounded but not always. A professional electrician can tell, or you can purchase a ground tester at a home supply store.

Security in Your Home Office

Keeping yourself healthy in your home office is your first concern. Once that's taken care of, taking the time to consider the safety of your home-office equipment is important. Here are a few simple guidelines:

- ✔ Make sure all electronic and other delicate equipment is stationed securely on your desk or another piece of furniture where it doesn't run the risk of being knocked over or down. Make sure it's safe from pets that may like to climb on your desk or knock into things with their tails.

- ✔ Be especially careful of food and drinks around computer equipment.

- ✔ Make sure your home office is reasonably secured against theft at all times. Even if you're just stepping out to run a quick errand, lock your house or apartment doors behind you.

✔ If your home office — and the equipment it contains — is easily visible from outside through a window or windows, consider securing those windows to make it harder for thieves to gain entry. Bars are only one way to secure a window. A stick or rod that prevents the window from opening is a simple way to greatly improve security, and you can remove the obstruction if you want to open the window while you're in your office.

✔ Consider a burglar alarm, if it's appropriate.

✔ If you're working with sensitive or confidential materials, you must also take a few steps to make sure they stay confidential:

- Obtain a lockable filing cabinet.

- Be sure not to leave sensitive materials lying around in the open when you're not in your office. This is especially important if people in your household are acquainted with people whose secret information (such as personnel files) you may have in your possession.

- Consider a paper shredder, if it's appropriate. Inexpensive paper shredders are now available for home offices through catalogs and office-supply stores.

Christine Doane-Benton: An office with a view

"When I worked as a journalist, I set up my home office in a loft in downtown San Diego," recalls former Windows Magazine software reviewer Christine Doane-Benton. She now works (on site) for Strategy Associates, a public relations firm in Silicon Valley, but has fond memories of working at home in her loft.

"There weren't separate rooms — only a lofted (second-story) bedroom that also had no doors," she notes. "So having an office in a separate room was not an option."

Still, she says, she created a clearly delineated office area in her living room by positioning her desks and bookshelves in three sides of a square. She ordered cherry wood furniture from a high-end office catalog, so it wouldn't look out of place with her living room décor. "I used plants to soften the look of all that plastic and metal hardware," she adds.

Originally, Doane-Benton had set up her desk with her back to the door, but a feng shui practitioner she hired to review her living and working space told her that was a mistake. (See the section on "Feng Shui" earlier in this chapter.) So she turned her desk toward the window, at an angle that had a good view of the door.

"I had a two-story cathedral window that spanned the height of the loft and looked out onto the San Diego Harbor. I enjoyed the view as I worked. It made working at home really pleasant." She adds, "I couldn't believe I had set my desk up facing the wall when I could have it face a view of the Pacific Ocean!"

Doane-Benton kept the whole area neat, with clutter stored away and one bulletin board of carefully placed inspiring quotes or images. The end result of all her work was a space few people could resist. "This area of my home became so welcoming that when I had guests, they'd want to sit at the computer," she recalls.

Chapter 7

Telecommuting Technology

*A*fter you've picked the perfect spot for your home office and you've found furniture that works for you, it's time to turn your attention to your office technology. Choosing these items requires some careful thought: They're the tools you'll actually be using to do your job.

Whatever office technology you wind up with needs to be comfortable to use, easy to understand, ergonomically sound, and sturdy enough for the amount of wear you'll be giving it. It must help you stay as connected as possible to your workplace. And it must help you maintain a professional and efficient workplace, even if that workplace happens to be in your basement.

Who Pays for What?

The issue of who pays for your home office equipment can be a tricky one. According to ITAC's Telework America survey, only 29 percent of employers pay all equipment and maintenance costs for telecommuting employees. Forty-six percent of telecommuting employees bear all these costs themselves, while the remaining 25 percent share the costs in some way.

These numbers indicate that a corporate practice for dealing with telecommuters' equipment needs has yet to be established. The question is up for discussion, and possibly for negotiation, when you create your own telecommuting agreement.

Complicating your negotiations are a wide variety of variables that are up for grabs when you tackle the question of who pays for what. Your employer can pay for all, some, or none of the following:

- Desktop computer, including drives, modem, monitor, and keyboard
- Printer
- Scanner
- Fax machine (It should be noted that multifunction printers that handle printing as well as scanning, faxing, and copying chores are available.)
- Laptop computer
- Copier
- Paper shredder
- Other office equipment
- Extra telephone for business calls
- Extra phone line for the telephone (along with features like voice mail and caller ID)
- Another extra phone line for the fax machine
- Yet another extra phone line for your Internet connection
- Cable modem
- DSL (high-speed Internet connection via phone lines)
- ISDN (Integrated Services Digital Network)
- Satellite service
- Cell phone
- Pager
- Wireless Internet device
- PDA (Personal digital assistant — hand-held devices such as Palm Pilot)
- Office furniture
- Rental of office space outside the home (see Chapter 5 for some possibilities)

Who gets home equipment?

What are your chances of getting your employer to pay for your home office equipment? It depends, in part, on how much available cash your company or department has for such expenses. But many aspects of your job and of your organization may make your employer more or less willing to pay for your equipment in your home.

Answers to the following questions may help you determine your chances of having your employer provide you with home office equipment and services.

✔ **Are you a full-time employee?** Employers may provide equipment for part-timers, but they're more likely to do so for full-time staff members. If you're a part-timer, you may have to sell them on the idea that you're really a member of the team before they'll consider providing you with home office equipment.

✔ **How much will you be telecommuting?** Your boss is more likely to recognize that you need high-quality equipment at home if you'll be working away from the office two or more days a week.

✔ **Does your organization favor telecommuting?** If your organization welcomes the idea of telecommuting, it is more likely to be willing to commit financial resources to help you set up your home office.

✔ **What deals are other telecommuters in your organization getting?** Find out whether others in your company are getting their home office equipment and services paid for before discussing this issue with your boss. You'll be in a much more powerful negotiating position if you just happen to know that Mary over in accounting has a new desktop PC, fax machine, and extra phone line, courtesy of your company.

✔ **Does your company have a formal telecommuting program or policy?** If so, you need to know about it because it may address the issue of paying (or not paying) for home office equipment.

However, keep in mind that *corporate policy* is just a set of rules that someone a few rungs up the ladder decided on at some point. It isn't necessarily engraved in stone. If the policy disallows paying for something and you really believe you shouldn't have to pay for it yourself, it's always worth asking if an exception can be made in your case. If you have a good argument for needing whatever it is, you may just be able to negotiate an exception to the stated policy, especially if you have some negotiating clout — for instance, you know your job would be difficult to fill if you left.

✔ **What about people with similar jobs at other companies?** Depending on what your job is, it may be more appropriate to compare yourself with others in your industry or profession with similar jobs than with others in your own company. If many of them are telecommuting with company-provided equipment, you may be able to use their situations as benchmarks, giving weight to your argument that you should get the same.

✔ **Does your job require that you be able to work from home?** For example, let's say that you're a customer relations person, and you have sole responsibility for your company's clients in Asia. You have a good argument for needing to work from home so that you can talk to your Asian contacts during their business hours. People with my husband Bill's specialty of online community often need to be able to work from home because most online interaction — especially chatting — takes place when company offices are closed.

A number of jobs have special requirements that create the need to be able to work from home. You can use these requirements as arguments in favor of your having special access to office equipment at home.

✔ **Are you an executive?** Rank has its privileges, in telecommuting as in everything else. If you're a high-level employee, you may be assumed to be more valuable, and your request for home office equipment may be taken more seriously.

✔ **Are you a techie?** For any number of practical reasons, technology people need access to better computer equipment than most other employees. You're also more likely to need access to the company's computer network.

At the same time, technology people are in high demand these days. So, depending on your expertise, you may be in a good position to get what you want from your employer. The irony here, of course, is that if you're the typical techie, you already have excellent computer equipment at home that you probably built yourself, and you may not be interested in adding anyone else's.

Are you sure you want it?

This may sound like a dumb question at first, but the fact is, some arguments find you dead set against letting your employer buy you office equipment. For example, Greg Breining, managing editor of *Minnesota Conservation Volunteer,* a magazine published by the Minnesota Department of Natural Resources, also works as a freelance writer, and for that reason, he decided not to have the DNR buy him a computer.

"My office was already set up with a computer and furniture," Breining explains. And he really didn't want to use two computers, switching back and forth from one to the other as he switched between his two roles. "It would have been a violation of our state employee ethics laws to use state-owned equipment for private business," he adds.

"Furthermore, the argument could be made that information stored on public-agency equipment becomes public information," Breining says. That would have raised potential problems for sources who wanted to remain anonymous, and conceivably could've raised ownership issues for Breining's copyrighted work. "I didn't want to get anywhere near that hassle," he says.

Here are some questions you may want to consider before you let your employer buy equipment for you:

✔ **Will you be keeping private information on your computer?** Will you be keeping material on your computer that you don't want your employer to see? (Love notes to co-workers? Cover letters for job applications?) Remember that if you have a problem with your computer, you'll likely find yourself sending or bringing it back to the office for repairs. Of course, ways to work around this include using two different computers, depending on what you're doing, or keeping all the private material in your own *external drive*. But you may decide that you'd prefer to use your own computer instead of bothering with any of these steps.

✔ **What software will you install on the computer?** Your employer has a legitimate right to know what programs you have running on your home computer, especially if shared files and other points of connection expose your company's computers to the danger of viruses your computer may have caught.

Many home computer users freely trade software with their friends, and use pirated copies of whatever they like without giving the matter too much thought. Using pirated copies of software can turn into a problem, however, if your computer goes in for maintenance and your employer discovers a lot of illicit software installed on it — especially if your employer has a no-piracy policy.

✔ **Will you be the only person using the computer?** What if your 10-year-old uses the computer to do homework or play video games? This may be perfectly fine with your employer. Or it can be a big problem. You should probably find out your employer's policy before letting other members of your household regularly use your company-owned computer. On the other hand, if the computer is yours, deciding who else can use it is up to you.

✔ **Do you want your employer choosing your equipment?** Of course, if you work in the company office, you're probably using equipment the company selected, no questions asked. But creating your own home office gives you the opportunity to do things the way you like. (I, for instance, would be pretty unhappy if I couldn't have the keyboard and monitor of my choice.) It may be worth getting your own equipment so that you can have it exactly the way you want it.

✔ **What if you leave your job?** In that situation, you'll have to return all the equipment that belongs to your company. Of course, you can always buy equipment of your own at that time. On one hand, the longer you wait to buy any kind of technology, the more value for your dollar you'll get, as prices go down and capabilities go up. However, you may be putting yourself in a position of having to make one or more major purchases at a bad time — right when you're between jobs.

✔ **Will you be using your computer for other paying work?** What if you, like Breining, do other freelance or contract work in addition to what you do on your job? In that case, using a company-provided computer can create a couple of problems. First of all, you may find yourself keeping information on the hard drive that you don't want your employer to see. And second, your employer may have a policy against using company equipment for outside work, even if the outside work itself isn't forbidden. In a case like that, using a company provided computer could conceivably wind up costing you your job.

✔ **Will you have to buy extra insurance?** The way many insurance policies are written, your employer's insurance covers the company's equipment while it's in your home. Even so, many employers who allow telecommuting are putting the responsibility on employees to make sure the equipment they use for work is covered by their homeowners' (or renter's) policies. If it isn't, the company often requires the employee to obtain supplemental insurance for the items in question. The company may also require that you agree to this as part of your telecommuting contract.

Selling your boss on the benefits

After carefully considering the drawbacks, you've decided that you'd like to have your company pay for your office equipment. How do you sell your boss on the idea?

As always, your best bet is to demonstrate that the idea is in the company's best interest, instead of your own. Fortunately, providing you with home office equipment can offer your employer many benefits. Here are a few:

✔ **Compatibility:** If your employer selects and purchase your home equipment, the company can ensure the equipment you're using is completely compatible with the equipment being used in the office. This will minimize problems when, for instance, you need to transfer files between work and home.

✔ **Upgrades:** These days, no one uses the same version of any software for long. If your company's IT people know you're running the same sort of box that you'd normally be using if you worked in the office, they'll know you have the same system requirements for any new versions or new software they may install throughout the rest of the company. That makes everyone's job a little easier.

✔ **Virus protection:** This is a particularly important piece of software these days, and whatever virus protection the rest of your company is running, your company has a vested interest in making sure that you have the same level of protection, because if you do contract a virus, it's only a matter of time before you pass it along.

✔ **Technical support:** If you have company-provided hardware and software, chances are the company's IT staff is familiar with it and can quickly figure out what to do if something goes wrong. They may be much less help if what needs fixing is something they've never seen before.

Even worse is the likelihood that if your company isn't providing you with a computer, it isn't providing you with technical support, either. That leaves you at the mercy of whatever support services you can drum up on your own. And the money the company saved by not buying you a computer can end up going right back out the door several times over because of productivity losses when you aren't able to use your computer for a few days.

✔ **Ergonomics:** OSHA may not hold your employer responsible for workplace injuries, such as carpal tunnel syndrome, but state worker-compensation laws probably still say that the company has to pay if you incur injuries.

In any case, nobody wins if you have to go on disability or cut back your work schedule because of a repetitive-stress problem. The best way for your employer to ensure that your workplace is safe and ergonomically sound is to provide you with the right kind of equipment. (See Chapter 6 for a much more detailed discussion of ergonomics and your employer's responsibility in case of a problem.)

Hand-me-downs

You may think you have only two choices: Either your employer buys your home office equipment, or you have to buy it yourself. But a third alternative may find neither of you shelling out a dime: hand-me-down equipment.

Finding good hand-me-down equipment may require a little research on your part. If your boss doesn't work in the IT department, he or she may not know where to find any spare computers or computer parts just hanging around. So you'll have to find out for yourself. Look around your company's various storage areas. You may find a whole pile of forgotten computer equipment in a corner. Ask your IT contacts if they have any less-than-new stuff they'd like to get rid of or any unused computers sitting around. You can always ask to take something home on a temporary basis, and offer to bring it back on a few days' notice, if it turns out someone needs it after all.

If you take a hand-me-down computer, keep in mind that you may be at least one generation of technology behind your colleagues at the office (and behind yourself, too, on the days when you work on an office computer). Try using software that works equally well in both situations. If you ask for technical support, make sure that whoever helps you knows exactly what vintage hardware and software you're dealing with.

Company laptops

It's highly likely that your company keeps a supply of laptops (or notebook computers) for use by executives, salespeople, and other employees when they're on the road. Asking to use one of these laptops in your home office may be a good solution to your home-office computer needs.

It may also be much easier for your boss to say yes to the loan of a laptop than to the purchase or loan of a desktop for your home office. Getting approval for a desktop for home use may mean filling out requisition forms and getting approval from upper management and/or the IT department. On the other hand, it may be a simple matter for your boss — or you — to sign out a laptop for your use.

What's more, if your company doesn't have a formal telecommuting policy — or worse, if that policy is *no telecommuting* — you may be a *guerilla* telecommuter. That is, you have an ad hoc arrangement in which you work at home one or more days a week, or at certain times during your work cycle. This is a private arrangement between you and your immediate supervisor, not a company-sanctioned deal. You obviously can't ask for corporate funds to equip a home office that you're not supposed to have in the first place. If that's your situation, signing out a company laptop may be your only alternative to buying everything yourself.

Your Personal Computer

Whether you're requesting equipment from your company or paying for it out of your own pocket, you must spend some time figuring out exactly what you need for your home office. What do you absolutely have to have to do your job? Are there things you want but can live without if you have to?

Unless your job is basket weaving or something equally low-tech, you'll need a personal computer to do it. In fact, you probably already have one. But is your home computer good enough for you to do your job?

Personal computer system standards change so often that it's impossible to have a state-of-the-art system without upgrading every few months. And you probably don't really need a state-of-the-art system to do your job. Basically, your home office computer needs to meet only a few requirements:

- ✔ **It must be compatible with whatever they're using at the office.** If your office is running on Macintosh computers, and your home computer is an IBM-compatible PC — or vice versa — you may have compatibility problems. Avoid setting yourself up for this headache by having the right kind of computer from the start. In fact, even if you're not telecommuting yet but just buying a family computer you might use to do work on in the future, it's probably a good idea to consider compatibility with equipment at work.

- ✔ **It must be powerful enough and current enough to run the same software they're using at the office.** This may actually mean that you need a *more* powerful computer than some of your colleagues. Why? If they're running on a LAN (local area network) at the office, every individual PC may not need to be powerful enough to run the software they all share. If you're not connected to the network from your home office, your computer needs to be powerful enough to run everything you need on its own.

✔ **It must be fast enough and powerful enough to use any Web applications necessary to do your job.** More and more of your business functions are likely taking place over the World Wide Web. Some may involve encryption or other features that dictate how powerful a computer you need.

✔ **It must have enough hard-drive space to store all the programs and files you need to do your job.** In these days of multiple-gigabyte hard drives, this is unlikely to be a problem for most jobs. But it may be a consideration if your job involves massive databases, heavy-duty graphics, or other hard-drive hogs.

Personal computer accessories

Of course, you need more than the computer itself. You may either absolutely need or want a variety of computer accessories. Some of them are essential; some of them are not so essential.

Monitor

If you're involved in serious graphics work, or intricate Web page development, you'll need a monitor equal to the task. The rest of us have much simpler monitor needs. The biggest concern is probably eyestrain. (For more on this issue, see Chapter 5.)

Keyboard

Once again, your biggest keyboard concern is likely to be ergonomics. (See Chapter 5 for a more thorough discussion of keyboards and repetitive stress injuries.)

Modem

You need a modem and an Internet connection of some sort. Your Internet choices may include a phone line, ISDN, DSL, cable modem, or satellite. Not all these choices are available in all locations, however. For a full discussion of Internet connection options, see Chapter 8.

Printer

This may be the digital age, but sooner or later, you're going to have to print something on paper. Once again, your printer needs depend on the nature of your job. If you have serious desktop publishing to do, or if your job is heavily graphics-oriented, you may need a printer that can accommodate special needs. For the rest of us, though, widely available and relatively inexpensive printers are perfectly adequate.

External storage

An external storage device (such as a Zip drive) can be handy for carrying work or software back and forth between the office and home. It also can serve the important purpose of backing up the files on your home-computer hard drive.

Several different types of drives are available. The common types plug into your computer and use special disks that can store anything from 100 megabytes of information to a gigabyte or more.

Other external storage options include external hard drives and tape drives. While these can be good for backing up materials, they're not well suited for carrying around.

Scanner

A scanner (which digitizes graphic images) can be a device you use all the time, or hardly at all, depending on the nature of your job. It can be useful, though, if you choose not to have a fax machine in your home office.

Single multifunction devices that act as scanner, printer, copier, and fax machine, all in one, are widely available. Some home office workers find them a satisfactory solution. Others report that they don't fulfill any of their multiple functions as well as stand-alone devices. Multifunction devices are probably a good idea if you do most of your sending and receiving by e-mail and your printing and faxing needs are relatively modest. If you do opt for a stand-alone scanner, the flatbed type (with a lid that opens, like a copier) is the more versatile and usually the best choice.

Microphone

A microphone attached to your computer can be useful for several different functions, among them:

- **Voice recognition:** If you use voice-recognition software that turns your spoken words into text on your computer screen, a high-quality microphone helps the computer properly understand your voice. Voice-recognition software is one of your best defenses against repetitive stress problems: The less you type, the better off you are.

- **Videoconferencing:** If your company uses videoconferencing to keep in touch with you while you're working outside the office, then you'll need a microphone so they can hear what you have to say. So far, videoconferencing is not used in most telecommuting situations, but it may become more common as high-speed Internet access becomes available in more places.

✔ **Internet telephony:** Also known as *voice-over-IP (VOIP)*, this technology helps you to cut long-distance costs by enabling you to make phone calls over the Internet. Some companies also use this technology to communicate with their off-site staff members. To use Internet telephony, you'll need to hear, as well as talk, and you may not want the other end of your conversation broadcast over a pair of computer speakers. A headset unit combining earphones and a microphone may be a good solution.

Personal-computer video camera

The PC video camera is the second device you'll need if you want to be able to videoconference from home. The camera typically is placed on top of your computer monitor and can shoot you while you sit at your computer. These cameras are relatively inexpensive and widely available.

Networking

Not long ago, creating a LAN (local area network) among several computers was the exclusive province of a few well-trained techies. Today, home networking kits make it relatively easy and inexpensive to network several computers in your home.

Why would you want to? Here are a few reasons:

✔ **Transferring information between laptop and desktop.** If you're fortunate enough to have a desktop computer to work on at home and a laptop to take with you to the office, you need some way to transfer files between the two. To do this, you can use floppy disks, if you have to transfer only a few document files. A direct cable connection from one machine to the other, or even e-mail, are a couple other options. But plugging the laptop into your home network is the easiest and quickest method.

✔ **Protection from hackers.** Whenever you're connected to the Internet, there's a chance that hackers can try to invade your computer. With high-speed systems such as cable modem or DSL, you're connected 24 hours a day, which means hackers have plenty of time to do their dirty deeds. Your best protection is a *firewall*, software that keeps intruders out of your system. A network setup, especially if it is equipped with a router, usually comes with a firewall built in.

✔ **Sharing devices and files among several computers.** This is especially handy if more than one computer and more than one computer user are in your household. With a network, for instance, your teenager can send documents such as school reports to your printer and thus doesn't need one of his or her own. The same goes for your scanner, if you have one. Better still, all the computers in your household can simultaneously share a single Internet connection.

Software

The most important thing to know about your home office software is that it is the same software they're using back at the office. It must not only be the same brand but also the same generation: If the office is using *Office 2000,* you shouldn't be stuck at home with *Office 98,* for example.

Generally, getting the right software from your company shouldn't be a problem. But you may have to borrow and bring home one or more CDs to install the software yourself, instead of having an in-house techie do it for you, as may have been the case back at the office. (See information on working with technology support later in this chapter.)

Desktop or laptop?

In an ideal world, your employer issues you a desktop computer to use while you're working at home, a laptop to bring with you if you're working elsewhere, and a network or cable to connect the two. Unfortunately, few telecommuters work in an ideal world.

If your employer is supplying your home office equipment, you may find you get either a desktop or — more likely — a laptop, and you don't get to choose between the two. On the other hand, you may be buying your own equipment, in which case you get to make your own choices.

Which is better? Laptops these days can give desktops a run for their money, and are more practical in many ways. On the other hand, desktops still retain some definite advantages over their more portable counterparts. Here are some of the better arguments for each.

- ✔ **Laptops are portable.** The biggest advantage of laptops — and the reason they were developed in the first place — is that you can take them with you almost anywhere you go. In Chapter 5, I describe a man who telecommuted from a water park, working in the shade while his kids rode the rides. Without a laptop, such things wouldn't be possible.

- ✔ **Laptops can be too portable.** This is especially true if, say, you're walking through a crowded train station and someone grabs it off your shoulder, takes off, and keeps running. That kind of thing is much less likely to happen to your desktop.

- ✔ **Laptops are easy to transfer between work and home.** If you're spending part of each work week at home, and part in the office — especially if your at-home days are Tuesday and Thursday — it can be a real nuisance to have to copy files you're working on back and forth every time. A laptop solves this problem: Plug it into an electric outlet and an Internet connection or network, and you're good to go. Use the laptop's *suspend* feature and you can start working precisely where you left off, without even having to start up your software.

- ✔ **But not that easy.** On the other hand, carrying a laptop back and forth to the office can get to be a real pain in the neck, not to mention the back and shoulders. So some telecommuters who started out carrying laptops back and forth have instead switched to e-mailing files back and forth between their home offices and on-site offices, or using a portable external disk drive to carry their work on.

- ✔ **Desktops give more bang for the buck.** All things being equal, a dollar spent on a desktop probably buys more computing power than one spent on a laptop. That's the tradeoff for the laptop's greater portability. Desktops also are more flexible: You can add memory and new devices more easily to a desktop than you can to a laptop. And because desktop components are easier to take in and out of the case, repairs and upgrades are easier on a desktop than they are on a laptop.

- ✔ **Laptops have bad ergonomics.** Laptop keyboards simply cannot, in any way, offer the same degree of protection against repetitive stress injuries that desktop keyboards can. And while laptop screens can be as good as desktop monitors, the fact that the screen is attached to the keyboard pretty much forces you to keep your neck in what can only be called a harmful position.

Just because you're using a laptop doesn't mean you're stuck with laptop ergonomics. Some laptops have *docking stations* available: If you purchase one, all you need to do is plug your laptop into it and you'll be working on a desktop computer monitor that you can adjust and a more ergonomic keyboard.

With many laptops, you can add the ergonomic benefits of a desktop computer by actually plugging a monitor and keyboard, or just a keyboard, into the laptop's own ports. If you decide to switch to a desktop, a different brand of laptop, or even a newer model of the same brand, you can probably keep using the keyboard and monitor. Docking stations usually work only with the specific model of laptop for which they're designed.

On the other hand, docking stations are in some ways a more elegant solution: It's quicker and easier to plug the laptop into them, and you'll have fewer wires lying around on your desk.

On balance, the best solution may be a laptop that plugs into a docking station or monitor-and-keyboard combo. But it really depends on your needs, your budget, and how portable you need your computer to be.

Your Home Office Phone (s)

When my husband Bill and I first moved into the house we currently live in, he was ten months into his current job. Because it's an Internet community role, he spends an enormous amount of time on the phone and online. At the time, I was researching and writing magazine articles, which meant I, too, was spending a lot of time on the phone and a fair amount of time online. I was also in the midst of working out the terms for this book. Bill's best friend Drew had been house sitting for us before we moved in and stayed on for a few weeks afterward. He was job hunting and looking for an apartment, which meant he also needed to spend many hours on the phone and online.

Unfortunately, our local phone company was just getting over a strike at the time. Orders were backed up, and our pleas for extra phone lines went unheeded. So everything we each needed to do, on the phone and on the Internet, had to take place over a single, shared phone line. All I can say is, "Don't ever let this happen to you."

How many lines do you need?

The number of phone lines a telecommuter needs can vary considerably, but you may need as many as four or more. Consider these possibilities:

- ✔ **An extra business line.** In my many years of working at home, I've never wanted a separate line for business and personal use because I can talk on only one phone at a time. I answer the phone in business mode during working days, and in at-home mode evenings and weekends. In any case, that always seemed like enough. On the other hand, I never have to share my phone with other family members, so there's usually no trouble getting or making calls.

  Yet several experienced telecommuters have told me they find it extremely important to have a separate phone line for the office phone. It helps them create a clearer separation between their work lives and their home lives.

- ✔ **A data line.** If you don't have cable modem or some other way of connecting to the Internet without using a phone line, you'll probably need a phone line for your computer as well. At best, not being able to use the phone while you're online can be a real drag. At worst, it can prevent you from effectively doing your job.

- ✔ **A fax line.** If you have a fax machine, it needs to be connected via its own phone line to receive faxes on. (See "To fax or not to fax" later in this chapter to determine whether you really need a fax machine and/or fax line.)

- ✔ **A personal line.** This line is exclusively for your own personal use, kept separate from business transactions. Of course, if other members of your family also work from home, or if you have teenagers, one phone line may not be enough for the whole family. You may need two, or even three.

Phone service features

These days, adding a phone line isn't as simple as it used to be. You have several additional decisions to make about various features. Here's a look at some of them.

Long distance

Long-distance service options are dazzling and confusing. New long-distance carriers are popping up every day with ever-more-confusing plans. Some home-based businesspeople I know like prepaying for minutes to various Internet-based long-distance companies that appear to give the better rates. The following sections describe a few more things to consider:

Call accounting

If you're making long-distance calls on behalf of several different clients, it can be a big nuisance to keep track of those calls for billing purposes. In fact, some freelance writers I know find this to be such a pain in the neck that they actually prefer to swallow their long-distance costs.

Many long-distance companies make keeping track of calls much easier by putting accounting codes on your line: When you dial, you hear a hum, and the call won't go through until you enter an accounting code of your own choosing. Your bill is then broken down by code. I find this feature invaluable when working on stories for several magazines at a time.

Local toll calls

If you've explored the jungle of long-distance charges, you know that some of the costlier calls you make are within your home state. This is something to be aware of, not only because you probably make many in-state long-distance calls, but also because your computer may, too. Your local phone book probably contains a diagram that shows you which calls in your area are *toll calls*. Depending where you live, when your computer dials your Internet service provider (ISP), it may be making a toll call, too.

You may or may not be able to fix long-distance Internet access problems. You can start by trying to look for a local ISP, to switch your local toll calls to your long-distance carrier (if rates are cheaper), and to look for a plan that offers lower rates on these calls. If you can find an ISP with a toll-free number, that might help, too, but be careful that you aren't charged for its use. America Online, for example, offers a toll-free number, but charges users 10 cents a minute while they're connected to it.

The important thing is to be prepared to deal with this issue. Too many Internet users I know have been hit from left field with phone bills in the hundreds of dollars that they didn't expect because they were unwittingly using an ISP access number that was a regional toll call.

Data long distance

Don't make the mistake of leaving your data line without long distance service. Having long distance available costs you nothing if you don't use it. And you'll need it if you ever send faxes via your computer's modem (assuming it's a fax modem) or dial into a computer network that's a long-distance call away.

Call waiting

When researching a magazine article or other piece of writing, I often find myself calling a long list of experts whom I'd like to interview. Of course, most of them aren't available, so I leave a message with my number.

When I had call waiting, what happened next was a real problem. The first expert called me back, and while I was interviewing him or her over the phone, the call waiting beeped at me. I'd ask expert #1 to hold on, answer the other line, and find expert #2. I'd tell #2 that I'd call right back and return to #1, only to have the line beep again for expert #3. By the third interruption, I would no longer put expert #1 on hold for fear that he or she would lose patience and hang up. That meant expert #4, or anyone else who called, would just hear endless ringing, but there wasn't much I could do about that.

Voice mail

My work life improved dramatically when voice mail became available from our local phone company. Now, if someone calls while I'm on the phone, they're routed to a professional sounding voice mail message, and I no longer have to interrupt important calls. Another option is to use the two features together: The call waiting rings through, but then the call is routed to voice mail if you don't pick up within a few rings. This enables you to take a business call if you're, say, chatting on the phone with your next-door neighbor.

Call forwarding

I find call forwarding useful in certain circumstances. In fact, I'm using it right now, because I recently moved. Calls to my old home office ring in my new home office. At my old office, which was in an old-fashioned town, voice mail was not available, so I set my office phone up to forward to my cell phone number. That way, callers could still get me if the phone was on, and otherwise the calls would route to the cell phone's voice mail, and I could get messages that way.

Caller ID

I've never used caller ID in my home office, but a few home-based business people I know swear by it. The question of whether it's useful to know who's calling before you pick up the phone yields a different answer from nearly everyone. Keep in mind that if your job involves a large number of phone calls from strangers, caller ID may not be of much use.

Three-way calling

Conference calls are a frequent occurrence for many telecommuters, but usually the conference-call technology is in use at your employer's office, and you don't need to have it on your own phone. But if you find that you must, for instance, connect a customer with a technical expert on the line to solve a problem, three-way calling may be something you need.

Telephone technology

Once you've decided what kind of phone service you want, you also need to decide what kind of phone you want. Once again, a wide variety of choices exist: phones with built-in faxes, built-in answering machines the list goes on. A few phone features that telecommuters may find particularly useful are described in the following sections.

Cordless

Before I had a cordless phone, if I received a business call while in the living room or kitchen, I'd ask the caller to hang on, race upstairs to my office, take the phone off the hook, race back down again, hang up the downstairs phone, race upstairs yet again and then sit down at my desk and take the call while trying my best not to pant out loud. Having a cordless phone means I can answer in another room and saunter along to my office without ever interrupting the conversation.

Speaker

One telecommuter I know equipped his office with a speakerphone and now wishes he'd gotten a headset phone instead. In nearly 20 years of business reporting, I've had countless conversations with people using speakerphones, and I can always tell. The sound quality makes it seem like talking to someone who's standing in a tunnel.

Nevertheless, I have one on my desk, and it comes in handy when I have to traverse layer after layer of automated response options before finally reaching the person I'm trying to call. It's also great when I'm on hold. I can sit and work with my hands free while the on-hold music plays.

Headset

Headset phones generally are a much better proposition than speakerphones, which is why they're rapidly gaining popularity. In fact, a cordless headset phone gives you maximum freedom with only a small handset to clip to your belt or stick in your pocket.

Headset phones make good ergonomic sense if you spend a lot of time on the phone or use the phone and type at the same time. You can keep your neck in a natural position instead of cradling the headset on your shoulder.

Mute button

A mute button lets you hear the other person but mutes the sound at your end. This feature can be invaluable if you can hear things like barking dogs or crying babies from your end. Practiced mute-button users actually unmute the phone just long enough to speak, then mute it again as soon as it's the other person's turn to talk.

Adjustable ringer

Most phones these days come with a ringer you can turn off, and that's a good thing, according to Christine Doane-Benton. "Otherwise, I would've heard the office phone ringing while sleeping at night." She works on the West Coast, and she recalls that East Coast business contacts regularly left messages early in the morning.

If you have voice mail, another option is to take the phone off the hook. That is what I do when I don't want to receive calls for whatever reason. The voice mail takes messages, and I return the calls at my convenience.

More Home Office Devices

The computer — with Internet connection — and phone are the most important pieces of equipment in your home office. But some other items you may want to think about using range from what is considered basic for any office to toys for technology junkies. Which ones are right for you? Only those that will truly help you do your job faster, more easily, or better.

To fax or not to fax

I've had a home office for more than 15 years, and in all that time, I have neither had nor wanted a fax machine. What bothers me isn't so much the cost of the machine itself (although, 15 years ago, they weren't cheap), but the expense and inefficiency of having to hook up a phone line just for faxes.

Times have changed, but my view about faxes hasn't. In fact, it's even easier in this day and age to get along without a stand-alone fax machine, especially one with its own phone line.

Of course, this may be a moot point for you: Your employer may assume that you can't operate a home office without your own fax machine and automatically provide one. Or you may have a job that requires a lot of faxing of *hard* material that has to actually exist on paper before you can send it out (documents requiring signatures, for instance). In that case, having a fax machine makes your work life more efficient.

Even if you need a fax machine (or one of those combined printer/scanner/fax/copier units or phone/fax units), it may not need its own phone line. Line managers are designed to screen incoming calls and determine which are voice calls and which are fax transmissions. Voice calls are routed to you or to your voice mail.

One drawback is that not every incoming call can be properly identified as a fax call, so your line manager may miss receiving the occasional fax. Another drawback is that people sending faxes are accustomed to doing so at their convenience, so you may encounter frustration if someone can't send a fax for an hour because you were on the phone.

In my early days of working at home, the solution was a neighborhood copy shop, where I'd send and receive faxes. Early on, I made sure the people at the copy shop knew me, so that if a fax arrived with my name on it, they'd know to call. (This saved me the embarrassment of asking business contacts to put my phone number on faxes addressed to me.)

As my computers evolved through the years, I found myself using Windows software, which has built-in fax software, and a fax modem that enables me to send faxes right from the computer. This was handy and became even handier after I added a scanner to the mix: Now I can actually scan pieces of paper and send them through the phone lines, pretty much as a fax machine does.

As an extra, somewhat sneaky step, I also scanned an image of my signature. After that, when I wanted to send out a fax that looked signed, I would simply insert that image at the end of the document.

All this worked great for *sending* faxes. *Receiving them, however,* was more of a problem. I considered setting up my computer to receive faxes through its modem line, but that meant senders would get a busy signal whenever I was on the Internet. For a few years, I sent faxes from my computer but received them at the copy store.

Then came eFax. EFax is one of several programs available on the Web that enable you to receive (and send) faxes via e-mail. EFax is particularly useful because if someone sends me a fax while I'm out of town, I can plug in my laptop and pick it up wherever I am.

I like eFax because it's free. On the other hand, if you use the free version, you can't choose the area code for your fax number. So I now have a fax number with an area code that appears to be in Utah, even though I live in New York. This doesn't faze people as much as you might think it would. If I'd been willing to pay a monthly fee (still much cheaper than an extra phone line) I could've had a phone number from one of several major cities.

So now I send faxes from my computer, receive faxes via the Internet, and never see my copy shop friends at all, except when I bring them bags of packing peanuts to reuse when sending packages. This is the best solution for me. A different one may be right for you.

Wireless

It's pretty much impossible to pick up a technology or business magazine these days without reading an article about wireless communications and wireless devices like phones, pagers, and PDAs. Everyone agrees they're the next big thing.

But next and now are two different things. Many people, including my technology-adoring husband, love wireless devices for their own sake and are constantly adding new ones to their collections. But unless you have a need to try out all the new gadgets, you're better off analyzing exactly what you need to do and then matching that use with the device.

Likewise, before investing in any wireless device, you need to carefully research the whole issue of signal and signal strength. Not all wireless devices work in every location, and in some areas, certain devices work beautifully, while others are a complete washout. Being aware of signal strength, at your home office and wherever else you may want to use wireless communications, helps you make informed decisions about various types of devices and signals.

Unfortunately, advertising for most of these products tends to focus on *nationwide networks,* without explaining that not all network signals work everywhere. And sometimes their customer service people aren't much help, either. My husband Bill recently found this out the hard way when he bought a nifty new text-based pager that enabled him to send and receive e-mail, and even instant messages. (If you're unfamiliar with instant messages, see Chapter 8 for more information.)

Because we live in a fairly rural area, with limited wireless signaling, he went out of his way to ask the company's salesperson whether it would work in our area, and was assured that it would.

It didn't. The nearest city we could find where the device picked up a signal was Albany, some 50 miles away. So he returned the device and demanded a refund.

With issues of signal and signal strength in mind, the following sections provide a quick look at some available wireless devices.

Phones

To my mind, a wireless phone is the single most useful of wireless devices. They're handy for any number of reasons: Callers can reach you when you're at the beach, and you can ask your spouse while standing in the produce aisle exactly what kind of fruit he wants.

Wireless phones also convenient in another way: Many come with calling plans that include free long distance. "I have a cell phone that I use almost exclusively for work. It is not attached to the family phone number, and my plan is such that 1,000 of my 3,000 minutes are available for anytime long distance on a nationwide basis for a monthly fee of $75," notes Donna Gettings. "I am able to not worry about calling vendors, co-workers, and contacts all over the country and parts of Canada at any hour during the day." Gettings' home has two phone lines, one of which is in use as her Internet connection for most of the day, she adds. Using a cell phone leaves the other phone free for family members who may need to reach her.

And wireless phones, like all technology, are evolving. My phone, purchased in 1998, is just a phone. Bill's phone, bought two years later, can bring him e-mail, stock quotes, and other information. It can also be used to page him, if calling doesn't work. In short, newer phones can blur the lines between a wireless phone and a text-based pager.

Pagers

If your job requires you to be reachable at a moment's notice, then a pager may be a great idea. You can often receive a pager signal in places where a wireless phone call wouldn't get through.

And today's pagers are becoming powerful machines, enabling you to receive voice mail, text messages, and even e-mail. The newest text-based pagers (like the one Bill had) are small enough to fit in a pocket, yet sport tiny keyboards that enable you to type e-mails and instant messages. They blur the lines between a pager and a PDA.

PDAs

A PDA (*personal digital assistant*) is a small, computer-like device that fits in a pocket or handbag. Some are designed for taking notes with handwriting recognition. Most can handle e-mail and simple word processing.

PDAs tend to be designed to do exactly what you probably need to do: carry schedules, contact lists, and documents back and forth between one office and another. That's why many telecommuters find them particularly useful.

When Things Go Wrong

If you were at your desk in your company's office and your computer started delivering error messages rather than e-mail, you'd know exactly what to do. You'd call for tech support.

But what do you do when you're in your office at home and something goes *kablooey*? That's a more difficult question, and one you need to consider when making telecommuting plans.

How you react depends a great deal on whether the equipment you're using belongs to you or to your employer. Generally speaking, if it's your company's equipment, your company takes responsibility for making sure it's working right. If the equipment is your own, the responsibility is yours.

Sounds simple, right? But you easily can find yourself in gray areas. What if you're using your own computer but having a problem with company-owned software you've installed on it? Or you're having trouble signing on to the Internet, and you can't tell if the problem is the company's computer, or your own phone lines?

If you've spent any time working with technology, you already know that sooner or later something is bound to stop working the way it's supposed to. As a telecommuter, your best defense is to prepare ahead of time so that you'll be as ready as possible when (not if) that happens in your home office.

Get to know your company's techies

Technical support people are people, too. Because their job is basically maintenance, they often feel disconnected from the companies they work for and are under enormous stress, facing competing demands from desperate co-workers, each of whom wants a problem fixed *now*. And the people they help out are rarely in a good mood. The nature of technical support is that you usually interact with people at their worst.

Keeping all this in mind, making sure you're friendly, and remaining calm can make you a preferred customer in your interactions with technical support folks. Better yet, get to know them before you need them. Some ways to get on the better side of the tech team include:

- ✔ Calling them to let them know you'll be working from home.
- ✔ Finding out who you should contact if you have a problem, and to introduce yourself to that person.

Taking these steps helps lay a strong foundation for getting the help you need when you need it.

Make contact with neighborhood techies

If you'll be responsible for your own equipment, you need to know whom to call on to fix it before you have a problem. Check out the computer repair options in your community, and introduce yourself, if possible, so they'll know who you are. Even if you have company technical support, this might be a good move because these options may serve as a fallback if the techies at the office are overloaded and can't take care of your needs.

Get to know your equipment

Every successful telecommuter I know has gained at least some expertise at working with personal computers. Most of your technical support will take place over the phone, meaning you can't step back and let someone else work on your computer. So the more you know about it, the better off you'll be. Your initial contact with the tech department is a good time to find out whether any quick training is offered in the use of your equipment, or whether you should watch out for any particular problems.

Try the obvious before asking for help

Okay, so you don't want to become a computer expert. I understand. But at least get to know a few basic steps that you can try before calling in the cavalry. When in doubt, always try by rebooting your computer, either a *soft reboot* or a *hard reboot,* using the reset button or on/off button. If the problem is with your modem connection, see if switching to a different phone line helps.

The phone jack in my office is inconveniently located by the door, and my desk is across the room next to the window. For several years I had a phone cord stretched across the floor (bad idea, I know) and every once in a while I'd catch my foot on it. Pretty soon, the connection didn't work so well, and as I'd try to sign on nothing would happen. It took me a while to catch on that the problem was the jack and not the computer. (I still have a line running across the floor, but now it's covered by a rubber line cover that makes it much safer.)

Keep up with upgrades

If everyone in the office has this year's version of your work software, and you're using last year's, you're setting yourself up for compatibility problems and general confusion. Staying alert to software upgrades in the office and requesting the latest version for your home office, too, is important. And, when talking to tech support, make sure they know exactly what version you're working on.

Back up your files

I know, I know, this is roughly equivalent to asking you to floss when you brush your teeth. Backing up your files one way or another is the only smart thing to do. If I thought it would help, I'd tell you an awful story about what happened when Bill's computer caught a nasty virus a few years back that wiped out his hard drive. It destroyed a gigabyte of information, including addresses of old friends and business contacts that were in his online address book. But enough said. Either you will or you won't.

Back up your computer

Having another computer on hand that you can work on in a pinch can save your tail if something goes wrong while you're trying to meet a deadline. This is especially important if you're responsible for your own equipment and you can't expect your employer to overnight you a laptop and bail you out. "A spare PC is an absolute must," notes Donna Gettings. "I've actually had both PCs break down on the same day and have had to drag out the old 286 for word processing while the other two were being repaired."

Chapter 8

Making the Internet Work for You

● ●

In This Chapter

▶ Choosing the right Internet connection for you

▶ Ensuring your security online

▶ Becoming an effective Internet user

● ●

*T*he development of the Internet has probably changed the way Americans do business more than any invention since the telephone. By some estimates, two-thirds of the economic activity in this country today has to do with information, and the Internet is the most efficient vehicle ever invented for moving information. It has made telecommuting possible for literally millions of people who could not have considered it before.

It can do the same for you. Using the Internet to properly communicate with colleagues in the office is one of the more important skills for a telecommuter. Do it right, and you can make an almost seamless transition between working in the office and not working in the office. Do it wrong and you can alienate co-workers, customers, and your boss. Do it *really* wrong and you can expose your company to a virus that can wipe out years of hard work, and turn its best customers into its worst enemies.

Making the Connection

One of your earliest decisions when setting up your new remote office is what kind of Internet connection to use. Basically, the faster it is, the happier you'll be. Indeed, you just won't be able to use some beneficial Internet applications without some form of high-speed access. Unfortunately, issues of cost and availability make high-speed access inaccessible for many people. The challenge is finding the right balance for you.

The following sections take a look at the more common Internet access options available for home offices at this writing.

How fast is fast enough?

Many Internet hot shots these days act as though having to use a traditional dial-up to an Internet service provider (ISP) is tantamount to having to write with a quill and inkwell. But the fact is, the vast majority of home offices use traditional dial-up connections. And those kinds of connections are perfectly adequate for many home offices.

Take mine, for instance. I'm married to an Internet professional, and he needs to have high-speed access in his home office. In our last home, he had a cable modem connection, and because he had networked our computers, so did I. (See Chapter 7 for more info on the benefits of home networking.)

It was great! I could listen to streaming audio from online radio stations. I could check my e-mail on a whim. When writing or reading articles with Web addresses in them, I could double-check the link by clicking on it without having to worry about signing on first.

Then we moved. No high-speed access is available at our new place. Do I miss it? Of course I do. Do I need it? No.

Don't think that I'm not a heavy Web user. I probably spend an average of two hours a day using the Internet — more when I'm doing a lot of research, less when I'm doing a lot of writing. On top of that, I use the Internet exclusively to send work back and forth to editors, and do extensive research over countless Web sites.

But the fact is that nothing I do actually requires a high-speed connection. Documents, whether prepared in simple text or word-processed form never take more than a few seconds to send or receive, even with dial-up connections. And most of what I'm looking for on the Web is text as well. So for me, high-speed access is a convenience but by no means a necessity. If this sounds like how you'll probably be using the Internet and your employer isn't offering to spring for higher-speed access, dial-up is probably your best choice.

A traditional phone connection can also have one huge advantage over the various modes of high-speed access: portability. If you use an ISP with a national or even international supply of access numbers, you can sign on from virtually anywhere. You may get the best of both worlds if you sign up with a DSL service that also allows some dial-up hours each month, but if you travel a lot, or use the Internet a lot while away from home, it may not be enough.

My personal Internet service provider is America Online (mostly because my husband Bill once worked there). Whatever its other advantages and disadvantages, AOL has one of the widest selections of available access numbers. It's one of the few ISPs with a number in my rural neighborhood. For family reasons, I spend a lot of time in rural Florida, and AOL has access numbers for me there as well.

Four years ago, a family member of mine died unexpectedly in Paris. I went there for ten days but still had deadlines to meet. Yup, they had a local number in Paris, and not only did I stay in touch with work e-mail, I also conversed for free with Bill and my friends at home via Instant Messenger, which was a huge comfort at a traumatic time.

AOL is only one of many service providers with national and even international access numbers. If you expect to spend time on the road, or want to be able to sign on from several different locations, pick a provider with enough numbers to connect in all the places you'll be.

Speeding up dial-up

A dial-up connection can never be as fast as a high-speed connection like DSL or cable. That said, you definitely can make your phone connection as quick as possible. Here are a few suggestions on how to do that:

- ✔ **Use a fast modem.** Using a dial-up connection is slow enough that you don't want to slow things down further with an outdated, slow modem. Assuming your phone line can handle higher speeds, use the fastest modem you possibly can.

- ✔ **Use a fast computer.** Computer users sometimes assume that their modems are the only reason their online experience can seem glacially slow. Not true. Besides a slow modem, two other factors can speed or slow your computer on the Internet:

  - • **Processor speed:** This is the speed of the processor, or the semi-conductor chip that runs your computer. It usually is expressed in megahertz. The faster your machine can think, the more quickly it can process Web pages.

  - • **RAM:** Random access memory (RAM) is your computer's short-term memory, which it uses while processing software of any kind. When RAM gets filled up, your computer dumps material it's working with into temporary files on your hard drive — a process that inevitably slows down your computer. Some computers are designed to use this *virtual RAM* as efficiently as possible, which helps somewhat. But the more RAM you have, the faster your Web experience will be (and the less likely you are to crash, too).

- ✔ **Check your phone lines.** If the connection on your phone line is poor, your fast modem automatically slows itself down to compensate. And what sounds like a perfectly good connection to your ears may still not be a good enough connection for your modem to work at its fastest rate.

And while you may not be able to do much about the quality of the phone lines to your home, you can make sure that the lines inside it are relatively up to date and functioning well. The modem in my home office routinely signs on at transfer rates in the 40 and 50 Kilobits per second (Kbps) range, close to 53K, which currently is the fastest dial-up speed. (Many modems in use nowadays are rated *56K,* but 53K is the actual speed over a phone line.) In my husband's office, similar computers sign on in the 20K to 30K range. What's the difference? Phone line quality.

✔ **Don't distract your processor.** If you don't have the fastest possible chip or as much RAM as you'd like, you can help your computer work more efficiently on the Web by only giving it one thing to do at a time. It's tempting to, say, switch back to word processing while that slow Web page loads. But if you don't have a powerful computer, you can end up shooting yourself in the foot. Your browser will work more slowly and may even time out or crash. You can use the wait time by straightening up your desk, reading a business magazine, or doing a crossword puzzle.

✔ **Go light on graphics.** Of course, not every Web page makes going light on the graphics easy. My personal favorite gripe concerns sites that put up an elaborate splash graphic — which can take minutes to load over a slow modem — before they let you actually enter the site.

Although things like that can be highly annoying, you can make them somewhat easier to contend with by setting your Web browser for low graphics, and by choosing *text only* versions of pages when given that option. (I know, I know: Bo-ring! But you'll get your work done a lot quicker.)

Speedier speeds

Dial-up Internet access is the cheapest and most portable solution, but sometimes it just won't do. This is likely to be true especially if you're working with a lot of graphics, using the Web for online meetings and/or presentations, or planning to access your company's network directly, via a virtual private network (VPN) or some other remote access.

If so, you'll probably want a higher-speed connection than mere dial-up networking can provide. Some of the options most widely available today are discussed in the following sections.

DSL

Digital subscriber line (DSL) Internet access is a high-speed connection that comes through your existing phone lines. Your local phone company, ISP, or any other enterprise may provide DSL service. One advantage to getting DSL from an ISP, especially one with national coverage, is that you may also get dial-up access as part of the deal. You may want dial-up access if, say, you and your laptop are in a hotel room somewhere and you want to check your e-mail.

DSL costs at least $40 or $50 a month. You will need a DSL modem, usually provided free of charge by service providers.

Advantages: Your connection is likely to be at least three times as fast as a regular modem, and it can be many times faster than that. In many cases, the phone line used for DSL can also carry voice conversation at the same time.

Disadvantages: DSL is not available everywhere. You need to be fairly close to a relay station to have access.

Cable modem

Cable modem Internet access is provided by your local cable television company, again at a cost of $40 to $50 a month. You'll need a special cable modem, which the company will usually provide, sometimes at an additional monthly fee.

Advantages: Speed. A cable modem provides the fastest access available today.

Disadvantages: Inconsistency. With cable modem, you're sharing bandwidth with many other users in your vicinity, and this can affect the actual speed you get. When we had cable modem in our last location, my husband Bill could always tell when neighborhood schools let out because the cable connection would slow way down. When strained by numerous users logging on at the same time, cable modem can actually wind up being as slow as dial-up connections. It's also less dependable than other types of access.

A second disadvantage may be the cable companies' policies, which in most cases require you to also order cable service for your television, regardless of whether you want it. This requirement can raise the actual cost of cable modem to $70 or more.

ISDN

Integrated Services Digital Network (ISDN) Internet service is a type of high-speed access available from your local phone company. The phone company actually puts two phone lines together creating a double line, running it into your home as a single ISDN line. You'll need a special ISDN modem, which the phone company probably will provide. The phone company will bill you for two phone lines, in addition to a connection charge similar to that for DSL or cable. That makes ISDN one of the more expensive available solutions.

Advantages: Dependability. And, if you set your line up in dual mode, you can use the ISDN line as a regular phone line at the same time you're using it to connect to the Internet.

ISDN also is available in most locations, making it the only viable choice for telecommuters in rural areas.

Disadvantages: It isn't that fast. ISDN lines in dual mode (which allow you to use it as a voice line) are only about twice as fast as traditional dial-up modems. ISDN lines without voice are faster, but not as fast as DSL or cable. Given its high price, you get less bang for the buck.

Satellite

Satellite technology can deliver Internet access through the airwaves. You'll need a satellite dish to mount on your roof, and a special modem inside. The dish may cost several hundred dollars. The service itself may be comparable in price to DSL. But, like cable companies, satellite companies may also require you to purchase their television services, which may bring the total cost to around $100 a month.

Advantages: Download speeds from the Internet into your computer are quite fast, comparable to DSL. Another major advantage is availability. Because satellites don't need wires or cables to reach your home, they're available in many places where other high-speed options are not.

Likewise, if you like watching TV, this service may be for you. Satellite Internet service typically comes as a package with TV satellite service that usually includes more than 100 channels.

Disadvantages: Upload speed (from your computer to the Internet) is slow — often no faster than a dial-up connection. What's more, with most satellite systems, you also need to have a dial-up modem and a phone line to send any information to the Web. Newer satellite services can send and receive, but the sending speeds are no faster than dial-up connections.

Whether slow uploading is a problem is dependent on what you want to do on the Internet. After all, quick downloads enable you to surf the Web most efficiently, so if that's your main need, it can be a good deal. On the other hand, if you're often sending graphics or other large files, it can be a real problem.

Cost is a second disadvantage. Satellite Internet service is one of the more expensive solutions available; however, the fact that it comes with TV service may compensate for some of that.

A third disadvantage is that you'll be somewhat at the mercy of the weather. Heavily overcast skies and other disturbances can slow or even interrupt your connections.

Safety on the Web

The growth of high-speed access for home use is a wonderful thing for those of us who love to work and play on the Net. But it also raises some important security concerns. Why? Well, most high-speed access options keep you connected to the Internet 24 hours a day. While this is extremely convenient, it also leaves hackers and other such miscreants 24 hours a day to try to break into your computer.

If high-speed access means you're less secure, telecommuting means the security stakes are higher. After all, if you have a security problem on your home computer, you may lose some digital photographs, some favorite recipes, or even the contact information for some long-time friends. But if you have a security breach with a work computer, the consequences can be much graver, and much more embarrassing.

A couple of months ago, I got an e-mail from a public relations contact that said, "Check out the new Web animated show," or something to that effect. A file was attached to it.

I didn't download the file. In fact, I didn't really believe I'd ever get a virus from a respectable public relations professional, but then I nevertheless generally don't make a habit of downloading attached files unless I have some idea of what's in them and that what's in them is something that I want. In part, this situation became a matter of impatience. Public relations people frequently send me messages with files attached, and if I took the extra minute or two to stop, download, and open each one, my workdays would be considerably longer than they already are.

Anyhow, it's a good thing I'm such a snob, because as it turned out, that download contained a virus. The PR person had received it in the mail, apparently tried to open it, and once exposed, the virus activated itself and sent itself to every name in the PR person's contact list. Imagine his embarrassment at having to contact all of us to warn us about the e-mail he'd sent, especially when, over the next few days, the virus sent the e-mail again another 10 or 12 times (although without the attached file). The virus continued sending the message until techies at the PR person's company finally managed to stop it.

Or imagine the embarrassment of an Internet CEO I know. He came from a bricks-and-mortar company and decided to try his luck at moving his operation to the Internet, even though he didn't know that much about it (or at least, not enough). A year into this new direction, he received a friendly e-mail, decided he liked the sentiment in it, and forwarded it to all his employees. Some of the more net-savvy ones smelled something fishy about it and didn't open it. But about a third of them did — and the virus it contained wound up disabling their computers for close to a week.

Okay, you're convinced: Security is a serious concern. What can you do about it? Here is some advice. Much of it comes courtesy of Matt Pardo, information technology director of TManage, Inc., an Austin, Texas-based company that helps employers work effectively with telecommuters. Many TManage employees are telecommuters themselves.

For the most part, you need to worry about two different types of attack when you're connected to the Internet: hackers and viruses.

Shutting out hackers

Hackers are people who use the Internet as a giant playground, sometimes to invade the privacy of other computers, computer networks and companies; sometimes to try to steal goods and services (for instance, when they use fake or stolen credit card numbers to log onto a paying service, such as AOL); and sometimes to create widespread havoc, such as with recent *denial-of-service* crashes.

Internet professionals like to point out that just as there are good cowboys and bad cowboys, there are also good hackers and bad hackers. The *good hackers* are coding geniuses who love technology and perform a vital service by exposing security weaknesses. They never actually hurt anybody. Good hackers often wind up being hired by the high-tech industry as well-paid security specialists.

On the other hand, *bad hackers* (some call them *whackers* or *wannabe hackers*) are less technologically adept, but they get a hold of a few bad programs and use them to unleash chaos wherever they can.

Bad hackers may attack your company's computer network, its Web site, your own home computer, or any of the information traveling among these locations just to prove that they can. In a now famous but embarrassing incident a few years back, hackers invaded the Central Intelligence Agency Web site, adding their own comments to the text and forcing the agency to take it offline for a time.

One of the better forms of anti-hacker protection is a firewall, named after walls built as an impenetrable barrier to prevent the spread of fire. A *firewall* uses software, hardware, or both, to keep hackers out by turning your Internet connection into a by-invitation-only deal. If you browse to a Web site, or check your e-mail, your system is inviting that connection. But a firewall rejects outside attempts to contact you — such as the *pings* that hackers send out in search of systems they can sneak into. Large companies and organizations, especially those with a substantial Web presence, typically use firewalls to protect themselves and their data. In fact, your company probably already has one.

Firewalls are not just for large companies anymore. Your home office may benefit from one, too. If you have more than one computer in your home, many good reasons exist for you to network them together. Here's one: If you use a router (a network device that assigns IP addresses to the different computers), you can get one with a firewall built right into it.

If you're not planning a network, you can still get a firewall simply by purchasing one. Firewalls are now available for home computer use.

Passwords make up another area where you can get into trouble with hackers — and other intruders. If you're like most computer users, you already have a host of passwords that you use at many points throughout the workday — to start up your computer, to sign on to your ISP, to enter your company's network, and even to read a newspaper online.

Although it may not matter that much whether someone else gets onto the *New York Times* Web site with your member name, it can matter a lot if someone who shouldn't gains access to your company's network — or gets into your account at an e-commerce site where your credit-card information is stored.

When you select passwords for things that truly matter, you want to make sure they are as difficult as possible for anyone else to figure out. Here are a few tips for making passwords harder to break:

- **Don't use the obvious.** Passwords based on your birth date, your maiden name, your children's names — or anything else that can easily be guessed by anyone who knows a little bit about you — are a bad idea. Be a little subtler.

  My ISP password is based on the pseudonym my paternal grandfather used when he wrote poetry many years ago. While you don't have to go that far, it's good to have a password that even people who know you probably cannot guess.

- **Don't make it all numbers.** A password that is nothing but a series of numbers is not a good idea, either. Some hacker programs are out there that can try numbers in sequence, and keep trying and trying, until they find the one that works. You're better off if whatever number finally works is someone else's password, not yours.

- **Don't make it a word.** Now imagine a program similar to the one above, except that instead of trying numbers, it goes through the dictionary instead.

- **Do mix letters and numbers.** A password that combines letters, numbers, and symbols is doubly hard for either of these two types of programs to uncover. It's worth it to give yourself this extra edge.

Avoiding viruses

A hacker is an actual person, trying to get onto your network for fun or thievery. A virus, on the other hand, is a purely technological foe. It's a bit of software written by someone, somewhere, who then unleashes it on the world purely for the pleasure of causing trouble. Some viruses are fairly innocuous.

One might, for instance, do no more than issue a message commemorating the birthday of its creator's favorite historical figure.

On the other hand, a virus can be highly destructive, wiping out all the information on your hard drive, damaging the drive itself, and sending itself on to everyone you know or have ever received an e-mail from.

Like a biological virus, a computer virus is self-replicating and keeps on spreading wherever it can, traveling along the Internet in a random path. It can keep going long after the person who created it has wound up in jail, died, or simply moved on and forgotten all about it.

Having one of these things get inside your computer is one of the worst dangers you face on the Net. To make matters worse, many viruses attach themselves to files that you send elsewhere — or that they themselves send — which means you can easily give a virus to hundreds of co-workers, acquaintances, and clients.

New viruses that can attack you in clever, unexpected ways are being developed even as you read this book. Several new viruses are discovered each day, and already more than 50,000 of them exist out there! The following sections offer you some ways to protect yourself against them.

Antivirus software

Most new computers come with some sort of virus protection, but if yours didn't, you absolutely need to get some before you spend another minute on the Internet.

Chances are, your company has virus protection software that it issues to employees in the office. You need to make sure you get it, too. Once you install the software, don't assume your computer won't ever get sick with a virus. New ones are being invented daily, and the only way antivirus software can be effective is if it is frequently updated, taking into account whatever new viruses have been discovered.

A monthly update is good. A weekly update is better. One painless way to do this is to set up the software to periodically connect with its manufacturer (Norton, for example) while you're on the Internet, and automatically download the updates it needs.

Be on your guard

One of the better ways to avoid a virus is to be exceedingly conservative about what you download. If, for example, I had downloaded that animated file the PR person sent to me, I'd have a great cautionary story to tell you right now about all the damage that it did.

As that incident illustrates, simply avoiding downloads from people you don't know is not protection enough. These things will send themselves out, and they can be incredibly sneaky.

A year ago, before starting his current job, my husband Bill sent an e-mail with his résumé in it to an executive at an Internet company who was looking for a community manager.

"Wow, the guy answered to me really quickly!" he told me happily that evening. The response read: "Dear Bill, thanks for your e-mail. I'll get back to you soon. In the meantime, here's some information for you to review."

Attached to the message was a zipped file. (Zipping is a method of file compression that allows large files or groups of files to be sent more efficiently over the Internet.) He tried to open the zipped file and — you guessed it — it immediately attacked his hard drive.

Turned out the guy had never e-mailed him at all. Instead, Bill had fallen victim to a particularly cleverly written virus. The executive whose computer had sent it was apologetic, of course. But the damage was already done.

If you receive an attached file that you aren't specifically expecting, even from someone you know well, your safest course is to contact that person, preferably by phone, to find out exactly what it is. In addition, be cautious about downloading software or other material from any but the trustworthiest Web sites. (If you're using a corporate computer, check out your company's policy relating to downloads.)

Beware of macros

A macro is an executable program that can run within other software applications, including popular ones such as Microsoft Outlook and Microsoft Word. Macros originally were intended to be a convenience, enabling users to compile a series of tasks and then execute them all with one single command. But because they run like any software, they also open a back door for viruses. For the first time, they made it possible to contract a virus simply by reading one's e-mail, although only in Outlook.

Your best protection is in how you set up the software you use. First, make sure your e-mail program is set up so that it does *not* automatically download files attached to e-mails. If you have Outlook, make sure it isn't set to run macros or visual basic code. The newest versions of Microsoft Word also allow you to limit or disallow its use of macros.

Keeping out Trojan horses

A Trojan horse (so named for the gift statue of a horse that turned out to be hiding soldiers inside) is a type of virus that claims to be software with a useful function but in reality does something else. Trojan horses can come hidden in games that you download or receive from a friend, supposed picture viewers, or animated graphics, to name just a few.

The reason is that Trojan horse viruses tend to be hidden in adult-oriented Web sites (possibly disguised as a picture viewer of some sort) and also in downloadable programs stored on badly monitored download sites.

In one of the more famous cases of a Trojan horse virus, visitors to various pornographic sites were invited to download a special viewer with promises that they'd be able to view titillating graphics once they did. Those who downloaded the software admired the pictures for a while, and then went on with their Web browsing, or simply left the computer and went about their business.

Yet, all was not well within their computers. Without their knowledge, the software they'd downloaded not only showed them the pictures they wanted to see, it also disconnected their modem from the Internet. It also muted the computer's sound, so they wouldn't be able to tell what was happening. Then it had the computer dial a telephone number in the Republic of Moldova.

What the heck is Moldova? It's a former Soviet Republic, and it's tiny and poor. So poor that the Moldovan phone company apparently agreed to collect the long-distance payments and kick back part of the money to the hackers who came up with this plan.

The computers stayed on the line with Moldova while the users continued to wander the Web. And even after the users had signed off the Internet and gone to bed, the virus maintained the connection to Moldova until the computer actually was switched off.

Victims of this Trojan horse virus received phone bills in the thousands of dollars. And because of international treaties governing international long distance, the long-distance companies were unwilling to remove the charges.

How can you avoid being caught by a Trojan horse? An external modem may be a good idea because they usually are equipped with lights that go off and on as it connects to and disconnects from the Internet. Even if you have an internal modem, you can also download free software from www.download. com that displays the same information on your monitor. (Download.com belongs to CNet and is a trustworthy site.) However, neither of these solutions will help you unless you also remember to keep an eye on the modem while you're online.

For the moment, being conservative about what you agree to download appears to be the best defense. Never download anything unless you're absolutely positively sure of the source — especially if you're on an adult site. Keep in mind, though, that anyone else who uses your computer can also put you at risk.

We found this out the hard way, when a houseguest used our phone line to connect his computer to the Internet. A few weeks later, a phone bill appeared showing a call to a place called Vanuatu. Mystified, we inquired with our phone company, and learned that Vanuatu is an island nation near Australia that apparently worked out the same sort of deal with some porn sites as had the Moldovans. The charge for the call was $25 and change. We figured we'd gotten off cheap.

Becoming an Effective Web User

Once you've put your Internet connection in place, and taken all the right security precautions, you can focus on getting the most out of the Web. When you telecommute, the Internet becomes an essential connection point between you and your co-workers. The more effectively you use it, the more you can keep the lines of communication open with everyone back at the office.

Network access

In the ideal situation, you can actually log onto your own company's LAN from wherever you are. Technologically speaking, among the several ways you can do this, the one that is gaining considerable attention right now is a new technology called virtual private network (VPN). *VPNs* use the existing network of the Internet to create a private network that is protected by encryption, and available only to recognized and password-protected users. The reason VPNs are so popular these days, Pardo says, is that they offer much greater security than the traditional firewall.

You may also be able to dial directly into the network, an older and less secure technology that can give you remote access. Or, if you can't get access to the whole network, you may be able to set up an area on the company's server where some of your work files would reside, and where you can have remote access via *file transfer protocol* (FTP) technology. This is simple technology used for moving files around on the Internet, and is commonly used for uploading or downloading to a Web site. FTP software is commercially available. This can be handy for a large work file that may not be so easy to e-mail or copy back and forth.

The advantage of being able to log onto the network is that you'll now be able to do from your home anything that you can do at the workplace. "VPNs have changed a lot of things for us," notes Pardo, who works from a remote office in North Carolina. "Everyone in my group can connect to the corporate network. We can use all the groupware applications on the company's intranet."

For one thing, it enables the members of Pardo's team to use Microsoft Outlook's calendar sharing feature to coordinate schedules and plan meetings with their distant colleagues. "VPN has made a huge difference in that area," he says.

If you're connecting to a company network, experts caution against staying on the network to work on files such as documents or presentations. Instead, downloading the material onto your own computer is recommended, so you can work on it there and then upload it back to the network when you're through. Doing so saves you considerable frustration and lost work if, for some reason, you unexpectedly lose your connection.

E-mail

These days, sending and receiving e-mail is a fact of corporate life. As a telecommuter, e-mail is an important tool you use to stay in touch, send work products back and forth, and communicate with those outside your company as well. It isn't the flashiest application on the Web, but it is the most useful — the Internet's *killer ap.*

As part of your adjustment to telecommuting, you probably need to make some changes in the way you handle your e-mail:

Multiple addresses

Once you have an Internet connection, you can make as many addresses as you desire, either through your own ISP or on one of the free services such as Yahoo!.

If you haven't done this already, now is the time to create different e-mail addresses for the different things that you do on the Web. You need at least two, one for work and one for family and recreation. And you may want more. For example, my husband Bill has a specific e-mail address he uses exclusively for shopping at online auctions and corresponding with the sellers there.

Keeping separate e-mail addresses helps you keep different parts of your life separate. It also can be handy in case you find yourself receiving correspondence (applying for a different job, say) that you'd rather didn't go through your company's system.

E-mail management

Once you've set up your multiple addresses, you may wonder how you can keep track of all your mail. Some Internet professionals favor e-mail software that simultaneously handles e-mail from several different addresses. On the other hand, some argue that using different e-mail readers for your different addresses makes them easier to keep track of. You decide.

E-mail filters can be another useful tool, sorting e-mail by subject line or by sender, and then placing it in different folders that you create. This can be useful for separating, say, a copy of the minutes of a meeting that has been cc'd to you as an urgent message from your boss.

E-mail response times

If you're working on site and one of your colleagues sends you an e-mail requesting information that you don't have at your fingertips, you might set the e-mail aside temporarily until you've had a chance to properly research the question. Then you can get back to your colleague with a complete answer a day or two later.

Delaying responses to e-mail is a viable way to work when you're in the office, but not when you're telecommuting. According to traditional social norms of the office, if you're not at your desk on site, you're not working at all. It can be easy for the most well-meaning co-worker to act as though your days away are days off. This kind of situation can quickly result in your being left outside of the corporate loop.

You risk reinforcing this impression if you don't respond immediately to your co-worker's messages. So telecommuting is one situation where it's a good idea to respond — even if you have nothing to say. "Got your e-mail. I don't have enough information to give you a good answer right away. I'll do some digging and get back to you by the end of the day tomorrow." This kind of message lets your correspondent know that even though you're not in the office, you're definitely on the job.

Instant messaging and chat

Instant messaging technology allows you to converse in text format with others on the Internet. Several different instant messaging networks are available on the Web. Two of the more widely used ones are ICQ and AOL's Instant Messenger. (Both are free.) You can give the software a list of user names for your co-workers (and/or relatives and friends), and whenever you're on the network, it tells you which of your contacts is on as well. Most software enables you to include links within instant messages (so you can send co-workers links to Web pages of interest) and to send files; however, some users prefer to turn this feature off for security reasons.

Net-savvy telecommuters report that this one piece of technology is the most useful tool they have for staying in touch throughout the day, answering questions and passing information back and forth, often between two people, but sometimes in a small group. Several mentioned that the rhythm of instant messages is exactly right for answering questions or providing help.

Most of the instant message programs have several other useful features. You can post a list of instant message user names for co-workers, friends, and others. Here are a few tips for working effectively with instant messages:

Work names and play names

As with multiple e-mail addresses, you may decide to create multiple names for instant message chat, because most instant message software enables users to see who among their friends and acquaintances is signed on. If you have friends who like to chat, and they see you online, they're likely to send you messages. You'll either have to stop what you're doing and chat with them or tell them you're too busy to converse, which can feel rude under some circumstances. Or else you can ignore the message and hope they assume that you've walked away but left your computer connected.

You can avoid all this by creating an instant message identity solely for work purposes, and giving the name only to colleagues and co-workers (and perhaps family members, for use in an emergency). On the flip side, your work contacts won't be able to message you with work matters if you're relaxing and chatting with your friends after hours, which may also be a good thing.

Spend some time "alone"

Although Donna Gettings spends her entire workday connected to the Internet, she says, "I do not leave instant messaging software open for the first few hours, preferring to be *alone.*"

Indeed, one of the great advantages of instant messaging is that it's easy to switch back and forth between an ongoing conversation and, say, reading your e-mail. But it's also true that messages popping in can be a real distraction when you're working on larger tasks that require focus and concentration. So it's probably wise to block out the instant messages for part of your workday. If someone *really* needs you, they can always pick up the phone.

Use short answers

In instant message chat, it's better to keep the conversation flowing by being reasonably quick when answering questions and comments. That's one reason why short answers tend to be a better choice than long ones. If you have a long response to convey, say it a line or two at a time, and write "more" or " . . . " at the end of each comment so that the person receiving the message will know that you haven't finished. What you don't want to do is spend ten minutes writing up your answer, and then hit the other person with a giant block of text that he or she has to scroll through to read.

Be patient

When you say something to someone in conversation, it's natural to want an immediate reply. Once they get comfortable with the technology, many instant message users expect the same sort of immediate reply.

But those desires and expectations aren't reasonable in this context. The person you're chatting with may have suddenly gotten a phone call (it's almost impossible to instant message and talk on the phone at the same time). Or the boss may have just walked into his or her office. So, rather than getting impatient, try turning your attention to other work for a few minutes. Most instant message programs give you some sort of audio signal when a new line of chat comes across.

Remember that text lacks personality

Many, many times, while instant messaging, I've written a line of text and then pulled up suddenly when I realized how it was going to come across. Comments that I would've softened by accompanying them with a smile or a shrug can appear stark when written in black on white. That's one reason many experienced chatters use *emoticons,* such as :-) or <g> (meaning grin). They let the other person know when not to take things too seriously.

Not everyone likes to use emoticons. And they may not be appropriate in every setting. But, regardless of whether you use them, be sure to give your comments a quick read, making sure you're not going to accidentally offend someone.

Keep a record

Some people still have trouble taking instant messaging seriously. Thus, if you have an important conversation, be sure to keep a record of it. You can do this by cutting and pasting the conversation itself into a document, text file, or e-mail. Most programs have a way of showing a date and time on the message as well. And it's a good idea to send a copy to the other person in your conversation as a reminder and a chance to review what was said.

Create an "I'm away" message

Sometimes you see people apparently signed on to their instant message software, and yet when you message them, they don't respond. They're not being rude; they've probably just stepped away from their computers to stretch their legs or get a snack, or maybe they've left the office for the day, but have a 24-hour Internet connection and have left their instant message software running.

To address this problem, instant message software now offers the opportunity to post a message explaining that the user is away from the computer, comparable to an answering machine message. That answer is automatically sent to anyone who sends an instant message to you while the "I'm away" message is in place. The person looking for you can also leave a message that you'll find when you get back to your computer.

But wait a second. A message you leave for a person to read when he or she gets back to the computer? Isn't that functionally the same thing as e-mail? "It seems much more immediate than e-mail," Pardo says. "E-mail, you read when you need to and reply when you can, not necessarily instantly. Instant messages have the immediacy of conversation."

Web-based conferencing

You may have heard that videoconferencing will be the next big thing. So have I. In fact, it has been about to be the next big thing for as long as I can remember.

While some organizations are making good use of videoconferencing today, it hasn't caught on across Corporate America. So far, the technology has not quite lived up to the promise of being able to sit down at your computer and wave hello to your co-workers in the next state.

The widespread use of videoconferencing, though, is getting easier all the time. Small, digital video cameras that can sit on a desk or on top of a monitor are now widely available and inexpensive. Videoconferencing software, such as CU-SeeMe and Microsoft NetMeeting, is available as well.

The big problem with videoconferencing is bandwidth. Videoconferencing requires fast uploads and downloads. Videoconferencing over a dial-up connection is so slow and cumbersome that it rarely works well, and when it does, the image tends to be unpleasantly jerky.

But the infrastructure to provide greater high-speed access to more locations is being built even as I write this, and it may not be long until enough bandwidth is available to make videoconferencing a viable tool.

Then, it may *really* become the next big thing. Or maybe not. Stay tuned.

Meanwhile, another form of Web-based conferencing is gaining much wider acceptance. Web conferencing uses collaborative browsing, which enables users in several locations to look at the same Web pages at the same time. With audio, which works better over slower access than does video, a speaker can make a presentation using the material on the page (a spreadsheet, for instance) as a visual aid.

With this *whiteboard* technology, users can actually write and draw on the screen, for example, making a circle around a particularly important number. Audio can be on, thus permitting other users to speak to the presenter and each other, either over the Internet or traditional phone lines. Or they can be *muted* during the presentation.

In a large group (one can have hundreds, and even thousands, of attendees at a Web conference) you can have a moderator filter questions at the end.

Ideally, one can even imagine combining videoconferencing and collaborative browsing, thus enabling Web users to see the speaker and the visual aid. But for now, Web conferencing appears to be the more practical solution.

Part III

Adjusting to Your New Work Life

The 5th Wave   By Rich Tennant

"Does our insurance cover a visit from Mike Wallace?"

In this part . . .

Your telecommuting job is in place. Your home (or remote) office is all set up. You're ready to start your telecommuting work life.

Be prepared for some big adjustments. Becoming a successful telecommuter means learning skills you may not have needed as an on-site employee. It also means overcoming obstacles you wouldn't have encountered if you'd stayed in the office.

Your new status as a telecommuter will mean adjustments for your boss, your co-workers — and the other members of your household. Use this part to help you make these changes as smooth as possible.

Chapter 9

Planning Your Telecommuting Career

*B*efore you start your telecommuting career, be sure to take some time to plan how your new relationship with your boss will work. Issues that won't ever arise if you're working together at the office can quickly become big problems when you're doing your work at another location.

The Pretelecommuting Conference

Clear and specific communication affords you the best chance for avoiding problems before they happen, so you and your boss need to spell out every aspect of your telecommuting work. This is the single most important step you can take to make your transition to telecommuting a successful one.

A better way to do this is at a pretelecommuting conference. A couple of weeks before you begin working from a remote site, ask to schedule a time so that you and your boss can sit down in a formal meeting with as few interruptions as possible. This in itself lets your boss know that you take your responsibilities as a telecommuter seriously and that you have a high degree of commitment to making the arrangement work.

You need to come to the meeting prepared to ask some questions. Take this opportunity to find out whether your boss has any particular fears or concerns about managing telecommuters. For instance, maybe your boss is especially afraid of not being able to find you when you're needed. If so, you can avoid that trouble before it happens by setting a frequent schedule for checking in and checking your voice mail or e-mail.

You also need to come prepared to take notes. You and your boss will nail down a vast array of details about your telecommuting work life during your telecommuting conference. After the meeting, you can set these agreed-on points down on paper, creating a telecommuting agreement that you and your boss can sign. This gives you a chance to make sure there are no misunderstandings.

Your Telecommuting Schedule

The first item you and your boss need to decide at your telecommuting conference is exactly when you'll be working outside the office. Will you work from home one day a week or four days a week? Will it vary at different times of the month or of the year? (For example, when you're working on monthly or year-end reports.)

How much time you spend working at home affects many other telecommuting issues. For instance, if you're out of the office four days a week, it may be important that co-workers and customers be able to reach you easily whenever they have questions or problems.

But let's say you're working from home only one day a week and using that time for writing, research, strategy planning, design, or anything else that requires long periods of uninterrupted concentration. In that case, you may want to approach the issue of access differently, giving your home number only to your boss and your assistant, if you have one. You must also make sure that your co-workers understand they're not to disturb you except for urgent matters and that they know how to get in touch with you, if they truly must.

One day here, one day there

If you're working from home more than one day a week, you and your boss may decide that you'll telecommute on alternating days — Tuesdays and Thursdays, for example. A schedule like this can be helpful from a workplace-relations point of view. Because you're only out of the office one day at a time, you may feel more in touch with co-workers, and they may not feel that you're as absent as if you stayed out two days in a row — even though you're absent the same amount: two days out of the week.

The trade-off is that alternating days telecommuting and days working in the office makes it harder for you to work efficiently. Telecommuters who shuttle back and forth between working in the office and working at home report that needing work materials from one place when they're in the other is a consistent problem. "It's easy to have someone e-mail me a file from the office, but not so easy if the forgotten file is on my home computer." That's how one telecommuter puts it. Finding yourself working in a different spot every day also can be unsettling.

If you try an alternating day schedule, it helps if you give some thought to how technology can make it easier. A remote connection to your company's network, for example, helps you coordinate your schedule smoothly and cuts down on worries about files that are left in the wrong place.

Using a laptop computer also can help because you're always working on the same computer. However, you have to lug it back and forth twice as often. Keep in mind that a keyboard-and-monitor setup, or a docking station, at each of your locations, makes this a more ergonomically sound option. (For a full discussion of laptops, see Chapter 7.)

One day now, more later

Another option is for you to start out telecommuting one day a week, with a plan to increase your time spent telecommuting in the future, once you and your boss see how it goes. Using this approach is a good way to ease into telecommuting, and it gives you a chance to find out whether you like working at home as much as you thought you would.

Assuming that you prefer to telecommute more, settling on an agenda for reviewing your telecommuting arrangement is a good idea. Doing so helps you answer how soon you and your boss will meet again to discuss the question of telecommuting more and what criteria your boss will use to make the decision.

Keep in mind that your boss is probably busy with many things, and once an arrangement is in place, taking the time to discuss the same issue all over again may be hard for him or her to do. So let's say you decide right from the start that in three months, if you've been able to produce written reports more efficiently from home, you'll change your current telecommuting schedule from Fridays to Thursdays and Fridays.

Three months later, you knock on your boss's door with a memo that compares the eight full-length reports you produced during your telecommuting period with only five you would've been able to finish had you worked in the office every day. You include some information about steps you've taken to keep up with other work that might normally be done in the office. And then you propose that, beginning in two weeks, you'll switch to a Thursday and Friday telecommuting schedule.

This strategy won't work if your telecommuting performance is not up to par, your co-workers are unhappy with your absence, or if your boss has been frustrated when he or she tried to reach you at home. But, if everything has been going well, it gives your boss the chance to rubber-stamp a prearranged deal, instead of giving the question careful consideration all over again.

Your Check-In Schedule

Once your telecommuting schedule is in place, your next order of business is deciding how and how often to check in with your boss. Here are a few of your many options:

- ✔ A daily phone call explaining to your boss what you'll be doing that day (and/or the following day) and receiving any special instructions or information.

- ✔ A daily e-mail in which you report the day's activities.

- ✔ A weekly report detailing what you accomplished while working at home and forecasting what you plan to accomplish the next week.

- ✔ Attending by conference call a weekly staff meeting.

- ✔ None of the above: You and your boss are in frequent contact anyway, and no special check-in is necessary.

As is true of many aspects of telecommuting, no absolutes exist. Some telecommuters report that with a daily check-in, they get the information they need to effectively do their work, and feel more *in the loop* than they otherwise would. In fact, one telecommuter I spoke with reports feeling dangerously cut off from the company grapevine ever since changing from a job with a regular check-in schedule to one with a different boss and no check-in schedule.

Balancing these views are reports from still other telecommuters who say that not having a set check-in schedule is just fine with them. "It shows that my boss trusts me," one says. "That's a good feeling. Also, because we don't call or e-mail just to check in, we each know that a message from the other is about something important, and therefore give it high priority."

Your use of chat technology also helps you determine whether you need a set check-in schedule. Let's say you and your boss have full-time Internet connections and chat software that is open most of the time. You may find that you have an informal ongoing conversation on and off throughout the day, whenever either of you has a question, problem, or idea. With this kind of constant contact, a formal check-in may be unnecessary.

Finding a check-in (or no check-in) arrangement that's right for your job, your working style, and your boss is important. Here are some principles that may help:

- ✔ **Don't let yourself feel cut off.** You may not really need to provide or receive information every day. But *not* checking in leaves some people feeling disconnected from their organizations. If you feel this way (or expect that you will), you must make sure that you get the daily contact you need. Explain to your boss that it's important for you to have a quick conversation — even if only for five minutes — on a daily basis. If your boss's schedule makes this impossible, perhaps you can select a close colleague to check in with instead.

- ✔ **Make sure your check-in meets your boss's needs.** You may be perfectly able to work effectively on your own for several days at a time. On the other hand, your boss may need the reassurance of a daily check-in. Remember that supervising someone who isn't in the office can be an uncomfortable challenge. Checking in daily may help your boss adjust.

- ✔ **Once you make an agreement, stick with it.** Telecommuters who don't check in when they're supposed to are a frequent cause of complaint among managers. One telecommuter who admitted sometimes skipping his scheduled check-ins reports that it has caused tensions with the boss.

  As a telecommuter, you're asking for your supervisor's trust. You need to show that you deserve that trust by living up to whatever check-in commitment you've made, even if it means calling when you don't really think it's necessary.

- ✔ **It's easier to stop checking in than to start.** Therefore, the best idea may be to start out your telecommuting life with a daily check-in schedule in place. Over time, as you and your boss become accustomed to your new working arrangement, the daily phone call or e-mail may come to seem like a formality. At that point, you may both decide that checking in isn't needed anymore.

Making Yourself Available

When managers and other on-site workers talk about their telecommuting colleagues or employees, one issue almost always comes up: availability. You can never find telecommuting employees when you need them, so the gripe goes.

I suspect the problem stems from the same qualities that can make telecommuting an efficient way to work. For instance, many telecommuters find that they can do more in a home office because they face fewer interruptions from their co-workers. By the same token, those co-workers aren't around to track that employee down for an impromptu meeting or to answer an urgent question.

Likewise, if you're on a long phone call at the office, your assistant or an office neighbor can poke a head in the door and whisper to you that your boss or an important client needs you *now*. On the other hand, a supervisor, colleague, or client, who calls and gets your home-office voice mail when you're working at home, has no choice but to wait for a return call. (For more on voice mail and other phone service options for your home office, see Chapter 7.)

Similarly, working at home can be ideal for jobs like research or report writing, which are done best with long periods of concentration. But those same long, nonstop work periods may mean you're not stopping that often to check your e-mail.

Nine-to-five or flextime?

The biggest reason telecommuters sometimes are unavailable when they're wanted is that they're not working on the same schedule as the rest of the office. Some telecommuting jobs require that you keep regular hours. For example, telephone and/or chat customer service people need to answer calls during specific hours of the day — although those hours may not be 9 a.m. to 5 p.m.

But for most other types of telecommuting-appropriate jobs, some flexibility in work hours may be perfectly feasible. In this mode of work, often called *flextime,* you make sure to put in a full workday, but you set your work schedule to take into account your personal schedule and working preferences.

In general, telecommuting workers are evaluated solely on their accomplishments, not the hours they spend on the job (more about that later in this chapter). So flextime may be a natural fit.

"It is fantastic to be judged on the work I do, rather than how I do it," notes one telecommuter who asked me not to use his name. He adds that he likes working in the morning and early afternoon, making any work-related phone calls then, taking some time off in the late afternoon, and then working in the evening. "It's just how I work best," he says. Even so, he tries to send his boss e-mails throughout the day to show that he's at his desk early and still there late.

"Bosses don't see you working at home at night," he says. "But they do notice if you slack off and read in the afternoon. It's nice not to be watched, to be able to make a personal phone call or do yoga for a half-hour at 3 p.m., instead of taking a coffee break, and still get the job done. Mine is an eight-hour *workday.* At the office, their eight-hour day is broken up by meetings, lunch, impromptu meetings, gossip, breaks, and coffee. Offices are terribly unproductive places."

Most of the telecommuters I've talked with take some sort of flextime approach to their jobs, making sure they're on hand for conference calls and other important phone calls during the day, but often doing their solo work outside of traditional office hours. While this can be an efficient way of working, it can cause misunderstandings and resentment and even derail your career advancement if you don't carefully work out this issue with your boss ahead of time.

"What I typically see happening is an agreement about *core* hours," notes telecommuting consultant and author Gil Gordon. "For example, between 9 and 11 a.m., and 1 and 3 p.m., the telecommuter commits to being at his or her desk and available during those hours."

How often will you check for messages?

Once you and your boss have settled on your at-home work schedule, and dealt with the question of flextime versus office hours, you'll have to tackle a second availability question: How often during the workday will you check for phone messages, e-mails, and faxes?

This issue is just as important. After all, you can sit dutifully at your desk from 8 a.m. to 6 p.m., and *still* get on your boss's bad side if the important phone call you missed at 10 (when you stepped outside to collect your mail) isn't returned until after 4.

Similarly, you may think it's perfectly reasonable to check your e-mail once when you arrive at your desk in the morning and again before you leave it at the end of the day. Yet your boss may think it's reasonable to expect you to answer an important e-mail within half an hour of receiving it. You're likely to run into big misunderstandings if you don't settle questions like these before your telecommuting work begins.

Once you've settled on a schedule for checking voice mail and e-mail, you may also want to discuss when you'll have your chat software open. For example, if you've made a commitment to be at your desk from 2 to 4 every afternoon, you may want to make sure you're online, and reachable by instant message during those hours. (Some flexibility is required, though, because even the most dependable Internet connections sometimes fail, and many people — including me — find it completely impossible to chat online while talking on the phone.)

What about meetings?

Another question you and your boss need to discuss is how to deal with departmental or staff meetings that you'd normally attend if you were in the office. In this context, it's worth noting that not having to spend time at meetings is unquestionably one of the reasons telecommuters are able to get more work done than their on-site colleagues. Indeed, the prospect of escaping at least some meetings is one of telecommuting's biggest appeals for many people.

Some get-togethers simply are too important to skip. In these cases, you have to bite the bullet and travel to the office, even if it's on a day you're normally scheduled to be working at home. The key is to choose these occasions wisely, because if you're constantly interrupting your work-at-home schedule to attend meetings, the promised productivity gains that probably helped sell the idea to your boss won't materialize.

How do you know which meetings are worth the trip? Here are some good ways to gauge:

- ✔ **How much do they need your input?** Your boss may assume you absolutely need to attend all-hands-on-deck company-wide announcement meetings. But if all you really need to do is listen, then announcements may be something you can listen to just as well over the telephone. On the other hand, if you need to present information, and especially if you need to answer questions, it's easier for you and your colleagues if you physically attend.

- ✔ **How much will you need to interact?** Let's say you need to make a ten-minute presentation that describes your department's activities during the past month. Afterward, you'll have to answer about five minutes of questions from supervisors in other departments. While doing this in person would certainly be better, you may be able to adequately provide the needed information and answers via a speakerphone, Web conference, or videoconference, so that a trip to the office may not be necessary.

  On the other hand, imagine that you're a member of an eight-person team engaged in a two-hour brainstorming session, trying to come up with new ideas for marketing your department's products. Your total input during this meeting may still amount to only the same 15 minutes required in the example above. But this second meeting requires much more in the way of intimacy, informality, and the free interplay of ideas. Being on site in this case is likely to be much more important.

- ✔ **Will your absence affect the team?** Let's say you're part of a team that turned in a disappointing performance this month, or made a costly error that embarrassed your company. Your manager calls everyone together in a meeting to discuss what went wrong. Your input won't be needed because the manager will do most of the talking, and everyone else will mostly be listening. So is it important for you to be there in person?. Absolutely. Otherwise, the rest of your team can easily become resentful, feeling that you've used your telecommuting status to duck out and dodge the issue, leaving everyone else to be called on the carpet without you.

✔ **Are you working with people for the first time?** It's much easier for your co-workers to work more effectively with you via the speakerphone at a meeting if they already know who you are. Your absence and not knowing who you are is doubly disconcerting for people who can't match a face to your voice. Thus, many telecommuters try to follow the rule that if they're meeting with someone for the first time, they need to be there in the flesh.

✔ **Are there political reasons to be there?** Sometimes, you need to show up at a meeting for no better reason than that you must be seen there. For example, your office is welcoming a new vice president who recently jumped ship from another company. Your team doesn't need you, your input isn't required, and you won't hear anything at the meeting that you couldn't hear over a conference call. So, you could meet the new veep next week, when your regular schedule brings you back to the office. Is it okay to skip attending this welcoming meeting? Maybe, and then again, maybe not. The answer depends on your particular company's culture and office traditions. In a situation like this, where you risk making a powerful enemy, make sure you know exactly what message you're sending before deciding not to show.

Attending meetings by phone

A popular solution these days is for telecommuters to attend important meetings by phone. One common scenario is having a speakerphone set up in the middle of the conference table where the meeting is taking place. The telecommuter phones in, or is phoned at the appointed time, and is connected to the speakerphone. This setup enables the telecommuter to hear and be heard by everyone in the room.

Some telecommuters secretly admit that they prefer attending meetings this way. "When it's over, I can just hang up and go back to what I was doing. I don't have to hang around schmoozing with everyone," one comments. "Meetings at company locations are often longer than they need to be," notes another. Having people call in to them tends to streamline the process."

Regardless of whether it's more efficient, this is a new way of working that at first can feel awkward to the person communicating via the speakerphone and to those sitting at the conference table talking back to it. For advice about how to make attending meetings by speakerphone function smoothly, I turned to my husband Bill, who spends several hours doing this every week. Here are a few of his suggestions:

✔ **Use a high-quality phone.** If at all possible, avoid using a cell phone or a cordless phone that makes static noises when too far from its base. For speakerphone meetings, you want as clear and fuzz-free a connection as possible.

✓ **Use the mute button.** Many telecommuters, especially those with babies and noisy pets, are big fans of the *mute* buttons that come on many phones these days. Muting is an especially useful feature during a meeting, where much of the time you need only to be able to hear and not to be heard.

During meetings, Bill uses a (high-quality) cordless headset phone with a mute button so he can roam around the house, pause to say a few words to me (if I'm on my way to the store, for example), and pour himself a glass of water or soda without the sound distracting anyone. In fact, he routinely keeps his end muted, turning the mouthpiece back on just long enough to say something when he has something to say.

✓ **Request handouts in advance.** If handouts are going to be provided at this meeting, make sure that you get a copy of your own. You'll be a step ahead of the game if you can get someone at the office to fax you a copy before the meeting starts. That way, you and your colleagues literally can be on the same page.

✓ **Visualize the meeting.** I know this may sound weird, but Bill swears it really helps. Try visualizing the group of people you'll be speaking and listening to seated around the conference table. He says visualizing is especially useful if members of the group go around the room, introducing themselves beforehand. That way Bill can mentally locate each person.

Bill does this in his head, but then he's unusually good at this kind of mental imaging. I'm not so good at it, so if I were trying to do this, I think I'd use a pencil and paper to make a quick diagram of where people are. That way I can refer to it as the meeting progresses.

Don't forget to visualize your own place in the meeting. Usually, you (that is, the speakerphone, which is your voice and ears) will be located in the middle of the conference table. Bill says it helps him to visualize himself there, too, peeking out from behind the phone.

✓ **Follow the whiteboard.** Things get much trickier if whoever is conducting the meeting is writing on a whiteboard as the meeting progresses. Unless you're using Web conferencing technology, you won't be able to see what actually is being written. Most of the time, though, you'll find that you can make a pretty good guess. For instance, if the speaker asks for new product ideas, and the people at the meeting make suggestions in response, the speaker is probably writing down those suggestions, or at least the more promising ones. Whatever's being written there, you also need to write it down at your end. If you're not sure you've gotten it right, you can always compare your notes with those of someone who was at the meeting.

✓ **Speak up often.** Obviously, you don't want to rudely interrupt someone who's giving a presentation. But during portions of the meeting where everyone is free to speak, it helps if you speak up more rather than less frequently.

Keep in mind that you're out of eye contact with other people at the meeting. If you were actually sitting there, you'd be sending out a constant stream of nonverbal signals as the discussion continued. You may fidget during a tedious part of the presentation, nod and smile at a clever suggestion, roll your eyes if you're certain something won't work, or shrug at an idea that's too new for you to know much about. Half the time, these signals are unconscious, almost involuntary, but they all serve as communication that is completely cut off when you're on the speakerphone. So you have to compensate by actually saying some of what you'd be communicating with all that body language. "Try to say something about as often as you would give a nonverbal signal," Bill advises.

✔ **Make sure you come through loud and clear.** This piece of advice doesn't come from Bill — but then he's a six-foot-tall barrel-chested baritone who doubles as a professional singer and has never had any trouble making his voice heard in any situation.

For the rest of us, who may tend to mumble or talk too quickly or too softly, it's important to remember that speakerphones are imperfect technology. They may make it possible for a whole roomful of people to hear you, but the trade-off is that none of them will hear you as well as they would if they had a receiver against their ear. Compensate by speaking more slowly, and perhaps a little louder than usual, and by properly enunciating.

✔ **Keep an eye out for new technology.** If promised increases in bandwidth materialize, videoconferencing and Web-based conferencing may become more available, even for small, garden-variety meetings. Seeing and being seen can make a big difference if you're feeling disconnected during a staff meeting. Likewise, if your colleagues in the office use Web conferencing technology instead of a physical whiteboard, you'll be better able to follow the action.

Getting the crib notes

Perhaps it's because attending meetings by speakerphone is a different way of working, but some people simply never are comfortable with it. "I personally *hate* doing it," one telecommuter confides. "I feel left out, I don't feel like I have valuable input, and it's hard to be heard as a disembodied voice over a phone."

In fact, he hates it so much that he's devised an alternate strategy. These days, instead of calling in to the speakerphone for a staff meeting, he gets the scoop after the fact. "I ask each person on the staff for an account of what happened at the meeting. That way, I get an overall picture of what was said."

Depending on the nature of your job, the nature of the meetings that take place while you're working off-site, and the expectations of your boss and co-workers, getting information after the fact may be an effective substitute for calling in. Here are some tips:

✔ **Find a *designated note-taker*.** It's probably wise to ask for several people's impressions of what happened at a meeting. You're likely to get a much more complete picture than any one of them can give you. (You may also be surprised to discover just how divergent their different descriptions will be.)

But it's also a good idea to find one person who will take notes with the specific intent of sharing them with you afterward. For one thing, most people take notes that are intended merely to jog their own memories of the meetings they attend. Whereas someone who's planning to share the information is more likely write it down more clearly and completely.

Of course, this means asking someone to go to a fair amount of extra trouble, so unless that person is your assistant and taking notes for you is part of the job, you need to consider finding some way of returning the favor.

✔ **Make sure you get a copy of any handouts.** Although in this instance, you won't be following along during the meeting, it's still a good idea to obtain handouts and background material as quickly after the meeting as possible. You then can look at it, along with whatever notes and other accounts you receive to paint a more complete picture of what took place.

✔ **Check in with the meeting leader.** As a matter of courtesy and office protocol, make sure you contact whoever is leading the meeting beforehand, to say that you won't be attending. The last thing you want is for your absence (even by phone) to come as an unwelcome surprise. Explain that you'll be getting detailed notes and other information from the meeting, and that you'll make sure you get a copy of any handouts. There's a small chance that your absence might even be welcome news for the meeting leader, who may be just as uncomfortable as you are with your presence as a disembodied voice.

✔ **Plan to give input.** Most meetings aren't a one-way street. You're expected to ask questions, help come up with ideas, and trade information with other people who attend. There's no escaping the fact that if you skip a meeting, you won't be able to do any of these things. So you need to compensate. Ask the meeting leader if he or she wants your input by e-mail after you've reviewed the notes from the handouts. Find out whether you need to address any specific issues or questions.

✔ **Make good use of the time you save.** Some of your co-workers would probably love to skip office meetings, too. So your best argument for retaining this special privilege is to demonstrate what the company or department gains by your absence. Use the extra time to write a needed report or fill out some paperwork that someone else in your department would have had to do instead. Taking on some of your team's *scut* work to make up for time that you didn't spend at the meeting may also help you avoid any resentment or jealousy from co-workers.

Getting called in

It's the first of your two telecommuting days this week. You crawl out of bed, and pad to the kitchen to make yourself some coffee. You're looking forward to a quiet day, alone in front of your own home computer, catching up on some of the work that distractions keep you from getting done when you're at the office.

Suddenly, the phone rings. It's your boss's assistant, calling to tell you that an unexpected emergency has arisen. You have to come in to the office as quickly as you can.

Depending on the nature of your office and your job, being called in to handle unexpected problems or emergencies can be something that never would happen — or something that may arise on a regular basis. Either way, you and your boss need to work out the details before you start telecommuting. That way, dealing with this situation won't come as a surprise to either of you.

Here are some issues to consider:

- ✔ **Under what circumstances can you be called in?** Does it have to be a true work emergency (a major system failure only you can fix, for example)? Can you be called in to cover for someone else who's out sick? To keep a visiting client entertained?

- ✔ **Will you *make up* the days you're called in?** If you normally stay home two days a week, but you're called in on one of those days, can you stay home three days next week? How will you catch up on the work you were planning to do at home?

- ✔ **How often can you be called in?** Of course, it's impossible to predict when or how often unexpected crises will occur — or they wouldn't be so unexpected. On the other hand, you won't be able to demonstrate the benefits of working from home if your telecommuting plans are consistently being superseded by one emergency after another.

- ✔ **How will you deal with dependent care?** Most employers frown on using telecommuting as a way to solve your child-care or elder-care problems, regardless of whether you might suddenly be called to the office. If you have dependents at home and being called in to the office is a real possibility, this probably is an issue you and your boss need to discuss up front.

In essence, making appropriate arrangements so that you can report to your workplace, if need be, is up to you. The exception might be if you have an emergency of your own, such as a child who's sick and staying home from school.

Moonlighting

One reason many managers resist telecommuting is that they fear telecommuters will wind up collecting their salaries but actually spend their time working at a business of their own or a second job. And, indeed, I've heard of telecommuters who actually took a second job while they were supposed to be working a telecommuting job — and, of course, before long were busted.

A more common scenario is for telecommuters to start a small business on the side. It makes sense if you think about it. The same qualities that make a good telecommuter — drive, self-motivation, self-sufficiency, and the ability to work well alone — also make a good entrepreneur. And the logistics are easier. If you want to take a few minutes during a coffee break at the office to make a phone call relating to your own business, you may have trouble finding the privacy you need. When you're working at home, that isn't an obstacle. And you already have a home office all set up.

If you're interested in moonlighting, how should you approach this thorny subject with your boss? Gil Gordon, on his Web site, www.gilgordon.com, suggests a useful approach. He points out that moonlighting is not unique to telecommuting workers. As a work practice, it's been around for generations, and unless your company is new, someone before you already has tried it.

Long-term decisions

Starting a side business while holding down a full-time job means making some decisions about your long-term career plans. You must give some thought to your ultimate goals before you get started. If your dream is to quit your current job once your business starts making enough money, then it may not matter to you if moonlighting cuts into your career advancement potential. On the other hand, if your side business is more like a hobby (say, you teach fly-fishing to tourists during the summer months), make sure that your employer knows that's all it is. If you just need a little extra cash, let your employer know that as well.

In some cases, starting a side business may be an effective means to a career switch within your current company. For example, you just finished training as a CPA, but your company has no corresponding job openings. Taking on a few clients at tax time can give you experience that will help you make the transfer when a job does become available.

Finally, don't take on a side business without first giving some thought to how it's going to affect your personal life. Starting a business while holding down a job can put a massive strain on your energy level, your health, your social life, your spouse, your kids, your budget, and your sleep patterns. You — and your spouse — need to consider all these factors before taking the plunge.

Whether it's a written, official, no-exceptions policy, or a more fluid, case-by-case approach, your company's management probably has a policy for dealing with the issue of moonlighting. Find out what the policy is and how your organization has dealt with moonlighting in the past. This gives you some idea of how to approach the issue with your boss.

In general, you shouldn't even consider moonlighting until you've successfully been telecommuting for a while; otherwise, you risk feeding into your boss's worst fears about telecommuters. Even then, before considering it, you need to take your company's policies, practices, and prejudices into account.

Moonlighting policies vary from company to company. But you're more likely to stay out of trouble if you observe the following rules:

✔ **Be honest.** Discuss your plans with your boss, and make sure he or she knows the moonlight work you do will not interfere at all with your current job.

✔ **Do your job well.** You're pretty much guaranteed to have a big problem if moonlighting is perceived to impair your performance in your main job.

✔ **Avoid conflicts of interest.** Your entrepreneurial business must not be in competition with your employer business. Neither should you work for a company that is. And don't work for a company that could be a customer, supplier, legal adversary, or have other direct or indirect dealings with your employer. You're probably better off working in a completely different industry, if possible.

✔ **Protect confidential information.** Your company's practices, technical information, marketing strategies, and even who its best employees are is confidential information that you must not share outside your company. In fact, if you signed a nondisclosure agreement, you may be legally liable if you do.

✔ **Make sure to be available.** Not being available when your boss, co-workers, or customers need you is a quick way to cause trouble for yourself at your current job. Make sure your outside work doesn't create this problem.

How Your Work Is Evaluated

Many years ago, I worked in a company known for developing and training young business journalists. The editorial director there had a whole system in place for evaluating us as we went along. One day, a man came to work for the company who was clearly brilliant but also seemed deeply troubled. It was obvious to all of us except the editorial director that he was having trouble with his job.

"He never leaves," the editorial director said to me once, approvingly, as the new man spent yet another late evening at his desk. The man rose rapidly within the company, until he landed in a job with heavy responsibilities he clearly couldn't handle. In the end, he was fired.

Almost all managers — even ones like this editorial director, with carefully constructed systems for judging employee performance objectively — have a hard time discounting how much time they see employees at their desks as a big part of their evaluation process. Employees seated at their desks must be working hard. Employees not at their desks must be sloughing off. These are deeply ingrained assumptions in the business world that can affect your evaluations and performance reviews — even if your boss doesn't intend them to.

What can you do? Talking about it is a good place to start. But cast the conversation in a positive light. For example, ask if you can discuss how your performance will be evaluated and whether your working outside the office will affect that process. It's in your and your boss's best interests to have a clear idea how your work will be judged.

Ideally, you need to come away from the meeting with answers to the following questions.

What specific achievements will mean you're doing a good job?

Finding out what specific achievements determine whether you're doing a good job is a question everyone needs to answer any time they start a new job or take on new responsibilities. In an early job of mine, I was given the task of writing magazine articles on a variety of subjects. I thought I'd impress my bosses by doing the best job I could, so I painstakingly researched and crafted each one. After a few months, I got my first job evaluation, which was decidedly lackluster.

It turned out that I had misunderstood the priorities of my job. As the new kid on the block, I'd been given the least important articles to do. My task was to show that I could quickly do an adequate job of them, making time to move on to more important and interesting stories and higher-level tasks such as editing other writers. Once I understood this, I never had a bad performance evaluation again.

Misunderstandings like these are bad enough when you're working in the office. They can be deadly if you're a telecommuter. For the days that you're out of the office, your boss has to judge you solely on the work you do. It's important for you to understand clearly what your boss expects you to achieve on your days out of the office, and which parts of your job he or she considers more important.

How will the boss measure your successes?

If possible, you and your boss need to find objective ways to determine the success of your projects and how they should be measured. For instance, let's say you're arranging a conference for clients of your company and important vendors to meet, learn about your products and your industry, and exchange information.

You and your boss may agree that the conference will be considered a success if the people at the conference fill out favorable evaluations, if many of them sign up for the next year's conference, if the event comes in under budget, or if the contacts made at the conference lead to new sales for your company. Of course, these are different and in some ways conflicting goals. And many aspects of the success or failure of the meeting are outside of your control. So you must determine beforehand which goals have top priority and try to build some flexibility into the evaluation process.

"When I talk to management about telecommuting, much of it is teaching them to shift their focus away from observing employees' activity and toward end results," Gil Gordon says. At the same time, he cautions, not every job lends itself to completely objective measures. The classic example, he points out, is programming: You can't just evaluate a programmer's output by counting the lines of code he or she writes.

So, he notes, although it's essential to know what your overall performance goals are, trying to come up with a numerical way to evaluate your performance may be a mistake if your job doesn't lend itself to that kind of measurement.

How will your boss decide whether your telecommuting is a success?

Asking your boss how he or she will decide whether your telecommuting is successful is an especially important question to answer, especially if your boss was reluctant or hesitant to allow you to telecommute at the outset. The two of you must agree on some criteria that tells you your new role as a telecommuter is working out, or conversely, warns you if you need to make an adjustment.

At the same time, it may be a good idea to set a time (say, three or six months down the road) to talk about your telecommuting, whether it's working as well as you each hoped, and any changes that need to be made to your schedule or working style.

Your Telecommuting Agreement

Most telecommuting experts advise you and your boss to sign a telecommuting agreement that specifies details of your telecommuting arrangement and serves as a legally binding document for both parties. While I think this is a great idea — if your employer initiates it — for you to do so as the telecommuter is a bit trickier. Some organizations are more formal than others and so are some telecommuting arrangements.

Depending on your boss's personality, and your organization's particular culture, you may simply want to type up a memo containing a few notes about your meeting, and send it back to your boss, to *confirm what you discussed*. Again, depending on your organization's norms, you may or may not want to ask your boss to sign it, too. However you decide to do it, it is indeed a good idea to put the details of your telecommuting plans in written form.

Your telecommuting agreement (or notes from your pretelecommuting meeting) may include some or all of the following:

- ✔ How many days a week (or month) you intend to telecommute and which specific days those will be.

- ✔ Your telecommuting start date and a trial time (say three or six months), after which you and your boss will meet to evaluate your telecommuting experience.

- ✔ Your contact information when working at home or at another off-site location. (For more on picking the right location for a home office, see Chapter 5.)

- ✔ Information on how you'll stay in touch (in other words, having your phone calls roll over from the office phone to your home-office phone, daily phone check-ins with your boss, chat, and so on) as well as any specific meetings or in-office events you'll make sure to attend.

- ✔ If applicable, a description of child-care or dependent-care arrangements you'll make while working at home.

- ✔ If applicable, a brief discussion of situations in which you may be called in to the office, what sorts of emergencies make this appropriate, whether you'll make up missed telecommuting days, and so on.

- ✔ A brief description of your office space (and/or a photo, if required).

- ✔ A list of equipment and furniture (if any) the company will be providing.

- ✔ A list of equipment (if any) you agree to provide yourself.

- ✔ Information about other additions you'll be making (such as a cell phone account, extra phone line or lines and/or high-speed Internet access, and added homeowner's insurance), along with information as to who is paying for what.

✔ Security information, including how any employer-owned equipment will be kept safe, how confidential work-related information will be handled, and how you'll keep your computer and network safe from attack by hackers and viruses.

✔ A general description of your job, and how it is evaluated.

✔ A brief description of those tasks (if any) that you plan to save for your at-home days.

✔ A brief description of your short-term, middle-term, and long-term goals for the job, and how telecommuting will help you meet those objectives.

This may seem like a lot of ground to cover, and it may not be necessary for you to address all these issues. Consider your own telecommuting situation to decide which of these areas (or others) you need to address and which you can safely skip.

Keep in mind that you're creating a binding document. It may actually be construed as a legal contract in some situations. It needs to reflect responsibilities and benefits for you and your employer and must include the elements each of you considers more important. Several telecommuters I know say they wish they'd "gotten it in writing" when they first worked out their telecommuting arrangements with their bosses, because their arrangements later were abruptly changed.

Don't forget that this document is binding on you, as well as your employer. So if, for instance, you write in it that you'll call your boss every day to check in, or that you'll buy virus protection software for your computer, make sure that you do it.

Telecommuting in a New Job

The issues addressed in your telecommuting agreement become particularly important when you're starting out in a new telecommuting job. In this situation, you and your boss will still be getting to know each other, so the more issues you clarify beforehand, during a pretelecommuting conference, and spell out in a telecommuting agreement, the less of a chance you have for misunderstanding later on.

Make sure you spend some time during your pretelecommuting conference nailing down the details of the job, exactly what your boss expects, which aspects of your job are most important, and exactly what criteria will be used in judging your performance.

You also must address the question of how you can create good relations with your co-workers, who may be tempted to regard you as only a partial member of the team. (For more on relationships with co-workers, see Chapter 12.)

Conventional wisdom among managers is that it's better to have an employee on site for a while, before he or she begins telecommuting. So you may find that, while you've been hired to do a job on a telecommuting basis, you're expected first to spend a certain period of time reporting to the office five days a week.

If you first must earn your wings at the office when you start your job, having a definite understanding with your boss up front about your telecommuting plans is important. Some managers tend to renege on these arrangements when it comes time to make the transition to a telecommuting schedule. It isn't that they're being heartless or underhanded — it's just that from a manager's point of view, it's so much easier to supervise someone who's in the office every day than it is to supervise someone who's working remotely. Because you've spent the last several months showing up at work, and everything's running smoothly, your manager may be reluctant to make a change, on the *if-it-ain't-broke-don't-fix-it* principle.

If telecommuting is important to you, try to work out the details of your transition right from the start. Ideally, you and your boss need to agree on a specific period (say, three months) after which you'll start telecommuting, unless there's a problem with your performance. If it's going to be a gradual transition — for instance, you'll start by telecommuting one day a week, and then increase it to two and so on — you need to work out a tentative schedule for making these changes as well.

As always, you must try to settle on criteria that are as reasonably objective and measurable as possible for your job. Find out which new tasks you absolutely have to master before you can telecommute, so you can concentrate on them.

And, as always, you must put whatever you've decided in writing. Either ask your boss to write up an employment agreement that you can both sign, or at least type up your notes of the meeting, and submit them to your boss as a confirming memo.

What if your boss refuses to be pinned down to specific plans and dates, preferring that you start out in the office, and then "see how it goes"? This can be a touchy situation for a person in a new job. On one hand, your boss needs to get to know you and get comfortable working with you before trying to manage you from a remote location. On the other hand, if you took the job specifically because you wanted to telecommute, you need some assurances that you'll get what you came for.

Your best bet at this point is to spend some time talking with co-workers who report to the same manager. You probably can get a good sense of whether the manager tends to stick to the agreements he or she makes. You also can find out whether the manager has worked successfully with other telecommuters in the past.

Likewise, you need to get as many specifics as you can from your new boss about exactly when the time will be right for you to start telecommuting. If not a specific time frame, is there a particular level of expertise that you need to reach? Do you need to consistently demonstrate that you can meet deadlines and turn things in on time?

Whatever measurements you and your boss are able to come up with, put them in writing and present them back to your boss as a telecommuting agreement or follow-up memo. That way you at least have some sort of commitment to specific criteria. Assuming you're able to fulfill these criteria satisfactorily, you'll also have a basis for going back to the boss in a few months' time and requesting that you start telecommuting, as promised.

Training for telecommuters

The idea of training before you start telecommuting may seem a little odd. After all, you already know how to do your job, and you know how to stay home. What's to learn?

The answer: More than you might think. When telecommuting arrangements fail or disappoint managers, a lack of understanding often is the reason why.

Training can help, claims Gil Gordon, telecommuting consultant, trainer, and author, whose most recent book is *TURN IT OFF: How to Unplug from the Anytime-Anywhere Office Without Disconnecting Your Career* (Three Rivers Press, 2001). "The main reason for training is not that it's terribly hard to get this telecommuting thing going. It isn't. But there are some areas where training makes the difference between trial-and-error and trial-and-success."

Gordon says he typically divides a one-day training program into three parts. The first session is only for telecommuters and addresses various aspects of working from home. The second is only for managers and helps teach them how to supervise someone working off site. The third session is for telecommuters and managers together. It addresses most of the issues that need to go into your telecommuting agreement as well as the agreement itself.

Although it's great having a professional telecommuting expert come in and train your staff, Gordon says a lay person within a company can learn enough about the subject to successfully train telecommuters and managers. "There are a number of Internet sites with enough information to help create a training program," he says. In fact, he says, so much good information is available about how to do it right, that "any organization that fails with telecommuting these days pretty much deserves to."

Chapter 10

Long-Distance Telecommuting

Long-distance telecommuting is like local telecommuting, only more intense. If you think it's easy to feel disconnected from the other people in your office when you show up there only one or two days a week, think how far apart you'll feel when your only contact is one week a month, or even less. The fact that your co-workers live and work in a different community than you can certainly increase your *sense* of alienation.

Availability issues become amplified as well. Bringing you to the office for an emergency meeting during an unexpected crisis is much more difficult, especially if getting you there means booking a plane ticket, rental car, hotel room, and kennel space for your dog. Scheduling meetings for the days when you'll actually be in the office also is much harder, and your opportunities to bond with the members of your team are much more limited.

In spite of these problems, long-distance telecommuting has grown rapidly during the past few years — in tandem with the rapid expansion of the Internet economy. It's easy to see why. In a tight labor market, employers benefit by hiring long-distance telecommuters because it makes pools of nonlocal talent available to them, vastly expanding their ability to hire the brightest and best.

In addition, most long-distance telecommuters live in regions where costs are lower than they are where their employers are located (usually a major metropolitan area). That enables employers to hire qualified people at lower salaries than they'd be able to offer if they had to bring them into their own backyard.

Employees also benefit from tight labor markets and cost-of-living differences. If hiring a long-distance telecommuter means choosing from a wider pool of talent, being a long-distance telecommuter means choosing from a wider pool of jobs. And working for a distant employer in a costly big city means pulling down a bigger salary than you can get at home.

Your Travel Schedule

How much time do you need to spend in the office if you're working long-distance? The answer seems to be as variable as long-distance telecommuters themselves. At one end of the spectrum are telecommuters like my husband, Bill, who has contracted to spend one week out of every month in his em-ployer's offices in California. In practice, it's often an eight-day week, too: He flies out on Tuesday, goes to the office on Wednesday, works through the following Wednesday and comes home Thursday.

At the other end of the spectrum is Sue Boettcher, also an Internet community expert, who works for WebCrossing.com. Boettcher says her company is completely virtual, and that it has no central office to travel to. "You may be surprised to hear that I've never actually met my boss face to face," she adds. Other long-distance telecommuters tell me they go to the office one day a month, a day or two every other week, or a few times a year.

In any telecommuting arrangement, much is to be gained by spending *face time* with your boss, co-workers, and customers. But added costs begin accruing when long-distance telecommuters come into their employers' offices.

When I say "costs," I mean it in many different senses, including the more literal: Bringing you to the office as a telecommuter means spending money on travel and lodging. But other costs also are incurred. A large amount of potential work time is spent traveling. You lose productivity because you're out of your usual work environment, as well as from exhaustion and possibly even jet lag. Being away from your home, your friends, and your family can also be wearing in its own way and can inhibit your productivity as well. (Later in this chapter, I look at ways to diminish these effects, but it's impossible to eliminate them altogether.)

Answering the questions posed in the following sections helps lead you and your boss toward decisions about how much time you need to spend in the office.

Should you set a schedule or come as needed?

In most long-distance telecommuting situations, good arguments exist for planning a schedule of visits to the office. Knowing up front that you'll be on site at least, say, three days each month may help your boss feel more comfortable with your telecommuting arrangement. You and your family may be more comfortable, too, knowing exactly when and how long you'll have to be away. You can plan your schedule to coincide with important meetings and company events. And you can save your employer big bucks by booking travel well in advance.

However, as with all aspects of telecommuting, one size doesn't fit all. Depending on the nature of your job, you may not be able to plan ahead when or how often you'll need to be on site. I see this frequently with telecommuting consultants, for example, who must travel to the office in response to client needs.

If you decide on making trips to the office as needed, rather than planning a schedule, you and your boss still must agree on how often you'll visit, on average, and how much total time you're likely to spend in the office during the next six months or year. This will prevent potential conflicts later on.

How collaborative is your job?

Do you need to interact with others in your company on an ongoing basis to do your job effectively? Or do you largely work on projects by yourself and then bring them back to the team? How often you need to work with other team members on communal projects partially determines how often you need to be in the office.

How good is your team at communicating electronically?

Some of the more successful long-distance telecommuters I know are Internet community experts who pretty much never work on their own. They spend their entire work lives interacting with others.

They make it work because the people they work with are adept at communicating over the Internet. They resolve problems, strategize, brainstorm, and build solid workplace relationships by chatting in a text box just as effectively as they do when they're sitting around a conference table.

Not everyone is as good at working over the Internet as these professionals, but how comfortable you and the people you work with are when communicating by chat, e-mail, and phone influences how much time you need to spend speaking to them face to face.

How good are your working relationships with your team?

How long you've spent working with members of your team may determine the quality of your working relationships with them. If, for instance, you've worked with them for several years, and you're now moving away because of a relocating spouse, you probably already have comfortable working relationships in place. You may not need to spend as much time building relationships as you would if you were new to them or to your job.

Are there other reasons you need to be in the office?

Good reasons that do not directly relate to your work may mean spending time at the office. One such instance may be if your company's formal telecommuting policy dictates that telecommuters must spend a certain percentage of their time in the office. Or, even though there isn't a formal policy, upper management expects everyone to attend a monthly staff meeting in person. Whatever they may be, it's important to take issues like these into account when planning your telecommuting schedule.

How much does it cost?

In most cases, the company pays travel expenses for long-distance telecommuters, so how often you come to town is partly a budgetary matter. If you can save your employer substantial sums by traveling to the office, say, once rather than twice a month, this can be a powerful argument for less frequent visits to the office.

How big a trip is it?

"The day that I travel is a lost work day," says my husband Bill in describing his coast-to-coast trips. "The following day, I may be in the office, but I'm still somewhat in a fog." So that second day is partly a loss as well.

In his previous job, he also lived in one place and worked in another, but in that case, his employer was only a three-hour drive away, rather than two long flights across three time zones. When he traveled to the earlier job, he could arrive late in the morning and still get most of a day's work in. On his return trip, he'd work a full day and then drive all evening, arriving home late.

Regardless of how far you have to go, the time you spend on the road is time you can't spend doing your work. And, transferring your workplace from office to office inevitably cuts into your efficiency, as does the stress and wear of traveling. The longer and more wearing the trip, the greater the negative effect on your productivity, even more so when jet lag is part of the deal.

Whatever travel schedule you and your boss settle on, it's important for both of you to remain flexible. Plan to reevaluate your travel after a few months. For example, Bill recently decided to try spending the last week of the month and the first week of the following month at his California office. He's still there for one week out of ever calendar month, as his work contract specifies. But now, instead of spending one week there followed by three weeks at home, he spends two weeks there, followed by six weeks at home.

The change benefits everyone. For Bill, it means fewer plane trips and less time spent adjusting from East Coast to West Coast times and back again. More full weekends in California give him more time to visit his brother and sister, who live a few hours' drive down the coast. As for me, though I hate having him away for two weeks, having him home for six weeks rather than three makes it more than worthwhile.

The company saves money by paying for one round-trip ticket, rather than two. And Bill says he's able to accomplish much more in one two-week visit than two one-week ones. "I spend the first week catching up with everyone and having them get used to me being there," he says. "The second week, we can really get down to work."

Coping with Travel

One of the hardest aspects of long-distance telecommuting is the long-distance travel itself. Obviously, traveling as a telecommuter is less fun than traveling as a vacationing tourist, but it can be even less entertaining than regular business travel. After all, you're constantly going back and forth to the same places, probably staying in the same hotel, and seeing the same people when you get there.

Being prepared

Dealing with the drag of travel is an individual matter, and you'll likely find out through trial and error what works for you and what doesn't. To get you started, the following sections provide a few miscellaneous travel trips from some of the long-distance telecommuters I've talked to.

Have two of everything

Many road warriors keep a bag with toiletries and a few days' clothes packed at all times, so that they can leave town anytime, at a moment's notice.

As a long-distance telecommuter, you'll probably know well in advance when and where you'll be traveling. But keeping a bag packed with some of the things you need still may be a good idea. Living and working in two places at once demands that you stay as organized as possible. Inevitably you'll need something in one location only to find you've left it behind in another. (As an example, Bill, who's in California as I write this, forgot the car charger for his cell phone on this trip. So he's picking up an extra one to keep there.) Having doubles of everything, and keeping one set packed, can help keep forgotten items to a minimum.

If you'd like to make life even easier, leave some clothes and personal effects at your work location so you don't have to carry everything back and forth each trip. Besides helping you stay organized and ensuring that you'll have everything you need while you're away, this can actually save you time at the airport (if you're flying) because you can make it so the few things you need to bring with you fit in a carry-on bag.

Find a comfortable place to stay

Finding someplace comfortable to stay means someplace comfortable as you define it. You may want to consider some nontraditional alternatives.

For example, I'm the kind of person who loves a hotel room. I'd be embarrassed to tell you how many cities I've missed the thrill of exploring, seduced instead by the pleasures of spending an evening holed up in my hotel. I think I like getting away from my home, which is a jolly, messy tangle of cats, plants, dishes, quilts, eccentric antiques, candles, and books, to a place where nothing is mine and I don't have to take care of anything.

My husband Bill is just the opposite. He dreams of RV (recreational vehicle) vacations where we can bring some of our things along with us. The thrill of the hotel room is lost on him, and the prospect of living in the same Ramada for a week every month struck him as dreary. He wanted a place to hang his hat and leave a few things, a place with a kitchen and room to roam around.

So he found an apartment share in the small town of Albany, California, about 15 minutes from his Emeryville office. His employer didn't object. After all, his share of the rent costs less every month than a week at the hotel would have. The other tenants were delighted — what's better than a roommate who's only home one week a month? As for Bill, he now has room to walk around, a kitchen to put cereal in, and a place to leave some things from month to month. And, just as important, he has someone around to talk to when he comes home from the office.

Plan travel that fits your own rhythms

Travel is stressful enough. Don't make it even more stressful by trying to jam yourself into a travel schedule that doesn't fit your normal patterns of high and low energies. If you're a morning person, accustomed to early bedtimes, don't agree to an itinerary that has your plane landing at 10 p.m. If you're a night owl, and used to staying up late, don't book a 6 a.m. flight.

Watch out for jet lag

Jet lag (difficulty adjusting to changes in time zone) can be a pernicious problem for telecommuters who must constantly switch back and forth across time zones. It helps if you're the sort of person who keeps to a regular routine. If you're used to showering at exactly 7 a.m. every day, then taking a shower at the new right time helps tell your body when 7 a.m. is. Anti-jet lag herbal remedies available in health food stores may also help.

Be aware that your jet-lagged brain won't work the same way it normally does. People suffering from jet lag typically are more forgetful and have a tougher time concentrating than usual. Being highly organized — and writing *everything* down — is especially important.

Stay connected to home

Being separated from your home and family can be one of the more stressful aspects of long-distance telecommuting, especially if you must leave home for fairly long periods of time. Bringing a picture of your loved ones along to put on your desk or in your hotel room makes you feel less separated.

It also helps if you have some sort of regular tradition for staying in contact. For instance, I know that when we're apart, Bill calls me right before bedtime every night. And, if your spouse spends time on the Internet during the day, he or she can use the same chat programs that keep you in touch with your co-workers to stay in touch with you.

Staying healthy

For many people, going on the road means going off whatever fitness and health regimens they otherwise follow while they're at home. Although this may be fine for an annual vacation or trip to an industry convention, it's a bad idea if you're going to be traveling every month. The following sections offer some ways of staying healthy during your trips to the office.

Look for ways to eat right

Keeping your refrigerator stocked with the healthy foods you like is easy when you're at home. However, doing so when you're living in a hotel room is much harder. Advance planning can help.

Consider choosing a room with a kitchenette, rather than a traditional hotel room. You may be able to make up the extra cost if it enables you to eat fewer meals in restaurants. If you do have to eat in restaurants, try to find ones with healthy offerings that you still find appealing.

Take note of whether your business schedule disrupts your usual mealtimes. Some long-distance telecommuters report that they wind up staying in meetings past their usual dinner times or skipping breakfast to make an early meeting. When that happens to you, try finding healthy snacks (such as fruit) that you can bring with you to the office. They'll help prevent you from pouncing ravenously on any junk food you find on hand and from overstuffing yourself when you finally do get to have a meal. In addition, excessive hunger is bad for your mood and hinders your concentration. Thus, healthy snacking can help you work more effectively while in the office.

Watch out for alcohol

Visiting your company's office can present you with something of a dilemma when you find yourself wanting to spend time outside the office, bonding with your co-workers. More often than not, that means drinks after work, or possibly a meal, usually with cocktails, wine, or beer. Before you know it, you can find yourself drinking substantially more than you would if you were at home.

What can you do? Remember that the days are long gone in most modern organizations when refusing to get drunk with your co-workers or your boss could mark you as a pariah. Given the large number of recovering alcoholics among us, for whom even a sip of alcohol is taboo, it's unlikely that any of your co-workers will give you a hard time if you choose to drink less — or not at all — when you spend time with them.

So nowadays, you're free to use your own judgment about when and how much to drink. You'll probably feel better if you stay within the bounds of your at-home drinking habits. For example, if you don't normally drink at lunch, doing so during your visits to the office is probably unwise. In fact, you'll probably feel better if you cut back your drinking a little from normal levels because the stress and exhaustion of travel can make you more susceptible than usual.

Look for opportunities to exercise

If you get regular exercise when you're at home, don't let your exercise program go by the wayside during your visits to the office. In this regard, it's an advantage that you're always making trips to the same location. If you scope out your exercise options on one visit, you'll know exactly where to go on subsequent trips.

If you love walking as I do, ask around among your co-workers for nice places in the area to walk or hike. Keep in mind that safety is a concern in some places, which may mean you shouldn't just go out exploring without first finding out whether the neighborhood you've picked is a safe one. If you're a gym person, find out whether any nearby gyms permit drop-in use, or have inexpensive memberships for infrequent users. If you like swimming, try staying in a hotel with a pool.

Whatever you do, make sure your exercise schedule is compatible with your schedule at the office. Don't plan an after-work visit to a gym that closes at 6:30 when your last meetings of the day never end before 6. Similarly, don't plan to get up at 5 a.m. for a pre-breakfast run when work-related social obligations keep you out past midnight each night.

Don't skimp on sleep

Which brings me to another important point: Try to get at least as much sleep as you do when you're at home — and ideally a little more. Travel is tiring, even more so if you've changed time zones. Constant interaction with your office co-workers may mean that you must be *on* all the time, which can be tiring as well. Your body and mind may need extra rest during these trips.

Managing expense reports

How many workers do you know who have ever bounded into their offices and flung themselves down at their desks all excited because they were going to . . . fill out an expense report? Of all the things you do during the course of a workday, dealing with expense reports is probably the least interesting.

But filling out expense reports has to be done. You can quickly find yourself in big financial trouble if you let your own bills pile up because you've spent all your money on reimbursable travel (or office expenses) and haven't filed a report to get any of it back.

This can turn into such a huge problem that when I asked one successful long-distance telecommuter if she now wished that she'd been told anything before she started out, she replied: "I wish someone had told me to stay on top of my expense reports."

Filling out expense reports is definitely drudgery, and not much can be done to make it more fun. But here are a few things that may make it easier:

- ✔ **Use only one credit card.** You can make expense reporting easier by using the same credit card for all your work-related travel expenses. That way, everything you spend is laid out on a single monthly statement that you can turn in to your employer as proof of what you paid. You can make life even simpler still if you also use that card to pay your phone bills, ISP charges, and other reimbursed office expenses so they show up on the bill, too. And you can really keep things simple if you make sure never to use the card for anything except work-related expenses. Then your credit card bill equals your business expenses for the month.

- ✔ **Use a trigger.** I think of a *trigger* as a reminder that forces me to remember some unpleasant task that I don't feel like doing. One simple trigger for me is the calendar. I know that around the tenth of the month, I must sit down and pay all my bills. A trigger for you may be the end of a trip to your company's location. As you unpack your things, you can gather all the receipts together, then put that stack of receipts on your desk as a nagging reminder that it's expense report time. Or, if you follow my first suggestion, the arrival of your credit card bill makes a good trigger.

- ✔ **Let them take care of it.** The easiest way to deal with an expense report is not to fill it out at all. In some cases, you may be able to have someone at your company, or at your company's travel agency, arrange air travel, car rental, and lodging for you, paid for directly by the company. Not only does this save you the trouble of expense reporting these items, it also saves you from waiting for reimbursement after you've already paid for them out of your pocket.

Long-Distance Work Relationships

The biggest challenge for a long-distance telecommuter is trying to create and maintain good relationships with co-workers from hundreds or thousands of miles away. Most days, you can't chat around the water cooler. You can't stick your head in someone's office to bounce around an idea. You can't invite your co-workers to lunch or dinner, admire the new photo of the kids they've put on their desks, or gauge by their body language whether they're in a good or bad mood today. For most of your working time, your usual avenues for creating bonds with the people you work with are unavailable.

Chances are, you benefit enormously from your status as a long-distance telecommuter. It enables you to live where you want, or where your spouse needs to be because of his or her career, or it saves you the hassle and expense of relocation while still allowing you to have a job that you really want. But for all these advantages, a few tradeoffs are required, and one of them is that you must find ways to build the personal relationships that normally occur naturally when you're otherwise working face to face with people every day.

Begin by accepting the fact that building relationships and keeping lines of communication open are your responsibility — not your boss's or your co-workers'. If you wind up missing an important piece of information because you aren't in the office, and no one who is in the office tells you about it, it's likely going to be a bigger problem for you than it is for anyone else. So you must do whatever it takes to make sure this doesn't happen. The following sections offer some ideas that can help.

Socializing during your visits to the office

Don't go back to your hotel and eat room service after work. The few days that you spend at your company are your best chances to form good relationships with your boss and co-workers. Invite people to lunches and dinners and go for drinks or workouts after work. If you're lucky enough to have an informal company event, such as a bowling outing or softball game, take place while you're there, make a point to participate.

Being available

Being easy to reach is of utmost importance for any telecommuter, but it's especially vital when you're a long-distance telecommuter and you go for weeks at a time without visiting the office. Otherwise it becomes all too easy for the co-worker who talks only to your voice mail simply to leave you out of the loop.

The most immediate way for the people you work with to reach you is by phone, and ideally, at least some people at work need to have your home office and home residence phone numbers so they can reach you about urgent matters. A cell phone (don't forget to have it on your person) also is a good idea for many reasons. One is that you won't be out of touch if you take a break to pick up some groceries in the middle of the day. Depending on the nature of your job, a pager may be appropriate as well.

Making a personal connection

One way you can make up for not being in the office often enough to get to know your colleagues as people is to make a personal connection when you talk to them on the phone. If you're talking to someone for business reasons, be sure to devote a minute or two to a bit of friendly conversation. This is especially important when you talk to someone you don't know, or don't know well.

Sometimes the best way to get to know someone as a person is to say something personal about yourself, thus opening the door for the other person to do the same, but without any pressure.

Needless to say, you must be sensitive to timing and time constraints. A casual, rambling conversation at the end of the workday may be a good time to get to know one of your colleagues. On the other hand, a co-worker who calls to ask you for information to be used in a meeting that starts in less than an hour may not have time for or want anything to do with a personal chat.

Making contact often

Successful long-distance telecommuters report sending e-mails to their colleagues and bosses more often than they normally would in the employer workplace. E-mail can be a comfortable and nonintrusive medium. At the same time, most e-mail correspondence is fairly casual, so it can be a good way to keep a friendly connection going. If you and your colleagues are comfortable with it, instant message chat can be another excellent way to stay open and in the loop.

Using distance to your advantage

Some long-distance telecommuters report that being a long way from the office actually benefits them in some ways. "Since I'm not a part of the office dynamic, I don't get involved in the interpersonal office huffs," says telecommuter Miriam Carey, who is profiled in Chapter 1. "I have the advantage of being able to remain neutral because I'm not in the mix, which makes me a friend to all."

Another way distance can work to your benefit is that it makes your visits to the office something of an event. "One of the great advantages of being an *outsider* like this is that people are happy to see you," she notes.

Carey makes the trip from Columbus to Cleveland once a month to attend a story meeting. "I make a point of complimenting everyone on their stories, bringing something to eat, and adding productively to the meeting," she notes. She also uses the opportunity to load up on office supplies and copies of the magazine. As a result, she says, if the on-site staff functions as something of a family, her role therefore is that of a favorite visiting aunt. (For more details on dealing with office politics as a telecommuter, see Chapter 12.)

Long-Distance Telecommuting in a New Job

Conventional wisdom has it that the most successful telecommuters spend a year or two working on site first. Unfortunately, that isn't an option in most long-distance telecommuting situations because the reason you're telecommuting in the first place is because you reside in a different region than the job and can't or don't want to relocate.

Starting out successfully in a new telecommuting job can be a challenge. The following sections outline some steps that can help you make sure it works out.

Making your first visit as long as possible

Your first visit to your new workplace is vitally important. If you get off on the right foot, you can start some relationships that will stand you in good stead later on. If your first visit is too short, you may not get to know your boss and your co-workers as well as is necessary to keep things running smoothly from a distant location.

Some long-distance telecommuters actually spend a month or two in their new employer's location when they start a new job. This can really help you get your feet on the ground before returning to the isolation of your distant home office. Of course, long visits aren't always feasible: You may not be able to leave home for that long, or your employer may not be able to afford travel expenses for such a long stay. But the longer you can make your first visit, the better.

Establishing relationships

Establishing strong relationships with your boss and co-workers also is vitally important for any telecommuter. But nowhere is it more crucial than when you're starting out in a long-distance telecommuting job. Make sure you get to know as many people as you can as well as you can during your visits to the office. Let those people know you'll be contacting them regularly in the weeks and months ahead. Find out how they prefer to communicate (e-mail, phone) and make a note of it for your future reference.

Making sure everyone understands that you're going to be working long-distance

Your boss is well aware that you'll be a long-distance telecommuter. But colleagues in other areas or departments may not get the message — especially if your initial visit is a nice long one. They may simply assume that you'll be in the office every day. When they don't see you there, they may think that you didn't work out, or worse, you're shirking your responsibilities.

Uninformed colleagues can result in ongoing workplace misunderstandings. Worse, such misunderstandings can lead to decisions being made without your input that affect your job. You can nip this problem in the bud by talking to your new colleagues about your plans as a long-distance telecommuter. Tell them how often you're going to be in the office, and how easy it will be to get in touch with you while you're not there. You can also tell them a little bit about your hometown, which helps establish a personal connection and makes remembering that you're not local easier.

Will Long-Distance Telecommuting Affect Your Career?

Unfortunately, with few exceptions, long-distance telecommuting affects your career. The few exceptions are a handful of heavily technology-oriented companies. In some cases (WebCrossing is a good example), the company itself is virtual, has no central office per se, and most or all employees work from home offices scattered around the country.

In other cases, an office exists, but technical ability is the standard against which everyone is measured, so that how well you code, for instance, takes precedence over how often they see you in person. In all cases, the people in the company are extremely comfortable communicating by telephone and over the Internet, making geographical distance less of a factor and less of a problem.

Employers such as these are few and far between. So, for most people, being a long-distance telecommuter means making a choice about your career potential. Long-distance telecommuters have the advantage of living where they like, but they limit how far they'll be able to climb their company's corporate ladder.

Advancement limitations are why Christine Doane-Benton left her long-distance telecommuting job at *Windows* magazine. "I love telecommuting, but I don't think there would've been a lot of growth opportunity for me as an editor," she says. "The executive editors were mostly in the New York office, as was the managing editor. For that position, you need to be near the production team and available at a moment's notice to make decisions. So, I started to feel that if I wanted to be promoted, I'd need to go into an office situation again, which is what I did."

For many long-distance telecommuters, limited promotion prospects are not a problem for one or more of the following reasons:

- ✔ **Their career path is out, not up.** Long-distance telecommuters may be at or near the ceiling for their particular jobs in their current companies. For instance, if you're a Web designer, already responsible for creating and maintaining your company's entire site, your best way to a better job may be to move to a different company with a bigger Web site.

- ✔ **The job is a *day job*.** Some long-distance telecommuters like their jobs mainly for the regular paycheck they receive while they pursue other projects that are dearer to their hearts. They may be starting a business of their own, going to school and hoping to switch careers, or trying to gain recognition as actors or musicians. Whatever the case, working toward a promotion isn't high on their list of priorities.

- ✔ **They plan to relocate eventually.** Every new job is an experiment, and long-distance telecommuting isn't any different. It can be a good temporary solution, with good arguments for delaying the trauma of relocating to a different area until after you're sure that the new job is really what you want — and that you are really what your employer wants. Once you relocate, your job prospects may widen.

- ✔ **They really like where they live.** Some long-distance telecommuters enjoy where they live so much that they willingly sacrifice career potential to be there. An avid skier on a mountaintop, or a sun worshiper on a tropical island, may prefer staying where they are and foregoing prospects for rapid career advancement.

In other cases, long-distance telecommuting is a matter of necessity rather than preference. Someone who needs to live in a particular location to be with a spouse or other family member may not have much of a choice in the way of a local job. In that situation, long-distance telecommuting may be the best available option.

Whatever your choices and priorities, when you start a long-distance telecommuting job, try to go into it with realistic expectations of what your career advancement is likely to be unless and until you decide to relocate. For obvious reasons, your boss may not be eager to let you know that your career path is limited, so besides discussing this with him or her, do a little research of your own. Find out whether other long-distance telecommuters have worked for your company, especially in jobs similar to yours, and if so, what happened to them. And try to find out what higher levels of management think of long-distance telecommuting. This gives you a truer picture of what your career prospects are.

Scott Decker: Is the boat still floating?

Scott Decker, professional services manager for TManage, Inc., knows first hand the difference between long-distance and local telecommuting. As a transportation expert (and telecommuting advocate) for the Washington State Energy Office, he spent ten years working from home one or two days a week.

In those days, *home* was a 42-foot boat moored at a marina, in Olympia, Washington. "I had a phone line on the boat, and I could plug in my laptop and get my e-mail," he says. "The rest of my work was really writing and telephoning." He particularly loved summer, when he could work on his back deck, with his laptop, looking out at the water.

Then, in 1999, Decker took his current job, as a long-distance telecommuter for TManage, in Austin, Texas. The biggest difference is "being on the outside," he says. "Things change quickly and often, especially in a startup company.

Being thousands of miles away, you miss a lot of that." To compensate, he spent a total of more than three months in Austin last year (2000). This year, he expects his visits to average three or four days a month.

Another big difference is that working at home five days a week means coming up with your own routines, he says. "You have to keep a balance in that routine and make time for yourself. Go to the gym, or have lunch with your friends once a week." It's important to make sure you get out of the house, he stresses.

Decker now is married and lives on dry land, and one of his favorite breaks is a walk to the marina, accompanied by his Labrador retriever. An admitted workaholic who starts reading e-mail at 5:30 each morning, he says he needs an excuse to get himself out the door. "My excuse is, I have to go see if the boat's still floating," he says.

Chapter 11

Balancing Home Life and Work Life

• •

In This Chapter

▶ Creating your own work routine

▶ Letting people in your life know you're working — diplomatically

▶ Making your home life work with your work life

▶ Telecommuting and parenting

• •

Your home (or remote) office is set up, you've put the equipment and phone lines in place that you'll need to do your job, and you've settled on a telecommuting schedule with your boss.

What comes next in the life of a telecommuter, in many ways, is the hardest part. Working alone in a home office, without supervision or immediate contact with colleagues can be difficult. In fact, some people find it impossible, which is one of the more common reasons telecommuting arrangements don't work out.

You can stack the deck in your favor with some careful planning. Spend some time thinking out what kinds of work arrangements work for you and talking to the people in your life about what you plan to do and how you want them to be a part of it.

Going into it with some forethought helps you ensure that your telecommuting life fits your job, your family, and your personal work style.

A Work Routine That Works for You

Seasoned telecommuters agree that getting yourself into some sort of work routine is important to your success on the days that you work at home. But one size definitely doesn't fit all, and the kind of routine that helps one tele-commuter work efficiently from home may not work well at all for another.

How will you know what routine works best for you? You may not know right at first. You may have to experiment as you go along.

Planning your routine

The following sections serve as general guidelines to use when planning your at-home work schedule.

Make sure your schedule fits your job

Before you start working from home, you and your boss need to come to some general understanding about what your work schedule is, or at least what hours you'll be available to communicate with the office. (See Chapter 9 for more information about how to discuss these issues with your boss.) Your flexibility in these areas varies depending on your job. For instance, let's say you're a purchasing agent, and you need to be on the phone negotiating deals for a large part of your workday. You'll have to be at your desk when the people you need to speak with are at theirs.

On the other hand, if you're a graphic designer, you may spend relatively little time on the phone, which enables you to work at odd hours that better suit you. In fact, if yours is a highly technological job that demands plenty of bandwidth and computing power, you may be better off working outside of normal business hours, at times when competition is less for network resources.

Whatever schedule you settle upon, it's essential for people back at the office to have ample times to reach you when they need you to answer questions and work on common projects. Creating a routine that gives them the access they need is important to your success as a telecommuter.

Take your own natural rhythms into account

One reason so many people work more efficiently and more happily as tele-commuters is that they can work at times that fit their own natural rhythms. Early risers can be at their desks at 5 a.m. Night owls can put in an hour or two after midnight. People who work best in shorter shifts can spend their mornings and evenings working, and take long breaks during the afternoon. Every-one can take advantage of high-energy times when they can get the most done.

It is obvious that you must take the needs of your co-workers and your family into account before settling on a schedule that differs too extremely from the norm. But, as much as possible, try to find a routine that takes advantage of your own work rhythms. And, be careful not to try to fit into a mold that isn't right for you. For instance, if your natural tendency is to be a late riser and to work late at night, don't let guilt feelings force you to set your alarm at 6 a.m.

Take your family's needs into account

Unless you live alone, you may need to take your spouse or family's needs into account when planning your work schedule. As an example, my husband Bill and I are night owls, and at various times when faced with deadline pressures, we tend to stay up late at night working.

But neither of us sleeps well waiting for the other to come to bed. So, at various times, each of us has complained bitterly to the other about this tendency to work on into the night, and we're still striving to reach some form of agreement that works for both of us.

Dinner times, child-care times, or family talk times may be among the activities that you simply shouldn't miss. So consider these issues as you plan your telecommuting routine.

Don't kill your social life

Plan a work routine that allows you plenty of time to spend with your friends and leaves you free at some of those same times. In other words, make sure you have a life, especially if you live alone. But even if you don't, getting out of the house regularly and maintaining an active social life to make up for the hours you'll spend working in isolation is vitally important.

Stay flexible

Once you come up with what seems like a workable routine, don't be too unyielding about sticking with it. There's a difference between self-discipline (which I discuss in the following section) and rigidity. You may need to alter your routine on various days to accommodate a special child-care situation, a sick family member, or a work deadline that can't wait.

You may also find that you need to periodically make adjustments to your routine to better accommodate work or family needs or to make a better fit with your own work style. Don't be afraid to try new routines to see what works best for you.

Staying motivated

Staying motivated and enthusiastic about what you're doing is much easier when you're surrounded by an office full of co-workers working on the same or similar projects and trading war stories in the hallways or over coffee. It can be a lot tougher to stay focused and enthusiastic when you're all alone in front of your computer screen. But it's vitally important to stay motivated.

Your performance as a telecommuter — and perhaps even the whole notion of telecommuting — will be judged on how well you do your job the days that you're not in the office.

Having someone back at the office to talk to and check in with every day about what you're doing and what you plan to accomplish can make a big difference, according to Christine Doane-Benton (a telecommuter profiled in Chapter 6).

"It helped to call into my boss daily and let him know what I was up to," she recalls. "That kept me accountable, and I'm still appreciative that he took the five to ten minutes each day to set up my day and help me get focused on what I was working on. After a while, you get into the practice of being disciplined, particularly because you notice that it feels much better to get your work done than it does to slack off."

To other telecommuters, she advises: "Get an *accountability buddy,* or talk to your boss to determine what you're going to do that day. Check in with that person at least one other time during the day." The right person for this role, she adds, is someone who you feel is supportive, and takes pleasure in seeing you achieve your goals.

In addition to helping you stay motivated, she notes, this approach "forces you to figure out what you're going to do every day — which is more planning than a lot of people do!"

Creating new networking contacts with others in your profession also can help. "It's especially important to stay in touch with your peers when working at home," says Xpedior's Robert Egert, who is profiled in Chapter 13. "You need to actively fight professional isolation." One good way to do this, he adds, is by joining a professional association and subscribing to e-mail lists that serve your special interests. In addition to helping you stay motivated, this kind of professional networking helps you make sure your career stays on track.

Avoiding the refrigerator

One big stumbling block for many telecommuters unaccustomed to working at home during the day is the easy accessibility of anything and everything that you may have to eat around the house. One telecommuter, when I asked about the temptation to nibble, answered, "Aaugh! I don't even want to talk about nibbling! I've gained about 20 pounds since I started working at home a little more than two years ago."

The following sections deal with different strategies that other at-home workers have devised for dealing with the dreaded fridge.

Locate your office far from the kitchen

When we lived in Massachusetts, our kitchen was on the basement level of our old house, and my office was on the second floor, so I had two long, narrow flights of stairs to contend with anytime I wanted a snack. The stairs were effective deterrents — although once in a while I'd override it by bringing a package of candy or cookies upstairs with me.

Stock up on healthy snacks

The disadvantage of having your kitchen nearby can be changed into an advantage if you stock it with healthier foods than you can easily get at the office. Fresh fruits and vegetables (which you can cut up in the evening for easy grabbing during the day), whole-grain breads, yogurts, and healthy soups in easy-heat containers are a few of the things you can have ready for good-for-you snacking. Pick things that are good for you and that you find appealing. That way, you're likely to reach for the right things if you do find yourself in the kitchen.

Give yourself non-eating breaks

I sometimes find myself sitting down to a snack not because I'm hungry but because I feel the need to stop working for a little while. Unfortunately, I'm conditioned to always be doing *something* — so if I don't feel like, say, washing the dishes, but just want to sit and relax a few moments, *needing* to eat becomes a convenient excuse. Once in a while, I succeed in catching myself in this behavior and simply try taking a short rest break instead.

If you're also used to always doing something, try finding ways to give yourself short, rewarding breaks during the workday. After all, if you were in the office, you'd occasionally stop to drink a cup of coffee and schmooze with your co-workers, right? Pick up a crossword puzzle, call up a friend, read a magazine article, turn on the radio and dance around your living room, or spend a few minutes with a favorite craft project. The point is to find something that you enjoy, and that you can spend 10 to 20 minutes doing, and then head back to work refreshed.

Compensate with exercise

"I like to nibble — a lot!" reports Tom Hoffman, an editor at *Computerworld* (an information technology biweekly) who works from home most days. "And I don't really curb my nibbling, but I've managed to keep my weight from ballooning by exercising at least three days a week, a bonus that telecommuting provides me." Hoffman says he likes to take his lunch hour and step out the door, go jogging, come back, shower, and go straight back to work. "I've also tried to balance my weakness for chocolate with less fattening foods such as pretzels, cereals, and fruit," he adds.

Of course, you don't have to go jogging if that isn't right for you. You may prefer going to the gym, taking a dance class, or bouncing tennis balls off a convenient wall. But cutting commuting out of your schedule — and being able to flex your work hours a little — may give you the opportunity for more regular exercise than you would have had at the office. Even if nibbling isn't a problem, extra exercise is always a good idea.

Beyond all these more-conventional strategies, Miriam Carey has found a method that works quite effectively for her. "Nibbling? Replaced that with lots of glasses of water," she reports. "Working at home means you can go to the bathroom 50 times a day and no one will look at you oddly. This is one of my favorite advantages of being at home. Drinking a lot of water keeps my skin looking great and stops me from snacking throughout the day."

Knowing when to stop

Most telecommuters report that the biggest problem with working at home is not getting too little work done. It's that it can be difficult for them to stop working, and get back to their home lives. "My problem is, I never stop working," Miriam Carey says. "I have to walk away from the desk at 6:00 for some down time." And other telecommuters report working on weekends or on into the night, unless they make a deliberate effort to take a break.

You may be thinking, "Great! I'll get a ton of work done." But working extended hours day after day without letting up is bad for your physical health, your mental health, your sense of perspective, your social life, your marriage, and your children (if you have any). You also run the risk of burning out on the job you once loved.

If you have a potential workaholic lurking inside you, it's important to find strategies that keep your work life from taking over your whole life. The sections that follow describe some of the strategies that helped the telecommuters I've talked to.

Schedule work time and nonwork time

"I struggled big-time to balance home life with telecommuting when I started," Tom Hoffman notes. He has been a telecommuter for the past six years. "I would often work later than I normally would at a *real* office and frequently checked e-mail and voice mail after hours." After a few months of this chaos, and after discussing the issue with more seasoned telecommuters, Hoffman realized his approach was a bad idea in the long run. "I decided I had to draw a line in the sand and stop work at a specific time, with the exception of one-time deadlines." That way, he says, "I can separate my work life from my home life as well as possible."

Don't pick a central location for your home office

WebCrossing's Sue Boettcher uses what used to be her home's formal dining room as an office. "It's awfully convenient, and it's in front of a set of four French door panels, so it's lovely. But I sometimes think it's too convenient — that I would have more of an *other life* if I put my desk upstairs in the spare bedroom."

"The mix of domestic issues and work issues can be confusing and stressful," Robert Egert concurs. "The more you can separate your office, the better." (For more information about how to pick the best spot for your home office, see Chapter 5.)

Organize your workday

You'll have an easier time setting regular work hours — and your work will go more smoothly, too — if you organize your workday into different times for different tasks, instead of simply trying to tackle everything at once. E-mail is a good example. Unless you're waiting for a specific e-mail that you need to deal with immediately, pick one or two times during the day for reading and answering your e-mail. When you first start work in the morning, or just before you stop for the evening, are a couple of good times to do this. Depending on your job, you may also want to pick specific times during the day for making and returning phone calls, leaving you free the rest of the time to concentrate on the work itself.

Schedule break times

Plan for at least one or two breaks during the day. Ideally, you can even leave the house for a few minutes, but even if you don't, find something to do that takes you completely away from your work for a little while.

"Keep the amount of prepared foods in the house to a minimum," suggests IBM's Chris Keating (profiled in Chapter 15). "This will force you to actually break away and cook lunch. For me, this is a nice mental vacation from work. It also helps to be firm with co-workers about lunch hours. Unless you like having lunch at four in the afternoon, it's good to know when to let voice mail do its job."

Have someone nudge you at quitting time

Chances are your spouse or other loved one will happily volunteer to let you know when it's quitting time. Bill, for example, knows he's likely to forget the time and keep working away in his remote office until the wee hours of the morning. So he frequently asks me to call him at some point during the evening and remind him what time it is and that it's time to come home.

Helping People Understand You're Working

Chris Keating was deeply involved in a conference call around 10 o'clock one morning when his home phone rang. He ignored it, but when it rang again only half an hour later, he feared it was an emergency. He excused himself to go answer it.

It was his mother, wanting to say hello, and wondering why he hadn't answered her first call. "Did I wake you?" she asked.

Making your friends, relatives, and neighbors understand that even though you're at home, you're also at work, is a challenge for all home workers. "It's as if something snaps in the minds of others when they find out that you work at home," Keating notes. "People who wouldn't think of calling you at the office have no qualms about calling you at home even when they know you're working there."

You must let friends, relatives, and acquaintances know that your home is now also your workplace, and that at certain times and in certain situations, contacting you is not appropriate. But remember that it may take some diplomacy to get the idea across without hurting anybody's feelings.

The following sections present some tactics that may help.

Keep a separate work line

Installing a separate work-only phone line is a good idea for many reasons. One of them is that having the work-only line helps you create a separation between your home life and your work life. Friends, neighbors, and relatives — as well as annoying salespeople — who call your home number during your working hours get an answering message just as they would if you were at the office. This may be more palatable than having you answer, and then telling callers that you can't talk because you're working. Close loved ones and immediate family members can have both numbers with the understanding that they can call the work line only concerning urgent matters.

Not only does this protect your work hours from interruption by social calls, it also protects your off hours from interruption by work calls. After all, just because the office is in your home doesn't mean you're available for work 24 hours a day. Colleagues who don't understand this may call you at whatever odd hour suits them, or customers in different time zones may call during their business hours. People who call the work line for business reasons during your nonwork hours will get an answering message — just as they would if you had gone home from the office.

Screen your calls

Are you one of those people who can't bear to leave a ringing phone unanswered — in case it's a loved one in an emergency situation? If so, you're not alone. But if you want to successfully balance your work life and home life, sometimes it's better not to answer.

Finding a way of screening your calls — Caller ID is one method — can help. An answering machine with the volume turned up, so you can hear the caller leaving a message, is another. Ideally, you need to be able to screen personal calls during working times and business calls during nonworking times.

When you have your call screening method in place, try to find the self-discipline not to answer every call every time. You may be surprised to find how often you're glad that you don't.

Screen your visitors

Screening visitors, on the other hand, is more difficult than screening your calls. But, if you live in a neighborhood where just dropping by is the norm, doing so may be essential if you want to work uninterrupted.

Ideally, your home office should afford you a view of the front (or most-used) door so you can see who is there before deciding whether to answer a knock or doorbell. Of course, this may be awkward, especially if a car in the driveway indicates that you're at home or — even worse — the person at the door can see you through a window. Keep in mind, though, that if you were on an important conference call, you'd not be able to open the door, and the person outside would simply have to understand.

Some successful home workers put a discreet note by the doorbell explaining that they work at home, and asking visitors not to knock or ring unless they're expected. This may be helpful because it lets drop-in visitors know that your not answering the door is a general rule, and not a personal rejection.

Dress for work (whatever that means to you)

Telecommuting is surrounded by myths of people working in their pajamas. Most telecommuters find this unworkable for a variety of reasons. One of them is this: If someone comes to the door and you answer in your bathrobe, you may have a hard time getting the idea across that you're actually hard at work.

At the other end of the spectrum, some at-home workers dress above and beyond the call of duty because they think it helps them take their professional selves seriously. I once knew a man who carefully dressed himself in a designer suit and elegant tie before sitting down to work in his rather cluttered home office.

You don't need to go that far. And, in my mind, being physically comfortable while you're at your desk is the most important element in dressing for work, whether at home or elsewhere. Beyond that, though, keep in mind that whatever you're wearing is sending out subtle signals to your family members and housemates, to anyone who happens to come through the door or look through your window, and to your own brain as well. Those subtle signals should unequivocally state that today is a workday.

Talk about what you're doing

Are you one of those people who doesn't really like discussing his or her work with family and friends? I can sympathize. I'm the same way. But talking about your job to your friends and relatives helps make it more real to them. If they know, for instance, that you're struggling to negotiate a contract, or launch a new product, or write a report, it may be easier for them to absorb the idea that what you're doing when you're at home alone is really work.

Be consistent

If your job is like most, you face different workloads, and different degrees of urgency, on different days. So you may be tempted to make yourself more available to neighbors and friends on days when you can afford to take slightly longer breaks. This can be a bad idea if it creates the expectation that you'll always be available when needed.

"It's hard to overcome the perception that you sit around the house all day, available for any errand a friend or relative may need help with," Miriam Carey notes. "Early and often, you need to remind people, 'I'm working,' when they call with requests. Turn them down on the small things, so they will be conditioned to this when the big things creep up."

Use deception — if all else fails

Sometimes the only way out of a sticky situation is to use trickery. While I don't necessarily recommend this, it is something you may want to have available, just in case. For example, one telecommuter who occasionally faces endless phone calls from friends recommends getting a phone that has a ringer that you can activate yourself. When the person on the other end hears it, you can tell them it's a business call that you've been expecting and have to take.

Managing Your Home Life

More than anything else, your home situation dictates what the experience of working at home is like for you. A parent with several small children running in and out of the house all day faces a completely different set of challenges than a single telecommuter who may not see anyone except the overnight delivery person.

Coping strategies vary with your home situation, as well as with your personality, the amount of time you spend working at home, and the nature of the job itself. Planning ahead may help you find a workable balance between your work life and home life.

If you live alone

Single telecommuters who live alone have some advantages over those with families. They can set their own schedules. No one cares if they work at odd hours, or spend too much time at their desks. And they'll likely face fewer interruptions while working than those with spouses or children.

But what is advantageous in one respect can become a disadvantage in another. With no one to pull you onto a regular schedule (especially if yours is the sort of job that accommodates a lot of flextime), you risk drifting into a routine that puts you out of sync with your co-workers — and the rest of the world, too. With no one to complain that you're spending too much time in the office, the temptation to work way too long may be hard to resist.

One single telecommuter I know reports that she usually quits work to watch a couple of hours of TV at around 9 p.m. But, she says, she often goes back to work at 1 a.m., when the shows she likes end. It's a pleasure, she says, because she loves her job. Yet it also leaves her with little time for a social or any other kind of life outside of work.

One way to fight the tendencies toward odd or unhealthy schedules is to establish a routine that interrupts your work — and, it is hoped, gets you out of the house — on a regular basis. One home worker I know uses an early evening dance class to give her life some structure. I try to use the sun to do the same for me. Every afternoon, right before sunset, I try to go outdoors, do whatever needs doing in the yard, and go for a walk. Sometimes I don't make it until after sunset, especially in winter when it gets dark early. But I still do the walk and the sunset gives me something to aim for. A yoga class, a weekly dinner with friends, a reading series at a local bookstore: Each of these can be useful ways to impose some kind of schedule on yourself.

Creating a schedule for yourself is an important task for single telecommuters. But there's another task that's even more crucial: Finding ways to fight the isolation that goes with working alone in an empty home. The most successful single telecommuters I know tell me that having an active social life makes up for time spent on your own.

Make sure to schedule time out with your friends as part of your normal week. Doing so keeps you connected to other people and gives you a mental break from the job once in a while. Having people come over to visit with you or share a meal can be particularly rewarding, and occasionally filling your living space with happy, laughing friends will likely make it feel less lonely when you sit down to work the next day.

While inviting friends and relations into their homes can be especially nice for single telecommuters, it also can be especially hard to say no to those same friends and relations when they want your time or attention during *your* working hours. Some telecommuters who live alone report that their friends and family members have a particularly hard time understanding that they're hard at work at home and ought not be interrupted. If friends and family tend to view you this way, being firm and up front about when you're available for social interaction, as well as when you're not, is a good idea.

Telecommuting with a partner or spouse

My husband Bill and I live in a 50-year-old house in a low-lying area next to a mountain. So when it rains (or when snow melts), large amounts of water tend to run into our basement. A sump pump keeps the basement from flooding.

At least, it usually does. One morning a few months ago, I went downstairs for something and discovered that our basement floor was under two feet of water. That's enough to flood the electrical works of our freezer and come perilously close to deactivating our water heater. I did what most wives do in this situation: I ran up the stairs looking for my husband.

The door to his office was closed — a *do not disturb* signal — but I let him know through the door that something was terribly wrong down below, and he needed to *do something*. He was on the phone and working on the Internet with people back at the office and didn't break away for a long while.

I was furious! He was abandoning me in an emergency. And he was adamant: What if he was away at the office? I'd have coped then, wouldn't I?

Well, yes, I would have. In fact, it turned out I was perfectly able to start dealing with the problem on my own. Eventually he took a break to help me, and between us, we got the basement cleared out in short order. (Why the pump temporarily stopped working remains a mystery, and it hasn't happened since.)

Setting boundaries with your partner or spouse as to when, how, and under what circumstances you can be interrupted while working at home is an uncomfortable process. But it's necessary for the success of your telecommuting career and for the success of the relationship itself.

The following sections serve as tips to keep in mind as you approach the difficult issue of setting boundaries.

Talk it out

Being able to discuss issues that are bothering you is a cornerstone of any healthy relationship, and your telecommuting needs are no exception. As the person who works at home, only you know the requirements of doing your job effectively, so setting limits and telling your spouse or partner exactly what will and won't work for you is up to you.

Yet this is where things can become uncomfortable because (as with our flooded basement) what you think is reasonable and what your spouse thinks is reasonable may not be a match. But talking about it still is important. At least then you'll know exactly what those disagreements are, instead of becoming resentful because you feel you're being interrupted too often, or having your spouse become resentful because he or she feels you're not available when you need to be.

It may help if you discuss what your home-working arrangement is before you actually start working as a telecommuter — and before disagreements about your availability create conflicts. Discussing arrangements when you aren't already annoyed with each other is easier, and working out as many details as you can beforehand means fewer misunderstandings later on.

Use do not disturb signals

Sometimes your spouse speaking to you or otherwise distracting you is okay, but other times — like when you need to concentrate or talk undisturbed on the phone — it isn't. Thus, letting your spouse or partner know which is which makes life a lot easier for both of you.

"I found it difficult when my boyfriend would stay over on days that I had to work at home," Christine Doane-Benton recalls of her telecommuting days. "He noticed that I became irritable. I much preferred telecommuting when I could have quiet around me, particularly because I would be deep in editing technology stories. What we found worked was to have *on time* and *off time,* meaning that he could interrupt me only at certain times, so I wouldn't lose my train of thought and could remain confident that I'd have time to work uninterrupted."

Doane-Benton now is married to her former boyfriend, and works full-time at an office. But, she says, "We still use this practice now, though in a different way. There are times when I'll be *off,* meaning that I get to spend time alone, uninterrupted, reading or doing whatever I want. I don't even answer the phone or respond if someone has called for me. I do that for about 30 to 45 minutes a couple of times a week and it's great."

In Doane-Benton's case, saying that she's on *off time* works as a *do not disturb* signal for her partner, which may have come about, in part, because she worked in an open loft apartment and couldn't use a common *do not disturb* signal — a closed office door.

For most people, when working at home as well as at the office, closing your office door means: *Don't bother me unless it's really urgent.* (This is one of the major advantages of having separate offices, with a door.) Bill and I use this signal ourselves, though a closed door can also simply mean one of us wants to block out household noises.

Whatever *do not disturb* signal works for you, make sure your partner or spouse understands exactly what it is and what it means. Then use it when you need or want uninterrupted time to work, plan, or think.

But do it nicely

Your style of communication is sometimes as important as what you're communicating. It's easy to become annoyed if you're interrupted when you don't want to be. Keep in mind, however, that sometimes your spouse can't read your mind, and that you need to politely let him or her know when you need to be left alone.

Set clear expectations

"When my fiancée comes home, she is often upset that I haven't done any cleaning," Chris Keating reports. "The assumption is that I'm home all day so I should be able to do things around the house. There is similar pressure to complete errands, such as picking up dry cleaning, during the day." Her assumption that he's available for these chores is "one big source of strife," he notes.

You sometimes (but not always) can nip attitudes like these in the bud by letting your partner know up front — ideally before you begin working from home — exactly what you will and will not be available to do. It may help to ask the question Bill asked me after the basement flooded: How would you handle this situation if I was working in an office?

The two of you may have different ideas about how much you can and should be available while working at home. But at least if you've clearly explained the boundaries you're setting, your partner knows what to expect.

Be reasonable

Of course, what's reasonable and what's unreasonable varies from job to job and from couple to couple. But sitting in your office with the door closed until midnight every night (unless completing a short-term *crunch* project) is not reasonable. Neither is expecting your spouse to handle all the cooking and cleaning if he or she has a two-hour commute to a full-time job. If you'd be embarrassed for your friends and neighbors to know what you expect your loved one to accept, that's a good clue that it isn't really reasonable.

Accommodate your partner whenever possible

Remember that you're not working in a vacuum. Your spouse or partner is along for the ride, and having you working from home may have disrupted his or her living space and work schedule in much the same way it disrupted your own.

So take your partner's needs and desires into account when planning your work routine. If it's important for your partner to sit down with you for dinner at 6:00 each evening, try to be available then, even if it means working earlier in the morning, or going back to work for a while after dinner. If you can easily perform chores or errands occasionally during lunch hour, then maybe it's worth it to do them.

The bottom line is that most people appreciate having their partners or spouses working at home. (I know I do.) This means your partner has a real stake in seeing you succeed as a telecommuting employee. So if you approach the issue in a collaborative spirit, it should be possible to find compromises that work well for both of you.

Telecommuting with Kids

Working at home takes on a whole new meaning when children are part of the picture. "If your job requires that you get anything done, you can *not* care for a child and work at the same time, period. You need a baby sitter or a non-working spouse dedicated to childcare," Robert Egert says.

This is one of the few absolute rules of telecommuting. So much so that it sometimes is written into a telecommuting contract: Telecommuting is not to be a substitute for dependent care.

Of course, like any absolute rule, this one comes with a few exceptions. Some home-working parents report that small infants who sleep most of the time can do so in a crib in their parent's office, or nestled in a baby carrier against the parent's chest. (This method may not work for a particularly fussy baby.)

Donna Gettings, community manager at OneMade.com, and a successful telecommuter of long standing, used to have her sons play on the living room floor near her desk when they were smaller. Still other telecommuters divide their workdays or rearrange their schedules so that they get their work done while their children are sleeping or being watched by the other parent. And, of course, most employers understand that you may wind up providing daytime care for your child if he or she is sick. (If you were working in the office, you'd have to stay home that day.)

Still, it seems wisest to assume that, if you have children, you need to plan some sort of day care for them, the same as you would if you were working in the office. A spouse who's a full-time parent may be the ideal solution, but it's one that isn't economically workable for everyone these days. If that's the case, remembering that childcare isn't your partner's job 24 hours a day and that a telecommuting parent needs to pitch in with childcare at least some of the time truly is important. Taking turns giving each other an evening off a few times a week is one way to ensure that both parents get the breathing room they need.

If you're working at home when one or more children also are home during the day, some planning is necessary to make sure your work can go smoothly. First, your children need to understand that your office or other working spaces are off limits, and that while you're there, you're working and not to be disturbed. From time to time, despite your best preparations, you *will* be disturbed, and often the disturbance will be the result of the other parent or baby sitter not giving the child what he or she wanted. You're being used as a court of appeal. Remember, not giving in to your child's demands in this situation is important for several reasons. For one thing, giving in undermines the authority of whoever said no in the first place. For another, it encourages your children to bother you again the next time they don't like something.

If you need to hire child-care help, you may be able to choose between having a baby sitter watch the children in your home while you're working there, or dropping your child at a day-care location outside the home. Each option has its advantages and disadvantages.

With in-home childcare, you can, to a degree, supervise the care of your child, peeking in on the baby sitter several times a day. You can visit with your child or children during work and lunch breaks, which is good for both of you. If your child is going through a separation anxiety phase, at least staying in the same house with you may be less upsetting than going to a completely different location. And, in general, you'll be able to spend more time with your child.

On the other hand, sending your child to day care enables you to work uninterrupted. You may get more done than you would if the children were still in the house — freeing you up earlier to play with them after your workday is done.

Visiting other places and interacting with other children may also be good for them, giving them a chance to learn to play well with others and to become more sociable at an earlier age. It may be an especially good idea if your child is an only child and doesn't get to interact with other children at home.

Tom Hoffman: "Daddy has to work"

Tom Hoffman is business feature editor for *Computerworld,* a weekly publication directed at information technology professionals. He began telecommuting six years ago, when his wife became pregnant with their oldest child. Today, Hoffman's wife is a full-time mom, and the two have worked out a child-care arrangement between them that seems to satisfy everyone.

Except on Thursdays. "I often work late on Thursday nights to help edit news stories for *Computerworld's* print issue," he says. "My wife gets frazzled from taking care of the kids all day and is looking for help and/or relief by this point. But Thursdays are really hectic for me, and there isn't much I can do to help out with the kids before 8 p.m." To help in general, he occasionally watches his 3-year-old for an hour or two so his wife can get to a doctor's appointment or do some shopping. "We also make sure

she gets out at least one night a week — more often two — to go out with friends to see a movie or just hang out." He adds that other fathers he knows — who often face a two-hour commute back and forth to work each day — are not as available to help out the way he is.

Occasionally, he finds himself slightly more involved with childcare than he intended. "Sometimes when my son, who's 3, doesn't get what he wants from my wife, he unlatches the gate that leads to the stairs and my office, and he comes in and pesters me.

"I've been working from home his whole life, so he generally knows not to pester me too much. When I'm not on an interview or if I don't have a pressing deadline, I'll usually gently remind him that Daddy has to work. Then I'll lead him downstairs and find him something to do."

Regardless of whether you choose a babysitter or day care, be prepared to reevaluate frequently and make different choices at later times. Children, especially small children, change rapidly as they begin to grow, and what was perfect for your 2-year-old may be the wrong solution for your 3-year-old. Staying flexible is the better way to ensure that your child-care arrangement keeps on working.

Chapter 12

Managing Your Work Relationships

. . . .

. . . .

*W*orking away from the office means many big changes for you. But it also requires big adjustments for the people that you work with. Some of them may have trouble communicating effectively with a telecommuter. If so, one of the more important aspects of your job is that you must do whatever it takes to keep those working relationships solid.

As a telecommuter, you're probably stepping outside the usual boundaries of how business is done in your office. So you need to put forth the extra effort to make sure the arrangement is as comfortable as possible for co-workers and to ensure that no important information gets lost between you and the office on days when you aren't there.

"Disconnectedness seems to be universal among the telecommuters who work for our group," one telecommuter I know says. "You're not there, and you miss out on things. It's just a part of telecommuting I accept."

Indeed, feeling disconnected and *out of the loop* is the single biggest complaint telecommuters have about their kind of work, and many of them believe it's a price they must pay for working away from the office.

At the same time, the single biggest complaint of those who work with telecommuters is that telecommuters can't be reached when needed.

Complaints about disconnectedness from opposite sides of the issue amount to failed communications. So it stands to reason that if you can keep communication lines with people in the office intact while you're not there, you can avoid some of the worst problems telecommuters encounter. That's why your foremost job is making sure the people you work with know exactly how and when they can get in touch with you, and when you'll be getting in touch with them.

By now, you and your boss probably have agreed on specific practices for your telecommuting, including how often the two of you will check in with each other and by what method. (If you haven't, Chapter 9 offers detailed information on how to do this.) It is hoped that you've already established a system that keeps you in communication with each other often enough to handle any issues, problems, or opportunities that arise.

Similarly, you'll probably schedule regular communications with anyone who reports to you so that you keep communications flowing smoothly. (For more on telecommuting as a manager, see Chapter 13.) Keeping communications clear with peers in your area as well as with peers in other areas or departments that you coordinate with is trickier and may require additional planning and strategy.

Getting Them to Pick Up the Phone

Kathleen "KC" Parrish, transient analysis section leader at Arizona Public Service Company, has a staff of engineers reporting to her. Many of them telecommute part of the week. Frequently, co-workers come looking for these engineers, and the following conversation (or something like it) takes place:

> **Co-worker:** Where's John?
>
> **Parrish:** He's telecommuting today.
>
> **Co-worker:** Oh, okay. I'll come back tomorrow.
>
> **Parrish:** No. Let's call him. That's what he's there for.

"Most people have to overcome the natural feeling that when they call someone at home, they're intruding," Parrish explains. "Your co-workers have to understand that their call is welcomed."

The benefits of coordinating communications between telecommuter and in-house co-worker are at least as great for you (as a telecommuter) as they are for your on-site colleagues. It may not sound like such a big deal whether someone looking to bother you with some pesky little matter has to wait until the following day. Yet that co-worker may have a legitimate reason for wanting your input. Or the issue may be one where you think it's important for your opinion to be heard. However, without access to you, it's likely that, rather than wait for you to reappear, your *co-worker-in-need* will ask someone else or simply go ahead and make an important decision without your input. You can wind up feeling — as many telecommuters do — out of the loop.

"It just struck me lately that co-workers might be hesitant to call me at home," *Ohio* magazine's Miriam Carey said after her first few months of telecommuting. "In the office, they can shout across a desk at each other with a question. To get in touch with me they have to pick up a phone. I worry that this could work against me in a subliminal way." (For more on Carey, see Chapter 1.)

You can improve the odds of having them phone you when needed with a few strategies that can help make your co-workers comfortable dealing with you by phone.

Forward your calls to home

Many phone systems can be programmed to forward calls to another number, even one outside of the system. If so, set (or have someone set) your business line to forward your in-house calls to your home office. "Many of my co-workers are unaware that they aren't calling an internal extension," notes IBM's Chris Keating, who has his calls forwarded in this way.

This simple tactic solves another problem that may arise for some telecommuters — ducking out on *random* calls. Here's what I mean: Many years ago, I worked for a trade magazine, where, a few times a day, we'd receive phone calls that could be dealt with equally well by any of us. These were usually annoying questions, or even more annoying requests (for a previously published article, for instance).

The operator forwarded these calls to each of the junior editors at random, or through some rotation of her own devising, so that none of us got too many of them, but none of us got to escape from them, either. Having calls forwarded from your office extension to your home office means you can continue to get your share of the random calls. Sure, it's a pain, but it saves you from resentment by your peers.

Leave a note

Forwarding your calls also keeps you in touch when co-workers phone you, but it won't be much help when they stop by your desk looking to speak in person. This is a shame, because someone who goes to the trouble of actually coming to see you may be someone with something important, complex, or sensitive to discuss.

That's why Kathleen Parrish advises all her telecommuting staff to stick notes on their computer monitors saying something like "I'm only a phone call away," and providing their home-office numbers. You might also leave a note on your phone itself, providing your home-office number (or better yet, indicating how to quick-dial it) and inviting colleagues to use your office phone to contact you.

Leave a picture

I know it sounds hokey and may not be appropriate in every corporate culture, but I think it's a great idea to leave a picture of yourself prominently posted in your workspace — or as your screen saver on your computer. Make sure the picture shows you sitting at your desk, at work, in your home office. After all, a picture is the most powerful possible form of communication, and in this case, the communication is clear: "I'm working. It's all right to contact me on work-related matters." Along with the picture, prominently display your home-office phone number and an invitation to call. This goes a long way toward helping people overcome their resistance to calling you at home.

Give them a mobile number

Assuming that your wireless phone works adequately in your home, try leaving a mobile phone number posted at your desk, rather than a home phone number. (You can also give this number on your answering message, if your phone can't be set to forward calls to your home.)

You may ask, "Why a cell phone?" Some people may hesitate less calling a wireless phone — when you're presumably out, doing something — than they would calling a home phone, when for all they know you might be taking a nap. If the connection is bad, or the cost of using the cell phone is prohibitive, you can always call back on a landline.

As an added advantage, if you go out but still want to be reachable, you can simply take the mobile phone with you. If you don't want to be reached — it's your lunch hour, for instance — you can always turn the thing off.

Set appropriate limits

Just as people don't always know when *to call,* they sometimes don't know when *not to call.* "It's as if something snaps in the minds of others when they find out that you work from home," Chris Keating comments. "You wouldn't think of calling another co-worker if you knew that person was at lunch, but people will call you from their cars on their own way to lunch."

Until she set appropriate limits, *Windows* magazine's Christine Doane-Benton says that people on the East Coast would call her for business reasons at 9 a.m. their time, forgetting — or not caring — that it was 6 a.m. her time. (Doane-Benton is profiled in Chapter 6.)

Rather than explaining what should be obvious — that just because you work from home does not mean you're available for work 24 hours a day — Keating suggests a better idea is to "let voice mail do its job." This is another good argument for separate work and home phone lines.

You can also nullify the effect of business calls outside of working hours by turning off the ringer on your work phone. If you think you must be reachable in case of a truly dire emergency, you can give your home number to your boss and/or your assistant, with instructions to use it only if the sky falls in, and never to give it to anyone else.

More Strategies for Staying in the Loop

Most telecommuters worry — probably rightly — that by being *out of sight* they're also *out of mind*. So while getting your co-workers comfortable with calling you (as well as contacting you by e-mail and possibly chat) is important, you also need to take a proactive role in making sure you aren't forgotten. Find ways to remind your colleagues — frequently — that just because they can't see you doesn't mean you're not on the job. The following sections provide you with some actions that can help.

Try nudging

Just as it's a good idea to speak up more often by speakerphone during a meeting, so that your presence isn't forgotten, frequently making contact with your colleagues, by whatever means best fits their work styles and your organization's culture, also is useful.

"I try to call key co-workers once a day, and get in touch with other members of the staff a few times a week," Miriam Carey says. Other telecommuters send out daily or weekly e-mails that subtly remind others that they're on the job. This is especially important when others in your organization are working on projects or decisions that can affect you and when you know it's important for you to be included.

Finding the right way to let co-workers know that you need to, say, be included in an e-mail list for a project, may be a simple matter, or a delicate diplomatic task, depending on the situation and the nature of your organization. And, of course, this is an issue that arises for on-site workers as well. But at least regular phone calls or e-mails to ask how things are going, or offer help, keep co-workers from forgetting that you're around and that you want to be included.

Don't miss important meetings

I know, I know. Not attending meetings is one of the biggest reasons you wanted to telecommute in the first place. And I'm certainly not suggesting that you show up for every possible meeting, or even every meeting you would've attended if you were at the office. On the other hand, you're guaranteed to feel out of the loop if a decision that affects you is made at a meeting while you're someplace else.

Likewise, trying not to be resentful if important meetings or other workplace necessities disrupt your work-at-home plans is important. "You really need to avoid making your telecommuting someone else's problem," Xpedior's Robert Egert notes. (For more on Egert, see Chapter 13.)

As an example, he says, not long ago, he was summoned to the office unexpectedly. He dutifully rearranged his schedule and made the two-and-a-half-hour trip by car and train from his home office in Sheffield, Massachusetts, to his company's office in Manhattan. "The meeting turned out to be only an hour long," he says. "It was a big pain, and I couldn't help feeling angry. But at the same time, I knew I had no right to be. They felt they needed me there in person. And I know I have to face up to the fact that if I want to live far away from where I work, I'm going to spend a lot of time traveling."

In fact, one ongoing danger of telecommuting is *not* hearing about meetings that you may want to or need to attend. For one thing, people planning meetings tend to prefer inviting a nontelecommuter rather than a telecommuter if they have the choice. That way they don't have to bother with planning the meeting around someone's telecommuting schedule or setting up one of those annoying speakerphones. One telecommuting department head told me his assistant is sometimes invited to meetings because they know *someone* from the department needs to be there. At times, he has gone back and insisted on being included in the meeting.

Stay on the grapevine

Making sure that you keep up with office gossip is at least as important as making sure you get official business information. How can you do this when you no longer hang out around the water cooler (or kitchen, or wherever people chat in your office)?

One good way is to view your regular contacts with co-workers and your boss (if appropriate) as mini-gossip sessions, too. "It also helps to have established your own communications channel before taking a mobile position," Chris Keating says. "For example, I got my present job from a recommendation from a co-worker who is now a peer of my manager. He is usually good for a heads-up." Other telecommuters also report having mentors at work, making sure to let them know what's going on behind the scenes."

Use the buddy system

"When I'm teleworking part-time (rather than long-distance), I have an agreement with a co-worker who acts as my eyes and ears on the days I'm not in the office — the buddy system," TManage's Scott Decker explains. "I reciprocate on the days when he or she works away from the office. A thank-you, and an occasional latte, go a long way toward making that person feel appreciated." (Decker is profiled in Chapter 10.)

This strategy works well not only during meetings — you ask someone who's present to take notes on your behalf — but also in the general day-to-day grind of office life. Whenever something seemingly important comes down the pike, or the place is abuzz with acquisition rumors, your buddy knows to pick up the phone and let you know what's going on. That gives you much less of a chance of being caught by surprise by unexpected changes, and it gives your buddy the satisfaction of feeling truly helpful, along with the pleasure that always accompanies passing along a good piece of gossip.

Make the most of your time in the office

One of my husband Bill's co-workers refers to the one week a month Bill spends in the office as "golden time." If you're a telecommuter, you should think of your time on site as golden time, too. Your time outside the office is when you'll likely get the bulk of your work done, and it's a good idea to plan accordingly. But your days in the office are the best time to renew ties, catch up with your colleagues, strategize or brainstorm with your boss or your co-workers, and generally get up-to-date on the goings-on and mood in your workplace.

How do you make the most of your own golden time? Strategies vary. Miriam Carey brings food for her co-workers. Other telecommuters I know make a point of meeting any new personnel, gossiping with everyone in sight, and making sure to have as many meals as possible with colleagues. "I pop my head in as many meetings and offices as possible without being a pest," Robert Egert notes.

Egert also uses the time to *synchronize* his computer with the company's network. This is a good idea, specifically because it gives you a chance to coordinate your schedule with the schedules of others (assuming your company uses some sort of network-based scheduling software), and particularly because you can find out if any meetings are scheduled that are important enough for you to attend.

Reach out to other telecommuters

If other telecommuters are in your work group, you may have to make a special effort to stay in communication with them — just as your co-workers must make sure to stay in communication with you. The fact that each of you spends at least some of your time away from the office may make it harder to keep in touch. Keeping communication lines open is as important with other remote workers as it is with on-site employees you may be working with.

Keep in mind that other telecommuters within your organization can be a terrific resource in helping you cope with telecommuting. You can compare notes, share work strategies, and find out which managers have a particularly hard time understanding telecommuting. You can learn from each other's successes and failures just what works (and doesn't work) well for you in your telecommuting role.

Given your other priorities when you're at the office, hooking up with other telecommuters on those days isn't always easy. But making the special effort is worth it to be able to keep in touch via an occasional phone call, an e-mail, or even a get-together. Keep in mind that you can meet away from the office — and that casual dress is probably just fine. "You should have a telecommuting support group within an organization," Robert Egert says.

Office Politics from Afar

"Politics are hard to deal with in, or out of, the office," Scott Decker notes. "I would rather have root canal work than deal with politics." Many telecommuters agree. In fact, many of the same qualities that make you a good telecommuter — the desire to work alone, be autonomous, and focus on the work — probably cause you to hate office politics with a particular passion.

Nevertheless, office politics are an unfortunate fact of most workplaces. And, as a telecommuter, you can be at something of a disadvantage because you're not there every day to notice who's holding closed-door meetings with whom, overhear whispered conversations down the hall, or take stock of the general mood in your office.

"Politics can be tricky, and you can be at some risk," Chris Keating notes. "You're often warned of organizational shifts too late."

"You tend to hear about things later, and you cannot tell very easily what the mood in the office is," Robert Egert adds. "It can be difficult to know what to say or do until you actually talk to a large number of people, or visit the office."

Having to deal with office politics from afar may seem even more odious than having to deal with them if you're in the office. But, like root canal work, they're a fact of life, and you ignore them at your peril.

Office politics is one reason it's particularly important to stay in the grapevine — making sure to hear gossip and rumors as often as possible — so you can avoid being blindsided by unexpected developments, or shifts in power.

"When I visited the New York office and saw co-workers, I wouldn't just go back to my hotel room at the end of the day! I made sure I dined with people from the office, just to be able to hang out in an informal setting and talk," recalls Christine Doane-Benton. "Sometimes we'd talk about work, sometimes not. But that was where I'd find out about what was really going on in the office, the kind of water cooler talk that keeps you from stepping on any political landmines."

Having a mentor — a higher-up who is helping nurture your career, advising you and helping you keep informed — is another approach that can help you find your way through on-the-job landmines when you're working outside the office. Having a mentor is important for any employee, but doubly so for a telecommuter, because you aren't always there to look after your own interests.

"I had a friend in an executive role at the magazine who took an interest in my career," Doane-Benton says. "He'd talk with me on the phone from time to time to let me know what was going on." That kind of inside information — and in-house advocate — can make a huge difference to your career.

Another strategy that can help is to go looking for trouble before it comes looking for you. "The most effective approach I've found is to take a proactive stance," Scott Decker notes. As he's starting any new project, Decker schedules a series of meetings, first with his own manager, next with any other manager who may be affected by what he's planning. He uses these meetings to ensure no problems or issues are raised by the project he's starting.

"It doesn't take long," he says. "And all managers appreciate the opportunity to discuss potential issues before they become problems." Not only is this good corporate politics in general, he points out, it also protects him from corporate maneuvering by any rival employees who like playing politics. Because he shows the consideration to ask these various managers to voice their opinions and concerns before he gets started, it is more difficult for anyone to convince them that he's stepping on their toes, or to enlist their help against him.

How telecommuting can keep you out of office politics

The following is a true story, although the name and some details have been changed.

Sally is a long-distance telecommuter, heading up the records department of a small insurance company. Her staff is responsible for archiving information on every insurance claim made by the company's customers. The information they store is kept in laborious detail, and includes every phone conversation or other contact that ever takes place between insurer and insured. Although this may seem tedious, Sally knows how detailed information can be helpful if questions ever arise — and essential in case the company ever faces a lawsuit.

Several months ago, Sally's company hired Jeff as the new (and on-site) head of its marketing department. Sally first became aware of Jeff when her staff began complaining that he was giving them work to do that had nothing to do with their jobs.

Then one day, Jeff appeared in Sally's office to tell her the way her staff kept records was all wrong. There was too much information, he insisted. It was too long and boring to read. Jeff's new marketing campaign involved letting some of the press read these records so they could report on how the insurance company had helped people in trouble. But reporters would never wade through the pages and pages of minutiae, Jeff insisted. The records would have to be shortened and made much more readable.

Sally explained the need for the current level of detail, but Jeff was adamant. Sally proposed that they keep two versions of each record, a detailed one for corporate use, and a shorter, more readable one for the press. He refused. Sally knew their boss considered the longer records indispensable and told Jeff so. He turned abruptly and stalked out of her office.

Sally was leaving to travel home the next day, and wouldn't be back for several weeks. She hated the thought of being on bad terms with a co-worker for all that time. So, on her way out that night, she decided to mend fences. After all, she reasoned, just because they didn't agree didn't mean they had to be enemies.

"I just stopped by to say goodbye before I leave town," she told Jeff. "I'll be back in a few weeks. I'm sure we can figure out something that'll work for both of us."

"You think this is over, but it isn't," he glowered. Sally sighed and went off to pack.

For the next couple of weeks, she worked from home, brooded about the situation, and brushed up her résumé, having come to the conclusion that the company wasn't big enough for her and Jeff. Meanwhile her problem solved itself. Jeff stepped on toes with practically every step he took. Eventually, he made one enemy too many, and was summarily fired.

Jeff had hired several employees for his department who were fiercely loyal to him, and they stayed on after his dismissal. With many of the company's other managers — especially the one who fired Jeff — they were openly resentful, but not with Sally. She was not known to be one of Jeff's enemies. No one had seen them disagreeing, or even interacting much, leaving the impression that she was completely neutral.

"In this case, being a telecommuter really kept me out of trouble," she concludes. "I had fewer opportunities to tangle with him because I wasn't there. And then I had fewer problems with the people he left behind."

How to stay neutral

Being a telecommuter has the definite potential to keep you out of trouble when it comes to the kind of intramural squabble that can confound on-site employees. If you play your cards right, you can wind up looking like Switzerland during World War II. Here are some tips for reinforcing your neutral status:

- ✔ **Avoid giving opinions.** When interoffice disputes come along, you'll probably have a strong opinion about who's right and who's wrong. You'll probably be sorely tempted to voice that opinion, especially when gossiping with your in-office friends. Don't! The fact that you favor one faction over another *will* get around.

- ✔ **Make friends with everyone.** Confound the status quo by inviting a co-worker from each side of a dispute to lunch or drinks at different times. Act like you have no idea there are different factions or cliques. What do you know? You're just a telecommuter.

  You can also try asking your different in-office friends for their advice about the projects you're working on. People usually love to have their advice solicited, and you may gain valuable information that way. And, of course, you're under no obligation to follow the advice if you don't agree.

- ✔ **Be a good listener.** As a neutral party, you're the perfect person to listen to everybody else's grievances. Be sympathetic, but be careful not to take sides. This can reinforce your in-office friendships, and may bring you inside information as well.

Managing Change

At one time, you could work the same job for the same boss without major alterations to your company's direction or your own career direction during many years or even decades. But those days are long gone. If you're like many employees today, the only certainty about your workplace is that it will be substantially different a year from now.

Here, again, your status as a telecommuter helps because, as one telecommuter puts it, "It keeps you out of the maelstrom. Imagine a large pile of rocks, with a large rock at the top. If you shift the one on top around, many of the smaller ones will shift around as well. But if you're a rock that's off to the side, it doesn't affect you.

Being out of the office can also mean avoiding some of the trauma that goes with workplace changes. "The print version of *Windows* magazine shut down when our company was acquired," Christine Doane-Benton notes. "The mood in the office was that of a mortuary for the six weeks prior to the shutdown because people could feel that something was going on. However, I was in my sunny flat and didn't have to deal with the emotional environment all the time. It definitely helped me."

But working outside the office during periods of major change is definitely a mixed blessing. You're insulated from anxiety and unhappiness when your co-workers have to deal with uncertainty, but you can also miss out on the information you need to make the right decisions on the job or about your career.

The danger becomes particularly intense if you find yourself with a new boss.

Although telecommuting gains more recognition all the time as a legitimate work option, not all managers are comfortable with telecommuters; neither do they know how to supervise them properly. A new boss who inherits the decision to let you telecommute may be uncomfortable making changes that are needed to deal effectively with an employee who isn't physically present. On some level — possibly even subconsciously — that manager may be happier seeing you leave than going through the difficult learning process required for dealing effectively with you.

Another interesting fact about being a telecommuter is that you may be more likely than most employees to find yourself reporting to a new boss. You may ask why? The answer is simple: Supervising an employee who is physically absent some of the time requires a skilled manager, confident in his or her ability to judge you on your work alone, and equally confident that you'll work hard and do a good job even outside of direct oversight. Not every manager has this degree of skill and confidence. Those who do are likely to be recognized — and promoted quickly to other positions.

Either way, some of the strategies in the following sections can help you prepare for changes in your work environment.

Keep checking for signs of change

Because you're not on site, you necessarily miss out on chances to overhear people's conversations, notice who's meeting with whom, or pick up on your co-workers' moods and anxieties. While not knowing these things can be a big plus for your attitude, and your ability to get your work done, it also can be a problem if change arrives when you're not prepared for it.

So you need to be especially vigilant. At your first inkling of clouds on the horizon, start asking your trusted associates whether they know if anything's happening, or sense that change is in the air.

Document your contributions

When a new boss takes over, or your organization is reshuffled, you won't be able to count on your old boss knowing and remembering what you've accomplished for your organization. So, wherever possible, it helps to have a written, concrete record of your achievements. Keep copies of reports you've written, in-house or professional awards you've earned, plans you've submitted, and any letters or notes of praise or thanks you may have received. Every six months or so, take a few minutes to jot down your own view of what you've achieved, and what recent contributions you've made. You may never need any of this material. But the need to document your contributions can arise at any time, and you're better off if you're prepared to do it.

Widen your circle

Making as many friends as is humanly possible inside and outside your own department also prepares you for any changes that may occur. In a corporate shakeup, you never know who'll wind up on top. And, if someone who's unfamiliar with your department winds up overseeing it, you'll want as many co-workers as possible to be advocates for you. The more people who know you and care about your work, the better off you'll be when change comes.

Get to know new players

If you wind up with a new boss, getting to know him or her as quickly as possible is extremely important. That may mean coming in to the office on the days you normally wouldn't, or making special trips so you and your new boss can meet.

"I make sure to schedule time with new managers, co-workers, and executives (when appropriate) to discuss my projects and what my telework experience look like, any problems I experience, and what benefits I experience," Scott Decker notes. "The point is to educate people at every opportunity about what I'm doing, and solicit responses about the effect, if any, on them."

Volunteer for new projects

A new boss or a shift in direction for your organization will likely mean that new projects are starting. Working on new projects is a great way to keep yourself front and center in your boss's mind, even when you're not around.

"Our company is shifting in a whole new direction, and part of that will mean building a new staff of specialists to work with our customers," one telecommuter reports. "That job could as easily have fallen to my department, or to a different department. But I made sure to get involved. It helps a lot if they can see positive contributions coming from me. It's more important in my case, because I'm not in the office most of the time."

Be prepared to change course

Another possible consequence of change is that a project that you've been working hard on may suddenly no longer fit with your organization's new priorities. Or you may simply need to take a different approach. Whatever the case, you always need to be mentally prepared to make changes, rearrange your plans, or drop what you're doing altogether and pick up something else instead.

"Being a teleworker is like working for a start-up company," Scott Decker says. "The key is to be flexible. Changes in the workplace are inevitable. So I have to take responsibility for staying informed about what's happening at the office when I'm not there, and what the changes mean to my work."

Keep your résumé handy

Having your résumé on hand is good advice for anyone, whenever change looms in the workplace, especially when you're a telecommuter. If you're committed to the idea of working from a remote location (or if telecommuting has allowed you to live where few local jobs exist in your field), you probably don't want to or can't take an on-site job if, for any reason, you leave your current position. That means you'd be looking for another telecommuting job — that may be harder to find than an on-site job.

So at least scoping out the possibilities earlier, rather than later, may be a good idea. After all, no rule says that you have to take a new job if you get it, or even apply for a job just because you find out there's an opening. But the more information you have about other available work that you can do as a telecommuter, the better position you'll be in when it comes to making decisions about your current job.

When Envy Rears Its Ugly Head

Most on-site colleagues of telecommuters are supportive of those who work at home. But every now and then, you may encounter some resentment from those left behind at the office. Remember the myth of telecommuting: that you're lolling around in a bathrobe, sleeping until noon, and watching daytime TV, collecting your salary all the while. No wonder some co-workers get jealous!

You must try to be as understanding as possible. Keep in mind, that although telecommuting should not be viewed as a perk, it's a privilege only accorded to successful and trusted employees. In most organizations, not everyone who wants to telecommute is allowed to. So your jealous co-worker may have been turned down on a telecommuting request of his or her own. And let's face it, you know how much more fun it is to work outside an office than in it.

What's the best strategy for dealing with an envious co-worker? Begin by trying to make friends with that person. Spend a little more time chatting with him or her during your times in the office. Make sure that the co-worker knows your home contact number and/or cell phone, and that you can be called any time during business hours. This may subtly get the point across that, while you may not be in the office, you're still at your desk and on the job.

You may also try discussing your work with this person; this is another subtle way of letting him or her know that you're not spending your days loafing around. If you're facing a work dilemma, impossibly tight deadline, or other problem, you may want to share your misery, or ask for advice. All these are other ways of communicating that just because you're away from the workplace doesn't mean you're avoiding the problems that go with it.

Finally, try finding out whether your co-worker would like to be a telecommuter, too. He or she may not have the right sort of job for telecommuting — in which case you need to be honest and say so. But if it seems like a viable option, maybe you can be of some assistance. Pass along tips about what worked and what didn't when you made your telecommuting pitch. Explain any techniques you've found to help you work more efficiently or communicate better with the office. Invite your co-worker to use you as a resource when launching a telecommuting career.

Finally, remind your colleague that your telecommuting success can benefit him or her, too. After all, if your telecommuting experiment is deemed successful, management is likelier to approve a telecommuting arrangement for someone else.

Chapter 13

When You're the Boss

*B*eing a good manager is a challenge for most team leaders. But being a good manager as a telecommuter adds another set of difficulties. "Management by wandering around," a method many management experts recommend, in which you can have casual, impromptu conversations throughout the day with the people reporting to you, isn't an option if you're not physically in the office. You can no longer use appearance or body language as clues to your team members' moods and emotions. Because most contact takes place over the phone and the Internet, you have to be much clearer in your communications and more alert to subtle vocal changes and other signals that may let you know what's going on.

If being a good boss in general means keeping communications clear — letting your reports know exactly what you need from them and staying aware of what they need from you — then being a good *telecommuting* boss means doing these things even better.

Hire with Care

Hiring the right people is essential for any successful manager. But because you'll be managing your team from a distance, having people on your team who can do the job well without direct supervision is especially important. So you'll need to make hiring decisions even more carefully than you would if you were in a traditional office setting. While in another situation it may be appropriate to hire an appealing candidate with borderline qualifications, as a telecommuting manager, that is probably something you can't afford to do. You have much less room to experiment than your on-site counterparts do.

Inheriting team members

As a manager, you don't always get your choice of people who report to you. If you take over a team from another manager (or if your organization has strict promotion guidelines), you may find yourself the boss of people you wouldn't have selected yourself.

This can be awkward for any manager, regardless of whether you're a telecommuter. It requires striking a delicate balance between taking a collaborative, team-centered approach and bringing inherited staff members in line with what you want to do.

In a previous job, my husband Bill inherited ten part-time, telecommuting staff members who, until he arrived, had a tremendous amount of autonomy. "Any time you take over an existing staff, it's going to mean big changes for them," he says. "Even if you're not trying to change their jobs, you'll do things differently from the manager who was there before."

But, in this case, Bill *was* making drastic changes to the job descriptions of members of his staff. Those changes required them to widen the scope of what they were doing and take on unfamiliar tasks that were definitely outside their respective comfort zones. The changes also meant limiting their autonomy and forcing them to function much more as part of a larger team.

It was a difficult transition for some of them. "I worked with their skills," Bill says. "Some really liked doing the new parts of the job, and others were uncomfortable with them. So, to some extent, I had people focus on what they were most comfortable with." But only to some extent. All the inherited staff members had to take on some new responsibilities and fundamentally alter and expand the way they did their jobs. Inevitably, some responded with resentment.

Bill is an outgoing person who has always made friendship a part of his management style, and this case was no exception. "I make friends with everyone, and I tried to make friends with them," he recalls. For most of the inherited staff, this strategy worked well, and they adapted quickly to their new roles. For two of them, the newly reorganized jobs were too much of an uncomfortable fit, and they wound up leaving.

When you take over a group of staff members, Bill says, "People will always come to you with complaints and concerns. You need to field these carefully. Some of their concerns might be valid. But, ultimately, you have to do the job the way you know how to do it, and they have to fit in with that."

That's why Xpedior's Robert Egert always asks colleagues to help select the people he hires. (Egert is profiled later in this chapter.) After writing a job description and getting a group of candidates from his company's recruiters, Egert screens qualified applicants with a phone interview. Once he has narrowed it down to a few that he likes, he asks two or three other Xpedior executives to conduct lengthy phone interviews with his choices. If they all agree, the person is invited to visit Xpedior's New York office, which usually involves flying the candidate in from elsewhere.

"I would always do it at the company office, not my remote office," Egert says. "The candidate would meet a variety of people, including some outside my organization." If the candidate seems right, Egert often makes an offer right away.

But, he says, "I've never hired anyone unless the choice was confirmed by at least two of my colleagues."

Building Relationships that Work

Once your team is in place, your next challenge is to create working relationships that enable the team as a whole to work effectively, even when you're not present to work with them directly. Many telecommuting managers find themselves in charge of teams whose members are also telecommuters, and may be geographically distant from the manager and their employers' office. In this setting, it's particularly difficult — but particularly important — to build effective working relationships.

Manage by objective

Regardless of whether they admit it, most managers depend largely on what they see employees doing (whether they're at their desk, whether they seem happy or stressed, and what their attitudes are) when evaluating team members' performances. Without all this information, you can wind up feeling in the dark when trying to determine whether the people you supervise are doing an effective job.

The only way around this obstacle is establishing specific objectives for your team members to meet, individually and as a group. You then can judge the team's performance, and the performances of individual team members, according to how well they meet these objectives.

"I would look for specific ways to measure performance for the people who report to you," says Robert Egert, when asked for his advice to other telecommuting managers. "Ideally, they should be numerical in nature. Find a set of numbers that defines how they are doing at their jobs."

It's crucial for you and your team member to agree beforehand exactly what his or her goals will be, he adds. "You need clearly defined objectives, and some way to measure a person's performance. Without that, it's difficult to know how that person is doing, because you're not in an environment with them, and you don't get to talk with them or about them."

Using clearly defined, specific objectives also is a big benefit to the workers who report to you. The better they know exactly what's expected of them, the better they're able to properly perform their duties — and the likelier they are to know without being told when they're excelling at their jobs and when they may need to make an adjustment.

This kind of information is important for all employees, of course. But as a telecommuting boss, it's especially vital for your reports, because they're not in constant contact with you as they go about their jobs. "In the office, if I go into my boss's office at 8 a.m., and the boss says, 'I want you to work on this budget revision today,' there will be many times that we run into each other as the day goes by. Each of those is an opportunity to fine-tune or clarify what I'm doing," notes telecommuting expert Gil Gordon. Without that frequent contact, it's vitally important to let the people on your team know in detail what you need from them.

Build a personal connection

I've often noticed that the people my husband Bill manages seem to love working for him. They seem willing to do almost anything for him. Several of them have followed him from company to company as he has changed jobs. One actually put us up in her house during a cross-country trip.

What makes this especially noteworthy is that most of them are spread out across the country, and one is in Canada. Most of them see Bill face to face only on rare occasions — and some have never met him at all. So I asked him recently how he manages to build so much loyalty with so little face-to-face contact.

"You have to really get to know them as people," he told me. "They know I take an interest in their lives, and that makes a difference when I tell them what the company needs from them." To prove his point, he gave me detailed accounts of his team members' lives — what their spouses did, what their interests were, who liked to talk on the phone a lot, and who didn't, and which team members were friends with each other.

Having that personal bond helps you be a better remote manager in many different ways. First, it helps telecommuting team members feel a closer connection to you, and that may enable them to feel more strongly that your work objectives are their objectives as well. Likewise, team members who think of you as a friend tend to feel more comfortable communicating with you and are more likely to let you know early on what problems or obstacles they're facing and to share their ideas and observations about their work. And they're more likely to pick up the phone or otherwise get in touch whenever they have problems or concerns, because calling you is a lot like calling a friend.

"Many managers feel more comfortable having a wall of sorts between them-selves and the people who report to them," Bill says. "I don't, and I feel that, as a manager, I'm a lot better off without it."

Trust your team

Trust is another important issue that is amplified for the telecommuting manager. Trusting the people who work for you can be a difficult challenge. But, as a telecommuter, you really have little choice. You can't watch what people are doing, how they're doing their jobs, or even how many hours they're at work. So if you can't trust them to do their jobs correctly, and give their best efforts, you'll probably face a great deal of frustration trying to check up on people from afar.

The issue of trust is one big reason to exercise extreme care when making decisions about hiring. Once you know for sure you've chosen the right person for the job, and given that person a clear idea of what goals to aim for, it should be relatively easy to step out of the way and trust the employee to get the job done. If you can't let go and trust the employee, you may need to work on your management skills.

You also need to give some thought to the management style that you use as a telecommuting boss. Because a high degree of trust is needed, you're prob-ably better off using a team-centered approach than a traditional supervisory role.

"I *trust* the team and empower them to be the experts," says Scott Decker of TManage. "I ask them how things need to be done and in that way act more as a facilitator than as a manager. I often play devil's advocate, challenging the process and decisions to ensure that we've explored all our options. Nine out of ten times the team has made the best possible decision." (Scott Decker is profiled in Chapter 10.)

Become an advocate

One of your more important roles as a manager is being an advocate for your team members. You must make sure they have the resources and support they need to do an effective job, and that once they've done an effective job, they're appropriately recognized and rewarded. And, in case of organizational reshuffling or other changes in your organization, you must watch out for their interests as well.

If the members of your team also are telecommuters, and don't spend much time working in the office, they may need an effective advocate more than most employees. Because they aren't on site, promoting their own projects or concerns, finding mentors, creating their own relationships within your company, or making sure that their efforts are noticed and valued may be hard for them. In addition, Robert Egert points out, your team may particularly need your support when it comes to technological problems. "If your team members are telecommuting, their telecommunications equipment is critical," he says. "You have to make sure the information technology department will service them properly."

That can be difficult to do from a remote location, he adds, and handling this issue on their own may be difficult for your team members. "As individuals, your team member can be seen as the odd man out," he explains. "As a boss, you can really advocate for your staff. So I'd recommend developing some service level agreement with the IT department on behalf of your staff."

Communicating with Your Team

As is true with many aspects of telecommuting, the key to succeeding as an off-site manager is communicating clearly and often with the people on your team. But, when it comes to this issue of communication, one size doesn't fit all. Some team members need and benefit from a daily *check-in* phone conversation, establishing what they're doing (or have done) that day, what their next tasks will be, and any problems they've encountered along the way. Others may really appreciate the trust implied in a less frequent check-in schedule.

The following sections outline some issues to consider when planning communications with your team.

Set a schedule you can live with

Whether it's once a day or once a week, set an individual check-in schedule with each member of your team. The schedule may be different for each team member, but whatever it is, make sure it's something you all can stick with.

Set a specific agenda for the check-ins. For example, have your employee report on new customers contacted, new research done, reports written, or whatever seems appropriate. Whatever the schedule, you and the person reporting to you need to have a clear idea of what information will be conveyed, and what issues need to be addressed when you check in with each other.

In general, starting out with a check-in schedule that is too frequent rather than frequent enough is wise. Why? For one thing, the potential for misunderstandings, missed signals, missed opportunities, or other unfortunate events is much greater if you communicate too little rather than too much. A second reason: If you must make an adjustment, reducing the frequency of check-ins is a lot easier than increasing them. Telling an employee to check in twice a week rather than every day sends the signal that things are going smoothly, everything's on the right track, and you trust the employee to make autonomous decisions. Telling someone who has been checking in weekly that you now need to get in touch every other day sends the signal that the employee is doing something wrong. Even if you explain that isn't the case, it's hard for the employee not to view increased check-ins as a criticism.

Consider different means of checking in

Different ways of checking in are appropriate for different team members in different situations. Some experimenting helps you decide whether you want team members to report in by e-mail or phone. In part, this depends on what forms of communication are most comfortable for you and your team members, and what medium enables them to communicate more effectively. Again, of course, one size doesn't fit all. Some members of your team may do well with one kind of communication while others do better at another.

E-mail

In general, e-mail allows you and the team members who report to you to choose your words carefully and provide well-thought-out information. If what you have to discuss involves a lot of detail, complex concepts or processes, or a lot of facts and figures, e-mail can be an especially useful tool. A further advantage is that saving e-mails or forwarding them to other team members who may need to share the information or take part in the discussion is simple.

Likewise, e-mail does not require you and your team member to be at your desks at the same time. If you both are telecommuting and creating your own work schedules, not having to coordinate with each other can be advantageous.

Telephone

A phone conversation gains in immediacy what it loses in detail and record-keeping value. Phone conversations enable you to respond directly to what your team members have to say, and to request more information or a clearer explanation, if anything is said that you don't understand.

On the other hand, a telephone conversation can be like a game of, well, tele-phone. You and your team member may come away with separate and different understandings of what was said and what actions each of you plans to take.

Ultimately, a combination of e-mail and phone contacts may offer the best of both worlds. For instance, you can have team members e-mail you once a day to report ongoing activities. You can then schedule phone conversations once a week to go over reports and discuss any issues that come up. Or, if you schedule weekly phone conversations, you may want to follow up with an e-mail that addresses the more important points.

Face-to-face

Depending on where each of you is located, meeting in person may be difficult for you and the members of your team. But, if it's at all possible, you need to do so whenever you can. Use business trips, conferences, or even vacations (if appropriate) as opportunities for visiting people who report to you, or have them visit you. If you don't know each other well, or rarely see each other, try scheduling some serious *face time,* including time to relax over a meal, go to a sporting or theater event together, or just hang out. Spending this kind of time can help you get to know each other as people and create a bond that can help you work well together when problems arise.

For those team members who aren't geographically distant, take advantage of having them nearby by getting together with them on a regular basis — at least once a month, and perhaps as often as once a week, depending on com-muting times and job requirements. Meeting like this gives you a chance to get to know your team members as people and to discuss in depth any issues that come up on the job.

Have an open door

If you're working at a home office, your staff members probably can't drop by to take advantage of your open door. So why not have a virtual open door instead? Let team members know they can call you any time during business hours — and outside business hours too, if that's appropriate to your work schedule.

Tell them that it's always okay to call, even if it's just to touch base, or get confirmation of something they already knew. If appropriate, give them a cell phone number, along with your home-office number, so they can reach you when you're not home.

Another way of keeping your virtual door open is making yourself available on instant message chat services. Staff members who are comfortable with using the Internet can sign on and see if you're there (online) any time they need you throughout the workday. If they have a question or problem, they can alert you with an instant message, and get an immediate answer.

Because instant message chats are one-on-one conversations, team members each can feel like they have your undivided attention. And it's easy for you to leave the chat box open throughout the day, going about your usual work but being available in case you're needed.

Helping Your Team Feel Like a Team

Helping the staff members who work under your supervision feel connected to you and to your company is vital to your success as a telecommuting manager. But that's only part of the job. It's just as important to make sure that team members who report to you feel connected to each other — and that they work together well as a team.

Laying groundwork for a remote relationship

Robert Egert specializes in information architecture — the art of creating Web sites that are easy and intuitive to use. Currently, he is chief creative officer for the startup firm The Learning Masters, a consulting firm focused on distance learning, which is education via the Internet. Before joining The Learning Masters, Egert was charged with bringing information architecture skills to a newly merged consultancy's practices around the country.

As a telecommuter, Egert traveled to the firm's New York City office one day per week and spent the rest of the time working in a home office in Massachusetts' Berkshire Mountains. His new role meant hiring practice leaders around the country. How could he establish a good working relationship with people he'd rarely see in person?

As part of the solution, Egert started each new employee off with an informal all-day meeting at his country home. The day began with Egert meeting his new hire at the train station and having breakfast at a nearby café. They would

work together for several hours, break for a walk or other activity, and then work a few hours more before he dropped the person at the train again.

These meetings fulfilled three important objectives, he says. "One was to develop a rapport that gives us enough momentum to sustain us through months of not seeing each other."

The second was to create a mission statement for the new person in his or her job. "We set goals for the next three months," he says. "After three months, we reassessed these goals."

The third objective, Egert says, "was for me to impart to them my knowledge of the company, my own mission and how they fit in."

After the meeting, the new person would formalize the mission statement and return a written copy to Egert. It was an important document, he adds. "I let them know that their bonus would be calculated according to how well they met those goals."

Because you're often away from the office, your team members risk feeling disconnected not only from you as their manager, but also as a team. This can be even more of a problem if, as often happens, you're managing a remote team, with each team member working alone in a different location. If so, making members of this widely dispersed group of people feel and function as a single team is an especially difficult task, but an especially important one.

How can you make a remote team feel like a team? Following are some strategies to consider.

Give projects to the team as a whole

Instead of giving each team member a specific task to do toward meeting your entire team's objective, give the team as a whole a view of the big picture. In addition to fostering a sense of unity among your team members, this actually can help you do a better job. Several heads are better than one. Team members who have a complete view of the goals you're trying to achieve may have useful ideas to help you reach them that you otherwise wouldn't have come up with on your own — and that they couldn't have come up with if they didn't already understand your overall objectives.

What's more, if the team as a whole feels responsible for team projects, they can work together to ensure that objectives are met. Scott Decker, for example, says he uses a work plan and an action log that enable team members to keep track of larger goals and day-to-day tasks. "The action log is posted in a folder on our network so staff can access and update it regularly," he says.

He notes that he has never had a disciplinary problem within his team — an accomplishment that he attributes to the work plan and action log. "The team knows if someone is not performing, and nobody wants to be the weak link," he explains. "If a team member is having difficulty, the rest of the team pulls together and asks if there is something they can do to help."

Assigning team projects can be a tremendous benefit for you in reaching your objectives as a manager. But some telecommuting managers report that this practice can prove dangerous as well: Once in a while, a team member can take on too much responsibility for team projects. He or she may log many extra hours doing other people's jobs, usually because of a real or perceived need to pick up the slack.

Nipping an overzealous team member in the bud is important. Otherwise, the employee who has taken on too much work can wind up feeling burned out and resentful. And the one whose work is being taken over may also be resentful of the intrusion.

Encourage communication within the team

You may find yourself acting as a central clearinghouse of information for the team, especially when team members are scattered in different locations. This is a natural tendency and can benefit you in some ways — for instance, by keeping you abreast of all new developments and potential problems. But by acting this way, you miss the opportunity to help your team work as a team by encouraging direct contact among team members.

So when team members come to you with reports of what they've been doing, or when they question how they should proceed, try to refer them to other members of the team who may be able to give them insight or guidance. Resist the temptation to deal with every question that arises, and instead encourage team members to exchange frequent phone calls, e-mails, and even visits.

Hold regular conference calls

In addition to communicating with each member of your team individually, communicating regularly with the team as a whole also is important. One simple way to do so is with a regularly scheduled conference call, which can function as a weekly staff meeting — as if you were all working in the same office. Conference calls can serve several purposes at once for your team. First, they give team members a sense of the objectives that the team as a whole is working toward and how their own projects fit in. Next, team members get to talk with (if not see) each other in a setting that allows for open discussion. It lets them get to know each other better. And, of course, it keeps you informed of team activities.

"We have two kinds of status meetings scheduled every week," Robert Egert says. "One is a half-hour meeting between me and each person on the team individually. They report what they'd been doing and chat about politics within the company and any obstacles they've encountered. The second kind of status meeting is a conference call where we all get together and do a round-table discussion of what we've been doing since the last time we met."

Conference calls are the usual mode of communication within the team headed by Scott Decker. So, he says, the meeting has some ground rules. First, only one person is allowed to speak at a time. Second, rather than a free-flowing, catching-up kind of discussion, Decker sets a specific agenda for each meeting. "If the discussion is straying, I let it go for a short time, until I feel it is no longer productive," he says. "At the end of the meeting, I recap what has been decided. I reiterate any actions the team has decided to take, and review when they are due."

Try online chat

Online chat is a difficult concept for many telecommuters and telecommuting managers to get used to. Unfortunately, many Internet users assume that chat rooms are for lonely teenagers, political fringe groups, or those with odd sexual preferences, and can't possibly have any practical use in the business world.

But they can. In fact, chat is an extremely useful way for a small group of people in several different locations to conduct a discussion. My husband Bill, for instance, regularly meets with his team members in a chat room and considers it a much better way to discuss issues with them than on a conference call. Of course, as an Internet community professional, Bill spends more time in chat rooms than most people, so it comes as no surprise that he's perfectly comfortable communicating that way. Not everyone feels the same way, and meeting by chat may not work in every situation. Still, Bill insists, chat is the way of the future, and most managers need to learn to be comfortable with it. Besides, he points out, chat offers some definite advantages:

- ✔ **Speakers are always identified by name.** Anyone who has participated in a conference call knows how hard it can be to tell who's saying what at any given moment. You can ask people to identify themselves by name before making comments — although you'll probably have to remind them repeatedly as the meeting goes on. In chat, no such problem exists: Every line of chat comes with the speaker's name in front of it.

- ✔ **People can't interrupt each other.** Scott Decker's rule that only one person be permitted to speak at a time is unnecessary in a chat room. The technology makes it impossible to speak any other way. People can't talk over each other. In a face-to-face meeting or conference call, less senior members of the group may stop speaking or back down when a more senior member decides to speak up. While this may satisfy those who are higher in the pecking order, it's counterproductive for the team because those who are lower in the pecking order may wind up not voicing their opinions or ideas.

   Situations such as this are much less likely to occur in a chat room because chat technology doesn't recognize corporate hierarchies. Once a comment is sent into the chat stream, it appears in the order that it arrived. Junior team members' views are thus much more likely to be heard. As Bill puts it, "Everyone is equal in a chat room."

- ✔ **A record of what was said is created.** If you want to remember what was said during a face-to-face meeting or a conference call, someone in attendance must take notes. But a meeting by chat creates its own record. After the chat session is over, everyone who participated can review a transcript of the chat. Doing so prevents misunderstandings about what was said, who said what, and what action the team decided to take. A transcript of the chat can remain in your company's archives as a record in case questions later arise.

✔ **Chat offers big savings on telecommunication costs.** Long-distance charges for conference calls can add up quickly, especially if participants are in various locations around the country. On the other hand, most Internet users pay flat monthly fees for unlimited use, so taking part in a chat doesn't cost anything extra. That can translate into significant savings for your company. It also may mean significant savings for you if you have to pay long-distance charges up front before being reimbursed by your employer.

✔ **You can bring the team together.** Although meeting by conference call or chat is a great way to keep your team feeling connected, it never will replace bringing people face to face whenever it's at all possible.

Help the team feel like part of the organization at large

Members of remote teams face the problem of not feeling as though they are part the organization at large. If you go out of your way to keep in regular contact with them, let them know you're interested in who they are, and make sure they know that they can always contact you for any reason, your team members may come to feel bonded with you. However, they may not feel that way about the organization they work for.

Feeling that they're not only part of your team but also part of the organization at large is important for your team members. Here are a few ways you can help this process along:

✔ **Foster communication between your team members and their colleagues in other parts of the organization.** Create as many points of contact as you can between other parts of your company and your team members. If, for example, someone asks you a question that can be answered in depth by a member of your team, you may give a short answer and suggest contact between the two parties. You may even ask the team member to get in touch. If appropriate, you can also encourage communication between outside parties, such as customers or suppliers, with members of your team.

✔ **Make sure they're *in the loop* for company communications.** Remote team members need to be included in companywide announcements or meetings. This may require having a speakerphone set up at company-wide meetings so that they can listen in. Gathering the information yourself and reporting back to them may be easier, but still keeps them one step removed from the rest of your company.

✔ **Get recognition for them wherever possible.** Other executives in your company must be regularly made aware of who your team members are and how they contribute to organizational goals. For instance, every time you write a report about what your team has been doing, be careful to identify by name each of the team members who took part in the effort and state exactly what they did.

Likewise, if the company is handing out commendations, recognition awards, gifts, or anything else that lets employees know they're appreciated, make sure your team members are included. These steps can be especially challenging — but are especially important — if you lead a team of remote staff members who rarely make appearances at the company's office. Keeping their contributions in mind is easy for you because you work with them on a daily basis. But others in your organization, who rarely see and have little direct contact with your team members, can easily forget that they're part of the larger team.

✔ **Bring them to the office.** "Trying to get to know a large organization from a distance is like trying to punch a cloud," Robert Egert says. That's why he brings remote staff members into his company's office as often as he can and especially when one of them is starting a new job. "If someone's going to be working in a telecommuting role, give that person the opportunity to spend a few weeks on site to meet people and create relationships."

When Problems Arise

Most managers hope the people who report to them will always do a wonderful job and that their only management task will be handing out kudos and raises. Unfortunately, for most managers, performance problems do arise at one time or another. Handling these issues well is what makes the difference between an effective manager and an ineffective one.

As a telecommuting manager, you may be at a disadvantage when it comes to first recognizing a performance problem. Because you don't see staff members every day, you can't read body language to identify any changes in mood or behavior, or gauge their interactions when working with others. That means you need to be especially alert to any changes you pick up on when dealing with them by Internet or phone.

"It can be harder to tell when there are problems," notes Donna Gettings of OneMADE.com. "But, the longer you work away from the office, the easier it is to *read between the lines* when interacting with staff members via phone, e-mail, and instant messaging." (Gettings is profiled in Chapter 4.)

Assume they're in the right

How should you proceed when you encounter a performance problem? Begin by assuming the employee is in the right and approaching them accordingly, Gettings advises.

In many situations, you can correct a problem by offering help, rather than imposing discipline. This was Robert Egert's strategy on two occasions when members of his team ran into performance issues, and both times it was an effective solution.

In one instance, he says, a team member became frustrated and began acting in an unprofessional way. "That was difficult to deal with," he recalls. "It turned out that person had started off with ambitious objectives. That employee was getting really stressed out and not having any fun at the job. So I worked with that person to identify the core requirements of the job and scale back the objectives so that they were more reasonable. That was the right approach in that situation."

In another instance, he found that one of his team members was not communicating effectively with people in other areas of the company. Working in Egert's department represented a big career move for the staff member, and although she was well qualified to do the job, she lacked confidence in her own judgment. "She would call me and say, 'Here's what's come up and here's what I want to do about it.' She needed me to reaffirm her decisions," he says.

That same lack of confidence was coming out in her interactions with others. "She didn't feel she had the authority to do what she needed to do," Egert says. "And people started treating her like she didn't have that authority."

Egert knew the solution was to use his own clout to support this team member, but he decided to make it her option, rather than imposing himself on her — and further undermining her confidence.

"The way I handled it was to offer to be available if she wanted me to sit in on meetings with her. She liked that. And she would call me in, and then I would come back her up." When the people at the meetings saw that she had Egert's full support, they began taking her more seriously.

Use clear communications, and document what was said

Whenever a performance problem arises, your first responsibility is to communicate clearly to your team member exactly what the problem is, and how you'd like to see it corrected. Ideally, you need to meet face-to-face with a team member who's having a performance problem. But if that isn't an option, you can still communicate the same information by other means.

If you address the issue over the phone or in an instant message chat, Donna Gettings recommends following up the conversation with an e-mail that goes over the main points (or contains pertinent parts of the chat dialogue). "That gives the employee the opportunity to challenge the details as you remember them," she notes.

"It has to be clear up front what the stages of discipline are," she explains. You also need to let the employee know whether repeated instances of the same performance problem will bring worsening and greater consequences.

"For instance, if there is a three-strikes warning system, you need to make it clear that a given e-mail or phone call is indeed a *strike.* As well, there has to be a known grievance process. If an employee is not satisfied with what you as a manager are doing, he or she needs an opportunity to say so and a clear route to your supervisor (if applicable) for resolution of the problem."

And, Gettings stresses, "Document, document, document. Documentation is the key and probably the most important aspect of all discipline, whether it's remote or not."

Asked if as a telecommuting manager she ever had to fire an employee, she replies, "Yes. It sucked. The person was not producing what she needed to stay employed with the company. She was given several warnings via e-mail, and we had several phone conversations to discuss her lack of performance."

The employee responded by saying she was resigning her job, but then continued working as though nothing had ever happened. Gettings responded by establishing a termination date for this staff member, and reminding her several times, as the day approached, that it would be her last day.

"She became angry, but her time with us was done," Gettings says now. "Once the decision is made, firmly, to let someone go, it doesn't matter whether it's face-to-face or remote. In these instances, documentation is your best friend."

Chapter 14

Telecommuting and Your Salary

. . . .

. . . .

*W*ill being a telecommuter mean having to accept a lower salary?

The answer to this question isn't as simple as I wish it was. In most organizations, telecommuters are treated the same as everybody else, as they should be. And it's what every telecommuting consultant I know recommends to his or her corporate clients.

Unfortunately, different employers view telecommuting in different ways. And some of them staunchly believe they have good reason to pay telecommuters less than their on-site counterparts.

Whether this is likely to happen to you depends a lot on your reasons for telecommuting, your employers' reasons for allowing you to telecommute, and the unspoken assumptions your employer makes about how telecommuting affects your job.

You can stack the deck in your favor, though, by going into the negotiation prepared with information that can help you support the notion that work done at home is no less valuable than work done in the office.

Making the Case for Equal Pay

Why should telecommuters earn less than their on-site colleagues? Ask most telecommuting experts, and the answer is simple: They shouldn't. So why do some employers believe that policy is the right one to adopt?

The following sections provide you with a look at some of the reasoning employers may use to argue for a lower salary — and some responses that can help you when negotiating a telecommuting salary.

Lower salaries are the norm

"Our chief financial officer insists that all he has read indicates it is customary for telecommuters to take a 10 percent to 20 percent salary reduction because this new work arrangement is to their benefit," reports one telecommuter who posted a question about salaries on telecommuting expert Gil Gordon's Web site (www.gilgordon.com).

I can't guess what this executive has been reading, but everything I've read indicates just the opposite. The norm is for employee salaries and benefits to be exactly the same as they'd be if the employee were in the office every day. And it's the norm for a reason. Any other way of doing things is unfair.

Telecommuting lowers employees' expenses

The truth is that working at home probably will save you money over working in an office. But using that as an argument for lower pay is akin to the one employers made years ago that it was right to pay a woman less than a man in the same job because he might have a family to support. The problem is that they didn't bear out their reasoning by paying single men less than men with families (or single mothers, for that matter). Each job has a value in the job market, and that value should be paid to anyone doing the job competently, regardless of gender or family status.

The same logic applies with telecommuting. Does your company pay the person with a two-hour commute a higher salary than the one who happens to live across the street? Does it pay more to a parent of small children because that employee has to arrange for day care? Or does every job have a particular value, a value that should be paid equally to anyone doing the job? That should be the standard for determining your salary.

The company will have to pay for your equipment, phone lines, and so on

Another argument for lowering the salary of a telecommuting position is that the company has to pay for equipment, phone lines, and such. Maybe so. But the company would be paying for your equipment and phone line if you were working on site — as well as for your office space, utilities, use of shared equipment (such as copiers and faxes), and a whole host of other expenses.

The fact of the matter is that your employer benefits financially by allowing you to telecommute. If you haven't done so already, preparing a cost-benefit analysis is a good idea, because it helps illustrate this point in an easily understood form. (For details on creating a cost-benefit analysis, see Chapter 3.)

Some actions can be taken to help defray the costs of having you work remotely. For example, instead of installing two phone lines and using one as a fax line, you can use a scanner and Internet-based fax service. Another way to save may include borrowing a company laptop and adding a monitor and keyboard for better ergonomics, rather than buying a whole new system.

You can also create greater cost savings at the office — if you're telecommuting most of the time — by offering your workspace to share with another telecommuter or use for temporary work. (This requires you to put everything away neatly and clear off your desk fairly well before leaving the office to telecommute, which is probably a good habit to form.) Better yet, you can free it up altogether, by telling your employer you don't need a desk of your own, and instead using a temporary workspace yourself when you're in the office.

Telecommuting is a perk

The argument that telecommuting is a perk is not true. A perk, short for *perquisite,* is something the company offers to valued employees as a reward for doing a good job, or as an incentive for staying on. Use of a company club, for instance, is a traditional perk. A perk is something that benefits the employee, and costs the employer.

Some managers reason that employees' and employers' interests are always in direct conflict. Therefore, if telecommuting is a positive for the employee it must automatically be a negative for the employer. But that is simply not true. By eliminating your commuting time, which is useless time for each of the parties, you and your employer gain. Telecommuting is truly an example of a win-win situation.

If you work at home, you'll focus on your home life, not your job

The preconception that you'll focus more on your home life than your job can be difficult to change, especially if you have small children or elderly family members at home who do need your attention, or if your reasons for telecommuting have to do with your family's needs. Part of the problem is a peculiarly American assumption that work life and family life are at odds and can only detract from each other. This assumption is not questioned as often as it ought to be.

Take me and my husband Bill. I'm a business and technology writer, currently at work on a book about telecommuting. He's a telecommuter employed in a technology-related field. Both of us are obsessed with what we do, and our work lives and married life overlap and interlock in more ways than I can count. We've spent hours brainstorming some business problem of Bill's or discussing some aspect of telecommuting. I help him with business writing. He keeps my computer running smoothly. Working at home has not made either one of us any less focused on our jobs.

But this is a personal observation, not something I think you should share with your boss. A better way to get the point across is to let your boss know what kind of working arrangements you've made. If you're setting aside a room that will be solely devoted to your office, then that may help demonstrate your seriousness about spending your days working with no interruptions. Letting your boss know your children will be at day care or with a baby sitter during your working times should also help your boss understand that you intend to be working, not fulfilling your parental duties during working hours.

All this information should help you explain to your boss that the fact that you want to work at home doesn't mean that you want to spend less time working. And explaining things can also keep you honest. For instance, if you find your working arrangement is something you'd rather your boss didn't know about (say, you're working at your dining room table while your toddler plays at your feet), that's a clue that you're probably not doing it right. A different kind of setup would probably be more appropriate.

Working at home means doing less work

Wrong, wrong, wrong. Study after study has shown that the opposite is true: Telecommuters get more done, not less, than their colleagues at the office.

Your boss may be skeptical on this point, and the only way to change his or her mind is by demonstration. Over time, you can show that you've gotten more done as a telecommuter than you would have in the office.

In the short run, you can use statistics to back up your statement that telecommuters are more productive than they would be in the office. (See Chapter 3 for some of these statistics. You can find more by visiting some of the Web sites described in Chapter 20.)

You may face a bigger problem, however, if your boss thinks you won't do as much work as a telecommuter as you would have done at the office — but won't say so in so many words. This belief that telecommuters are really goof-offs who spend their days watching soap operas underlies many of the problems with telecommuting — from colleagues who may be reluctant to call and "bother you at home" to managers who may assume you can no longer be counted on to get your work done.

An unspoken objection is harder to overcome than a spoken one, so your first job is to get this belief out into the open where you can discuss it rationally. Ask your boss directly to voice his or her worst fears about your telecommuting performance. Again, statistics about telecommuter productivity may help. But you'll probably have to prove it by showing your boss how much you actually can accomplish.

You'll be spared meetings and other tasks you could only do in the office

This argument bears some truth. But rather than penalize you by paying you less, you and your boss ought to figure out ways that you can make up the in-office work that you're missing. For example, you can and should contribute to meetings, even when you won't be there, either attending by speakerphone, or at least giving the meeting leader the benefit of your ideas and input before the meeting takes place.

You can also look for ways to pitch in on or compensate for in-office tasks that otherwise fall disproportionately on your non-telecommuting colleagues. Let's say your department receives a daily stack of correspondence that is directed to the department as a whole and not to any specific team member. Sorting through and answering this correspondence is a piece of *scut* work all members of your department must share.

If your telecommuting schedule puts you in the office only one day a week, then you can make sure that you handle the mail on that day, so that you don't miss your turn. Another option maybe to change the parameters of the job. Because you can't participate in sorting the mail, you might offer to take the letters that require responses home with you once a week, where you can answer them quickly in the uninterrupted atmosphere of your home office, saving the other members of your team from a particularly onerous task.

The point is to work with your boss and your co-workers, making sure that you're not getting away with missing shared work and that your productivity gains don't come at the expense of jobs you're skipping out on and leaving for your colleagues to pick up the slack. Coming up with a division of labor that seems equitable to all should be possible. Otherwise, if working away from the office finds you missing a significant part of your job that can't easily be made up, you may not have the right job for telecommuting after all.

You'll be changing jobs

Changing is about the only situation in which it makes sense for your salary to change when you begin telecommuting. If you decide to switch to a job with less responsibility or fewer hours than the one you had before, a corresponding reduction in pay may be perfectly appropriate.

But that doesn't mean you need to accept whatever salary you're offered. Regardless of what your new job is, other people in your organization are bound to be doing similar, or at least comparable, jobs. You and your boss need to use the salaries for those positions as benchmarks to determine what an appropriate pay scale is for you. And that pay scale needs to reflect your actual responsibilities, not the fact that you're fulfilling them from home.

Paying telecommuters less is perfectly legal

Well no, not perfectly. Although a specific law may not protect the rights of telecommuters the way other laws protect minority and disabled employees, that doesn't mean your employer can get away with offering unequal salaries for equal work. Companies can be, and have been, successfully sued for such discrimination.

Regardless of whether you have a viable suit if your employer refuses to pay you equally depends on a wide variety of factors, from where your company is located to the circumstances of your telecommuting. And, in the real world, suing, or even threatening to sue your employer, works against your best interests in the long run. But knowing you may have the law on your side, and perhaps finding a subtle way to let your employer know too, can be a big help during salary negotiations.

Should You Become an Independent Contractor?

When you make the switch to a telecommuting job, one option you and your employer may want to consider is whether your status should change from employee to independent contractor. Even if your employer winds up paying you somewhat more than the salary you're earning now, making this change represents a huge financial benefit for your company. First of all, it saves the company from paying health insurance, retirement, disability insurance, and other benefits that most employers offer full-time employees. It also saves the company on taxes. Perhaps even more important, it gives your employer the flexibility to do the following:

✔ Let you go, permanently or temporarily, if the company doesn't need you.

✔ Cut the amount of hours you work for the company without notice.

✔ Change how much the company pays you for your work in the future.

But, as I said before, just because something is good for them doesn't necessarily mean it's bad for you. The following are some questions to ask yourself if you're thinking of making the switch:

How badly do I need employer-funded health insurance?

Because no national health-care plan exists in the United States, most people must get health insurance from their employer, a spouse's employer, or else pay for it themselves. If you've ever priced private health insurance, you know the cost can be prohibitively high. You may be able to get a somewhat better deal through a trade association or other group, but insurance, nevertheless, still is a huge expense. Don't consider being an independent contractor until you've found a solution to this problem.

How badly do I need disability insurance?

What would happen if you were unable to work? Chances are, your job provides some form of disability insurance that is superior to government-sponsored disability programs. Do some research to find out what benefits you're eligible for, and determine whether you need private disability insurance (or some variant, such as mortgage insurance) before you strike out on your own.

How badly do I need a steady income?

As an independent contractor, fluctuations in your income are certain to be more volatile than when you were a full-time employee. Some of the time, you may find you're making more than your old salary — at least before you factor in the benefits portion of your compensation. On the other hand, there's no guaranteed paycheck anymore, so if your old employer doesn't need as much work from you as before, you may find your income drastically reduced.

However, if you're in an industry that tends to be unstable, you may find a tradeoff because what you lose in steadiness, you gain in diversification. As an independent contractor you can — and absolutely should — work for several different employers, whom you will now call *clients*. Diversifying may offer some protection in case of major upheaval at any one of them.

I remember one terrible year in the magazine publishing world when three different magazines where I was a regular contributor ceased publication, and a fourth was cut to half its original size. Each time this happened, I lost a portion of my income, but only a portion. I was able to strike out in new directions and find new sources of revenue. My friends who had full-time jobs at these publications were left scrambling.

Can I do without paid time off?

Working without paid time off may be easier than you think because people who are self-employed usually manage to take more time off than their salaried counterparts. I remember that the first full year I worked for myself, I not only made more money than I'd been making as an employee, but I also took six weeks of vacation rather than two. (And worked hard the rest of the time.)

Still, it's worth noting that, as an independent contractor, you won't be paid when you're not at work because you're sick, caring for a sick family member, prevented from working by a storm or natural disaster, or taking a vacation.

How does being a contractor fit my career plans?

If your dream is climbing the corporate ladder, then striking out as an independent contractor probably doesn't make much sense, except, perhaps, to tide you over while you look for a real job. On the other hand, if you're hoping to start a business of your own, being an independent contractor may offer you the freedom you need to do that.

Or perhaps your aspirations lie in a completely different direction. For instance, your real dream is to be a professional actor. In that case, being an independent contractor may be a good idea because it enables you to make your own schedule so that you can take the time you need for auditions and short-term acting jobs.

Do I have the right personality to be my own boss?

If you have the right personality to be a successful telecommuter, the answer is probably yes. In each case, you need to be driven, self-motivated, and able to work well in relative isolation.

But becoming an independent contractor means taking one big step further outside the fold than you did when you began telecommuting. You lose some of your camaraderie with co-workers, an overarching employer watching over you, and the opportunity to be promoted. As an independent, the only promotions you're likely to get are the ones that you create yourself by seeking higher-level, better-paying, more interesting work than you were doing before. You also need to be even more self-motivated than you were as a telecommuter and to give careful thought to these issues before striking out on your own.

Will I really be independent?

If your boss wants you to become an independent consultant, make sure he or she is also willing to give you the freedoms appropriate to that status. Some employers seek out the best of both worlds. They don't want to pay for employees' insurance or vacations (not to mention Social Security and other government payments), but they still want to exercise control over their ex-employees' work lives.

For example, your ex-employer may forbid you from working for other companies or demand that you fulfill a certain quota of work every week. Neither demand is appropriate for a true independent contractor. If you're truly an independent contractor, every job has an agreed-on fee (calculated either per task or per hour) that is fair to you and your client. You may need to finish some of your work on deadline. If you're writing programming code, it may have a specific completion date, but you have the right to accept or reject each separate job.

Likewise, you're free to take on work from other clients, if you so choose, though you may have to avoid direct competitors. Indeed, your survival as an independent contractor depends on your having a wide base of clients to work with, so demanding that you work for only one client is setting you up for failure.

Such demands can set your employer up for failure, too. Unemployment offices and other government agencies have been looking closely at independent contractor arrangements that are simply excuses for employers to avoid paying benefits and taxes. So if you're going to go the independent-contractor route, having a fair arrangement is better for everyone.

Long-Distance Telecommuting and Equal Pay

If you're a long-distance telecommuter, your employer may offer you a lower salary than your on-site counterparts based on two pieces of reasoning:

> ✔ The company has to defray the cost of your travel when you come to the office.
>
> ✔ A cost-of-living discrepancy exists between where the company is located and where you are, which enables you to live as well on less.

Some truth is in both of these arguments. My husband Bill is among many long-distance telecommuters who have accepted lower salaries than they might have made on site because of cost-of-living differences. But, as he points out, "If I were telecommuting from San Francisco to a company in Upstate New York (the opposite of his current long-distance telecommute), I guarantee they wouldn't pay me a *higher* salary to make up for the cost-of-living difference."

As a long-distance telecommuter, you probably have compelling reasons for living where you do, either because of a strong preference for a certain kind of lifestyle or because family ties require you to be there. And, chances are, finding a comparable job in your area would be difficult, which is the reason you became a telecommuter in the first place.

For all these reasons, you may decide accepting the offer of a lower salary from your distant employer is best. Even so, the following sections provide some questions you may want to ask.

Will my salary go up if I relocate?

Your employer's reasons for paying you less will vanish if circumstances change and you find yourself able and willing to relocate to your employer's location. So it's worth finding out what would happen if this change were to take place. Would your employer be committed to bringing your salary in line with the local market? And if not, why not?

Does my salary truly reflect travel expenses?

Because you're the one who's traveling, you have an accurate view of exactly how much you're costing your long-distance employer in travel expenses to the office location. The cost of other travel to conferences or to meet with customers doesn't count, because you'd be doing that anyway.

So, if your company claims that it must pay you less because of travel costs, comparing the difference between your salary and the salary for an on-site worker with with what you're actually spending on travel is worth the effort. If you're spending $800 a month on travel to and from your employer's site, but earning $20,000 less than you would be as a non-telecommuter, you have good grounds to question why.

You may also have a negotiating point if you can make some adjustments to your travel costs. You may be able to save on airfare by booking your flights well in advance or using a low-cost, no-frills airline. You may be able to save on your bill for lodging and meals by choosing an adequate but inexpensive hotel or perhaps a room with a kitchenette where you can prepare your own food. If you're able to cut travel costs by $3,000 during a year, ask if the company will give you a bonus reflecting at least some of those savings.

How does my status as a remote employee affect my perceived value in the company?

Finding out whether your status as a telecommuter affects how the company views your status as an employee is difficult to pin down, and your boss may not know how to address it. Or he or she may insist that the fact that you're telecommuting from someplace far away makes no difference.

Depending on the nature of your organization, this may be perfectly true. However, your status as a long-distance telecommuter may also mean that you're seen as less of an asset. If so, legitimate reasons for this treatment may include the following:

- ✔ You're not available to come in to the office on short notice to deal with an unexpected crisis, or to meet with an important client.
- ✔ You can't pitch in with in-office tasks.
- ✔ You can't participate in team projects the same way you can if you're at the office on a daily or weekly basis.
- ✔ Promoting you to certain positions isn't possible unless you're willing to relocate.

Most of these items you can't change. But at least by discussing your status, you can bring the issues out into the open. At the same point, you may find ways that you can participate more fully in team activities, work more closely with your associates, or adjust your travel schedule to increase your value to the team and the company.

Demonstrating Your Worth

Regardless of whether you're getting the same salary as a telecommuter that you would if you worked full time on site, finding ways to demonstrate your contributions to your organization is extremely important. Your boss won't always be able to watch you sitting at your desk, and you won't be on hand to speak up in team meetings, explaining what you've been doing or making immediate contributions to the discussion.

Because of these shortcomings, you need to compensate by finding objective ways to demonstrate that you're doing a good job. If it's appropriate for your job, try to find a numerical means of measuring what you do, so you can show what you've been doing. Of course, not every job lends itself to that kind of measurement, and other factors and circumstances often affect these metrics. Yet even an imperfect form of measurement is better than no measurement at all.

As a telecommuter, keeping track of your own achievements and making sure others do the same is important for you. So every few months, you need to stop and make a note to yourself about what you've recently accomplished and what you soon hope to accomplish. If appropriate, you may also want to send occasional progress reports to your boss.

Assembling this information can be especially useful when you know you're due for a performance review. You can prepare for the review by giving your boss a report on what you think your achievements have been. (In many companies, you will be asked to do this.) When you started your job, and/or when you started telecommuting, you and your boss should have agreed on specific objectives. (See Chapter 9 for more on how to work with your boss to establish these objectives.) Review how well you've met your objectives so far, what the response has been among customers and co-workers, and what you plan to do next.

Can Telecommuting Increase Your Salary?

It's certainly more common for telecommuters to earn less, not more, than they would if they were on site full time. But, in some circumstances, working outside the office can actually lead to higher pay than if you work on site.

How? Consider the possiblities presented in the following sections.

Telecommuting can increase your productivity

If your workplace is a *meritocracy*, where your work is likely to be recognized and appreciated, then the fact that you can get more done as a telecommuter may be noticed, and may lead to a better raise than you otherwise would have gotten. *Ohio* magazine's Miriam Carey reports that this is how things appear to be working out for her.

"I find I'm more productive at home than I've ever been in a workplace environment," she says. "My boss thinks so too, and she's asking me to think about slowing down! That's a first. I'm up for a six-month review, and I believe I will actually get a better raise because of the high level of productivity I'm able to achieve in the at-home environment."

Telecommuting can advance your career

Intuitive workplace thinking indicates that telecommuters are likely to get left behind when it comes to career advancement. In fact, however, the opposite appears to be true. Telecommuters are more likely, not less likely, to be promoted than their on-site counterparts. Obviously, if you have a greater chance of being promoted, you have a greater chance of making more money. (For details on how and why telecommuting can help advance your career, see Chapter 15.)

Telecommuting can lead to new skills

The job market, like any market, is governed by laws of supply and demand. The more demand you have for what you do, the greater the salary you can get for doing it.

To a large extent, these issues are determined by realities you can't change. For example, it's a reality of my work life that writing is a highly competitive business, with many more writers and aspiring writers on the market than available paying work for them to do. And it's a reality of Bill's work life that the available supply of Internet community managers is low (although rapidly growing), and that for the moment, a greater supply of jobs exists that demand the skills he possesses than people with the skills to do those jobs.

But you can always tip the odds in your favor by acquiring skills that enhance your marketability. In my case, I have an edge over many other writers because I've learned enough about technology to write about it for a lay audience. In fact, many career experts advise constantly upgrading and developing your skills as a replacement for the job security that once was assumed in most large corporations.

If you want to develop your skills base, telecommuting puts you in a perfect position to do so. First of all, the fact that you're telecommuting alone may mean that you've had to practice and improve your business communication skills, and perhaps learn some new technology skills. (For example, you may have mastered chat, Web conferencing, or videoconferencing.)

And working from a remote location also puts you in a great position to add to your education by taking courses or attending workshops, conferences, or industry meetings. As a telecommuter, you'll probably have an easier time getting to these events because you're less likely to get stuck in the office, or to have to conform to a rigid work schedule.

At the same time, attending classes or educational events now serves a dual purpose for you. Not only do you get to learn new skills or enhance existing ones that can help increase your value on the job, but it enables you to get out of the isolation of your home office and engages you in human contact and interaction that you need with others in your field.

Part IV
The Long-Term View

The 5th Wave By Rich Tennant

"It's the crew Captain Columbus—they want to know what our flat-world contingency plan is."

In this part . . .

After you've settled in to a new telecommuting position, you may find yourself wondering about the
future. How will telecommuting affect your long-term
career goals? And will you be able to continue to telecommute in years to come? Is this a growing trend, so that
more and more opportunities will become available over
time? Or is it a fad that will disappear, leaving you to
choose between returning to the office or being sidelined
in your career?

You need answers to these questions if you're considering
telecommuting as more than a short-term arrangement.
Use this part to gaze into the future and decide if it's the
right long-term choice for you.

Chapter 15

Telecommuting and Your Career

··

··

Does being a telecommuter mean saying goodbye to any prospect of career advancement? Many employees believe that it does. They fear that being out of sight means they're out of mind — that they'll be forgotten when opportunities to take on bigger projects or move into higher-level jobs come along. In fact, it's a testament to telecommuting's enormous appeal that so many people ask to do it, even when they believe their career advancement will pay the price.

Jack Nilles, sometimes seen as the father of telecommuting — a term he invented — finds telecommuting is not necessarily the career-stopper many think it is. As president of the Los Angeles consulting firm JALA International, Nilles shows that in many cases, telecommuters actually received quicker raises and greater career advancement than they would if they'd stayed in the office.

"It depends on the nature of your job, your personality, your company's personality, and your career plans," he comments. Ideally, he adds, your current job and the one you want to be promoted to need to work well as telecommuting positions. Then, you have to be good at telecommuting, and your company has to be one that truly recognizes and rewards performance (rather than skilled office politics or personal connections). If all that is true, he notes, "Your chances of promotion are excellent."

"One of the problems I've had in evaluating telecommuting programs is that telecommuters keep getting promoted out of the telecommuting project, thereby reducing the size of our database," he adds. Typically, those promoted represent a small minority of all telecommuters during the period being studied, he notes. "But it demonstrates that telecommuting is not a career dead end."

Several of the telecommuters who've advised me for this book report that telecommuting has, if anything, enhanced their career advancement.

Why Telecommuting Can Be a Career Booster

If you think about it, employers have many good reasons why they're quicker to give telecommuting employees promotions than their non-telecommuting counterparts. Consider those reasons in the following sections.

Telecommuters are more productive

Ample evidence supports the notion that telecommuters get more work done in their home (or remote) offices than they do when they're in the office. (For more details on increased productivity among telecommuters, see Chapter 3.)

If your company is well managed, the fact that you're more productive as a telecommuter is something your boss needs to notice and reward. The fact that you can handle your own job efficiently is an indication that you may be ready to tackle bigger and better things.

"I know of telecommuters who insist on telecommuting, knowing it will allow them to shine out among their colleagues because of their improved performance," Nilles says.

Telecommuters' work is measured objectively

Does this mean that, as a telecommuter, your work is measured more objectively than that of your on-site colleagues? Well, yes, it might. Most managers, regardless of whether they admit it, rely at least in part on how much time a person who works for them spends sitting at a desk when deciding whether that employee is doing a good job. This isn't so much laziness as it is just plain human nature. It's a difficult habit to change.

But, if you're telecommuting, your manager cannot know during much of the workday whether you're at your desk — and in any case, your workdays may follow a different schedule than that of your non-telecommuting colleagues. That being so, your boss has no choice but to focus on the work you do when judging your performance. Assuming you're doing a good job, and working hard, that is likely to work to your benefit.

Telecommuters are in the spotlight

Although telecommuting is becoming mainstream, it's often still considered an experimental way of working, and many corporate telecommuting programs are called *pilot programs*. If this description fits your company, then telecommuting brings with it one big benefit — visibility. Being part of a popular experimental program means that upper executives in your area or department watch what you do closely. And the whole point of a pilot program is that if it's successful, it will be expanded throughout the company. That means executives from other areas will watch you closely, too.

Successful telecommuters have shown they can be trusted

Trusting employees to do their jobs without constant supervision is difficult for most managers. If you've been telecommuting successfully — and especially if your productivity has gone up since you began — you'll have proven to your boss that you can be trusted to be self-motivated and disciplined. Again, this makes you look like a good candidate for increased responsibility.

Telecommuting is considered a plum assignment

In a way, being allowed to telecommute is similar to landing a coveted plum assignment and an indication that the company values and trusts you. And, like any plum assignment, doing it well puts you in a good position to be considered for advancement. And, like any plum assignment, it carries its own forward momentum. Because your company has trusted you to be a telecommuter, you may feel more strongly motivated to work hard and show that you can succeed.

Telecommuting means learning new skills

Learning new skills, or simply demonstrating some that you already had that were going unused is an important part of telecommuting. As a telecommuter, you almost certainly need to communicate more in writing than you did when you were in the office. So if you happen to be a brilliant wordsmith, telecommuting may be your chance to shine.

Telecommuting also means working with technology more intimately than you might if you were in the office. If you weren't using the Internet already, you'd have to become adept at using it to share information and work on communal projects. You'd probably have to go beyond simple e-mail skills and learn about Web conferencing, FTP transferring, working with files or materials on the Web, live chat, or videoconferencing.

Telecommuting also means you're probably much more familiar with your computer than you were back at the office. If something went wrong there, you could simply call on a tech support person and go get a cup of coffee while the techie magically returned your machine to working order. Now, however, when you call for tech support, you probably find yourself working over the phone, entering different commands, and trying different solutions to solve, or at least diagnose, the problem.

Telecommuters probably would have been promoted anyway

Every piece I've ever read about picking the right employees to telecommute gives the same advice. Only your best and brightest, self-motivated, driven employees with a will to succeed should be given the opportunity to telecommute.

This creates something of a chicken-and-egg question: Are telecommuters promoted because telecommuting makes them look capable of greater responsibility, or are the more promotable candidates chosen to telecommute in the first place?

It's a good question, but the answer doesn't really matter. Maybe you were on the fast track toward promotion before you started telecommuting. Or maybe, by successfully telecommuting, you seem like a better candidate for bigger things. Either way, if you're interested in climbing the corporate ladder, chances are telecommuting is a good way to go.

How Telecommuting Can Sometimes Undermine Your Career

Yes, working remotely is a step toward the fast track for many employees. But, remember, it also can work against you. If you're committed to advancing your career and deciding whether telecommuting will help or hurt, take note that telecommuting can stop you or slow you down on the way to your career goals, if what's described in the following sections turns out to be true.

You're not cut out for it

Not everyone has the right personality to be happy as a telecommuter or to operate effectively while working at home. This absolutely does not reflect on your ability to do your job — or a higher-level job — in general. Many extremely successful executives out there have failed miserably as telecommuters — or have never tried it because they know they can't handle it.

If you don't have the right personality to be a telecommuter, you're probably better off not trying it than having it go badly. So give some careful thought to whether you'd truly be happy working on your own before signing up to telecommute. And if you decide to try it, be prepared to change back to an on-site working style early on, if you see that things aren't going to work out. (For help determining whether telecommuting is right for you, see Chapter 2.)

Your manager doesn't like dealing with telecommuters

Managing a telecommuter is tougher than managing an on-site staff member, and many managers have a hard time doing it. Some supervisors say they support telecommuting but aren't really ready or able to make the necessary adjustments that it requires. If this describes your boss, you're likely to run into trouble. Training for you and your manager can help prevent these kinds of problems, but, unfortunately, if your manager isn't fully supportive of telecommuting, or doesn't have a clear understanding of how to make it work, you and your career can wind up paying a severe price.

Your company doesn't believe in telecommuting

Some companies create telecommuting programs only because upper management has heard *it's the thing to do,* not because they recognize how having employees working in remote locations can help them reach their corporate goals. Or they may allow only specific employees to telecommute under specific circumstances to accommodate health issues or family needs — because it's a way to help employees — believing the work won't be done as well as it would be if they were in the office.

If this describes your company, you're taking a risk by telecommuting. Over time, you may be able to show your boss and your boss's boss that, far from doing your job less well, you're actually more productive when working away from the office. They suddenly may realize they've been wrong all along and decide that telecommuting really is a situation that benefits both parties.

But perceptions are difficult to change. And it's just as possible that upper management will see you working less productively, not because you really are but because that's what they're expecting. Much as you may want to telecommute in this situation, you need to be aware that you'll face an uphill struggle convincing your company that you're as valuable an asset telecommuting as you are working in the office. If climbing the ladder at this company is important to you, telecommuting may be the wrong choice.

Your job isn't right for telecommuting

Although you may have exactly the right personality for telecommuting and although your firm and your boss are completely supportive, your telecommuting experience still can wind up going wrong if the job you're doing doesn't fit your telecommuting plans.

If you find you're missing out because you don't have enough face-to-face contact or because the people who work with you have trouble with the fact you're not always around, telecommuting may be a mistake. Simply adjusting your schedule so that you spend more time in the office may be enough to solve the problem. However, if telecommuting impacts your ability to do your job effectively, it can without a doubt damage your career.

You aspire to a non-telecommuting job

For many telecommuters, the upward path is a path back to the office full time. Management jobs that require coordinating many team members at once require plenty of face-to-face contact that communications technology can't always replace. So, in most organizations, the higher up the ladder you go, the greater the presumption that you have to work on site.

"If the job you want to get promoted to requires substantially more location dependence, then your promotion is likely to make inroads on your telecommuting," Nilles says. "I know of telecommuters who have refused promotions for that reason."

Of course, if career advancement is important to you, you may be quite willing to give up telecommuting as part of your pursuit of that corner office. The problem is that successful telecommuters often are reluctant to go back to working in the office full time, and your boss may assume that you feel the same way.

So let your true feelings be known. Tell your boss that, while you love telecommuting, you're committed enough to your career to give it up with no regrets if the right opportunity comes along. When job openings arise that you think may be right for you, make sure to remind your boss (or whoever is hiring for that position) that you're interested, and that you understand it means a return to an on-site position.

You're a long-distance telecommuter

If you're commuting hundreds of miles or more, getting to the office for emergency meetings is difficult for you. You may be working remotely for several weeks at a time. You can't easily step into a more senior position that requires you to be on site more often, or even full-time. So in this situation, it's possible that telecommuting can and will hold you back in your career.

One obvious tactic is informing your employer that you'd be willing to relocate (assuming you would be) if the right opportunity came along. The problem with that is you're asking your employer to take on a certain amount of risk. Knowing for sure ahead of time that you'll be happy living in a new environment isn't easy, and if you're not happy, you may leave after a short while, leaving a senior post empty again, and possibly having cost the company thousands in relocation costs as well.

Another option, if it feels right, is to volunteer to relocate in your current job, so that you'll be in a better position to take advantage of future opportunities. Whether this make sense depends on your willingness to move, your commitment to your current company, your current prospects for advancement, and other job opportunities in the area.

But even if you're not willing or able to relocate and therefore can't climb the ladder in your organization, long-distance telecommuting can still be beneficial to your career. My husband Bill is a perfect example. Although we love it here, the region of New York State where we live simply does not offer the kind of specialized, high-level job that he can do — and is doing for his California employer. So although his career path there may be limited, he's still gaining important experience and credentials in his field — and a higher salary than he'd be able to get from a local employer.

Getting Ahead While Staying at Home

Telecommuting, in and of itself, may or may not be a good way to give your career a boost. Either way, your career is your responsibility, and, if you're interested in climbing the corporate ladder, it's up to you to do the things that help you get there.

Your status as a telecommuter means some of your career advancement strategies are a little different than they'd be if you were in the office full time. The following sections deal with some areas that may require special attention.

Fighting line-of-sight assigning

"One of the risks with telecommuting is that the person can become better and better at doing less and less," telecommuting expert Gil Gordon notes. That's because an employee who isn't actually in the office can be forgotten when the boss hands out new work. "Let's say there's a project coming up," Gordon says. "It's easier to pick someone who's in the office right now than someone who won't be in till Wednesday."

Kathleen Parrish, of the Arizona Public Service Company, calls this phenomenon "assigning by line of sight." Unfortunately, line-of-sight assigning may mean you aren't offered some of your department's more challenging assignments, or that you wind up with less *on your plate* than your on-site co-workers. In either case, your career can suffer.

In an ideal world, dealing with such shortcomings wouldn't be your problem to solve. The best way to prevent line-of-sight assigning is training managers how to work effectively with telecommuters before they have to do it. Unfortunately, according to a recent American Management Association survey, less than 10 percent of companies that sanction telecommuting offer any training to telecommuters, let alone their managers. So the odds are, you're on your own.

If your boss is disproportionately assigning projects to people who are in the office, while giving you less than your fair share of the workload, chances are he or she is doing it unconsciously. According to Parrish, most managers drift into working this way, unless they make a particular effort not to do so.

With that in mind, a good first move may be to sit down with your boss and talk about what you think is going on. Make note that line-of-sight assigning is a common phenomenon for managers of telecommuters, and be sure to ask whether your boss has been handing out work recently by looking around the office and seeing who seems available. Keeping the conversation on friendly and nonthreatening footing makes recognizing the problem and committing to do something about it easier for your manager.

Beyond that, you may have to take steps to ensure that an appropriate amount of work is coming your way. The best first step is making sure the work you have to do is completed quickly (which may be easy to do in the no-distractions environment of a home office). Don't fall prey to the human tendency to allow available tasks to fill the time you have to do them. Showing that you have your current projects under control is important so that you can say you're available for something new.

You also can volunteer for new projects, something that's likely to impress your boss and may be good for your career in any case. Use your regular check-in phone calls to ask what new projects are underway and to ask your friends at the office for updates about what's going on. When you hear about interesting new initiatives, ask if you can take part in them.

Coordinating your telecommuting schedule with an eye to your boss's assigning schedule may also help. For example, if you've noticed that first thing Monday morning is when your boss tends to hand out new projects, then Monday may be a good day for you to pick as one of your in-office days. After all, line-of-sight assigning can work to your advantage if you actually are in the line of sight.

If all else fails and you find your co-workers taking on more projects while you're getting fewer of them, consider offering to help out. After all, if you're not getting your fair share of work, that means those left in the office must be picking up the slack, and some of them may be feeling swamped. True, you may not get the visibility or credit you would have if the project were yours. But you'll be demonstrating that you're a team player, and that you can work effectively with others, even while telecommuting. Plus, you'll be building good will with your colleagues. And you never know when that may come in handy.

Building key relationships

Speaking of good will, your second strategy for telecommuting career advancement is building as many personal relationships in your workplace as you can. The wider your network of friends in the office, the better your chance of finding out ahead of time about workplace changes, power shifts, new initiatives, and anything else that may affect you and your job.

As a telecommuter, it's especially important to have as many allies as possible because the fact that you're physically absent some of the time may mean you'll miss out on important information, conversations, or hallway rumors. If you can, try to expand your network to include friends in other departments, other locations, and/or other areas of your company. Doing so gives you a broader base and can help put you in line for higher positions in areas you may not otherwise have known about.

Finding a mentor within your company, if you can, is especially helpful. A mentor is someone in a more senior position, and usually older than you (and usually not your immediate boss) who takes an interest in your career and is willing to spend time offering you guidance and advice. Having a mentor in your corner is useful for any aspiring corporate climber, but here again, having someone powerful looking out for your interests as a telecommuter is nice because you're not always in the office yourself.

The best mentor relationships arise naturally, with both parties falling into conversation and finding each other easy to talk with. If you find someone who seems like he or she would be a good mentor, and you want to test the waters, ask for advice on a problem currently before you. The quality (and quantity) of the answer you receive tells you whether this executive is interested in you and has the smarts to help you, and whether the two of you are on the same wavelength.

Raising your professional visibility

Asked whether telecommuting had helped her career, *Ohio* magazine's Miriam Carey answers by describing her activities *outside* the job. "I'm very involved in networking groups," she says. "I serve as vice president of membership for the Press Club of Cleveland, and serve on a number of boards as a volunteer."

In part, she says, participating in other activities is possible because she doesn't have to adhere to the usual office schedule. "In an office environment, a two-hour board lunch would be frowned on by co-workers who take only one hour of lunch every day — even though I would rarely go out for lunch in exchange for the one or two long lunches a month. At home, nobody is tracking my time in this way, so I can attend the meetings, give the organization my full attention, and work thoroughly at my job as well."

Thus, she says, "I'm able to truly manage my time, getting as much impact for the outside work that I do for the press community here as I do with the paid work that I do. This really helps my career overall."

Most successful corporate climbers can attest to the value of participating in trade or professional groups as part of their career strategies. Professional groups, and the events they sponsor, are sources of tremendous opportunity. You can make networking contacts in other companies (which can help you find a better job by changing employers, if you so choose), raise your own professional visibility, and learn how to do your job better, all at the same time.

Participating in a trade or professional association has even greater benefits for telecommuters. Working alone at home can leave you feeling personally and professionally isolated — out of touch with the people who do the same kind of work you do. Going to industry events helps you reconnect with others in your field.

Working at home provides the freedom to attend industry events without being stuck at the office. And it may also provide the motivation: After a long day in front of the computer, you may want to get out and mingle.

When Moving Up Means Moving Back to the Office

It's a quandary many corporate climbing telecommuters must face sooner or later: What do you do if the promotion you covet means that you have to go back to working in the office? Or worse yet, if changes in your job or your organization mean telecommuting is no longer an option?

The telecommuters I've talked to all agree that the benefits of working at home are extremely important to them — important enough that they won't automatically give them up just for a bigger or better job. "I've been telling friends that the only way I would go back to a company office is kicking and screaming," IBM's Chris Keating declares. "The worst part about going back would be ironing and commuting. Then there's the fact that the cafeterias aren't always open exactly when I'm hungry or that I might have to share an office."

Others say they might consider it if the right position came along. But it would have to be an appealing job.

"Giving up the freedom would be the hardest part," Miriam Carey notes. "The freedom is worth a lot of salary dollars to me, so it would have to be a big career move with a very large salary jump." And that's not all. "The employer would have to prove to me that they have a well-managed, 'we all get along' kind of work environment."

If that turns out not to be the case, she adds, "I don't think I'd put up with the office nonsense for very long. Now that I've walked through the grass on the other side in my bare feet, I *know* it's greener."

From losing the freedom to make their own schedules to having to wear pantyhose on a daily basis, telecommuters I talked to had no shortage of things they thought would be hard to adjust to if they went back to an office job.

Chris Keating: Mobility and Entrepreneurship

Ask Chris Keating how being a telecommuter has affected his career, and he'll tell you it has been a big help. Keating is an Information Technology Architect for IBM. "My job is to gather requirements for IBM's own information technology projects and help implement them," he says.

This is his second telecommuting or "mobile" position at IBM. His first job entailed providing technical support for one of the company's all-mobile sales groups. He soon was promoted to his current job, and, he says, telecommuting is a big reason why.

"Being a mobile worker has improved my prospects for a few reasons," he comments. "First, working remotely seems to indicate to managers that I am more tolerant of change and more willing to travel. It also opens up opportunities where I can report to a manager in another state, although I suppose an employee in an office could do this as well.

"I don't think that I would have gotten this (job) so quickly if I were physically located at an office," he adds. One reason: Because he worked remotely, his former manager made comments in his evaluation that reflected the skills needed for a more responsible position. "Mobility put me at an advantage," he says.

"One more word about being managed from a distance," he adds. "After accepting this position, I soon realized my manager knew very little about what I did day to day." If a major problem arose, he notes, "We would have to spend a lot of our time bringing each other up to speed, and the problem would either fester or become moot."

For that reason, he says, "It's often better to be as autonomous as possible and solve problems on your own. So I think this is a situation which fosters entrepreneurship. That may help explain why telecommuting benefits one's career."

Chapter 16

A Look at the Future

What is the future of telecommuting? In one way, the future doesn't really matter. You're one person, with one career, and the fact that a larger trend is headed one way or the other may not matter much when you consider how you as an individual do your job. Telecommuting may keep growing rapidly, but if you're stuck in a company or an industry that insists on doing things the old-fashioned way, your opportunities to telecommute may be extremely limited.

Conversely, if telecommuting as a whole is on the decline (though I don't believe it is), but you're in an industry or company that's committed to new technologies and new ways of doing business, you may find you have lots of telecommuting opportunities.

The bottom line is that there are and will continue to be millions of telecommuting jobs in the United States. And all you need is one of them.

Will Telecommuting Continue to Grow?

According to the Bureau of Labor Statistics, between 13 million and 19 million telecommuters worked in the United States in 2000. Telecommuting estimates for 1990 were around 4 million, so the number of telecommuters has grown rapidly and maybe even quadrupled during the last ten years. Given these figures, you may think that the number of employers allowing staff to telecommute was growing, and you'd be right. A 1999 study by the Society for Human Resource Management found that 28 percent of organizations surveyed allowed telecommuting, up from less than 20 percent three years earlier.

Many telecommuting experts believe rapid growth will continue. Telecommuting consultant Jack Nilles, for example, believes that by 2025, almost half of the U.S. workforce will be working remotely at least some of the time.

Some, however, are naysayers. A survey in 2000 by the consulting firm CareerEngine.com found that 62 percent of employers planned to hire fewer telecommuters than in the past. And *Los Angeles Times* writer Bonnie Harris reported that "most personnel managers and experts in the field say that the ranks of telecommuters nationally are declining and that a majority of companies are planning to allow fewer people to work from home."

How do you reconcile these two views? I believe that at the same time telecommuting has been a management fad, it also has been a serious, business-driven trend. Because it was a fad, many companies jumped on the bandwagon with pilot programs that were intended to study telecommuting, but they lacked a good analysis of how telecommuting would be of benefit to the business and failed to provide proper training and preparation for telecommuters and their managers. That led to disappointment with telecommuting, at least among managers. A second problem is that some organizations actually imposed mandatory telecommuting on staff in an effort to lower real estate costs.

That is a terrible idea because telecommuting is definitely not for everyone. People who need the social contact of the office or who need to be out of the house to concentrate on their work are unlikely to make successful telecommuters. And even if you have the right personality for it, feeling the drive and motivation required for making it work when you didn't want to telecommute in the first place must be hard. I find it is no surprise that programs like these have led to frustration and disappointment.

Overall, it simply isn't true that the numbers of telecommuters is on the decline, or that telecommuting is a passing fad, destined to be forgotten. Having employees work from remote locations simply makes too much sense in too many situations for it to go away anytime soon.

I believe telecommuting will continue to grow over the next ten years, although not as rapidly as it did in the last ten. A few factors that I think make that growth inevitable are described in the following sections.

Transition from a manufacturing to a service economy

We're in the midst of a giant shift away from producing physical products and toward producing services and information. It's obvious that the less your job requires you to deal with physical objects, the less you need to be in any one place. (Factory workers and delivery truck drivers are unlikely telecommuting candidates.)

On the other hand, if your job deals with information, whether it's statistical analysis or writing code, you can do it from pretty much anywhere. So the more we become an information-based economy, the less need there will be for people to physically travel to a workplace.

Acceptance of the Internet

Not everyone is comfortable with working over the Internet today. But this rapidly is changing. As a larger and larger segment of our population gets wired, business managers won't have any choice but to become fully comfortable using the Internet — and for more than just e-mail.

Here's an example: As I researched this book, noting the different attitudes that businesspeople had towards live online chat (including instant messaging) was interesting. Younger and more technology-oriented telecommuters were comfortable with it and found it an extremely useful way to keep in communication with co-workers throughout the day. But older and less technology-oriented managers (including many telecommuting experts) insisted that chat is a distraction that cuts into the concentration telecommuters need, and that if you have something to say, you're better off picking up the phone.

I can attest to the usefulness of text-based chat for business purposes. In fact, it has been the primary means of communication between my agent and me throughout the writing of this book. When we try to get in touch by phone, we almost always wind up leaving voice mail for each other. If I see her name on my instant message list (meaning she's online), I know that she's there and at her computer, and will see and respond to my message right away.

I believe that as time goes on and the Internet evolves, more and more people will become more and more comfortable with a much wider variety of ways to make contact online. The more that happens, the easier it becomes for telecommuters to stay in touch.

Disintermediation

This fancy-sounding word refers to the current trend toward eliminating intermediaries of every sort. Disintermediation is why many people buy car insurance directly from a national company like Geico instead of using a local insurance agent, open an online trading account rather than calling a broker, or order pay-per-view movies instead of visiting a local video store.

Disintermediation is good news for telecommuters because it tends to reduce the need for face-to-face interactions with customers — who may not want to leave their homes, either. If the trend continues, it may contribute to telecommuting's growth.

Labor shortages

During the past few years, unemployment levels dipped to historic lows. In the process, some industries, like the high-tech industry, faced paralyzing labor shortages. Unemployment may rise somewhat in coming years, but not enough to solve what is a growing problem for many employers: You just can't get good help these days.

That's good news for telecommuting too. Although properly managed telecommuting arrangements benefit employer and employee, overall, employees are by far the more interested of the two groups. In fact, many businesspeople still insist that telecommuting is a perk.

A tight labor market gives more employees the opportunity to demand what they want from their employers. And, for many of them, what they want is telecommuting. According to International Telework Association & Council (ITAC), millions of on-site employees would prefer to telecommute if only they could, and reading through posts on telecommuting message boards, you'll find that most of them are from people desperately seeking work-at-home jobs.

Aging of older and younger managers

As a broad generalization, managers of the older generation tend to be more uncomfortable with newfangled workplace concepts like flextime and telecommuting. They also tend to come from an earlier era where a command-and-control style of management was more the norm.

Younger managers may be more comfortable allowing employees to set their own schedules and/or work outside of direct supervision. They've grown up in a modern work environment, where freedoms like these are commonplace.

During the next ten years, many of the older managers will reach retirement age, while many of the younger ones will rise to positions of power. After that, we may see a growth spurt in telecommuting that makes the last decade's growth seem like a practice run.

Urban sprawl and pollution

New York City's population recently topped 8 million in the census for the first time. Other American cities are seeing the same phenomenon — a burgeoning workforce, overcrowding, and suburbs spreading wider and wider. Two-hour commutes to work are becoming commonplace, and three-hour commutes are not unheard of.

Commutes like these are a staggering waste, especially if they are spent driving and thus making it harder to catch up on your reading or your e-mail. A two-hour commute each way means an employee is away from home 12 solid hours, even if all he or she does is work an eight-hour shift. No matter how much they may dislike telecommuting, employers must understand that those lost hours benefit no one.

Some high-smog urban areas already are mandating that local companies allow employees to work from home or reward them for doing so. And this situation will only worsen. Although the United States is one of the few nations on earth that doesn't officially recognize the reality of global warming, I believe that during the next several years we'll have no choice. Eventually we'll be forced to take even more serious steps to reverse its effects. At that point, keeping people out of their cars will become a high priority.

How Will the Economy Affect Telecommuting?

How will an economic slowdown affect telecommuting? I believe it will slow, and possibly even stall, telecommuting's growth for a few years, depending on how bad and how long of an economic downturn you're talking about.

Less competition for employees

The reason I feel certain competition for jobs will be reduced is that telecommuting still is something that employees want more than their employers do, at least in the majority of cases. Until recently, telecommuting's rapid growth has been fueled in large part by stiff competition for capable employees, especially in technology-related fields.

My husband is a perfect example. Bill's current employer wanted to hire him, but he was on the East Coast and reluctant to move to California. His current long-distance telecommuting arrangement is a compromise that both sides can live with, and Bill has shown that he can do his job effectively despite the distance. But what would the company's management have done if they'd been able to find an equally qualified candidate living locally? Without a doubt, they'd have hired the local person.

The labor market for technology and technology-related fields is different today than what it was then. Many companies have either laid off parts of their staffs or closed down altogether. Those who are job-hunting today are finding they can't write their own ticket as easily as they did before the bubble burst. The fact that fewer employees can negotiate the work arrangements that they want means fewer of them will be able to cut telecommuting deals.

This effect will be temporary, at least for the foreseeable future, as long as unemployment remains relatively low, the labor market remains relatively tight, and (as it seems likely) the need for highly skilled workers continues to outpace the supply.

Likewise, as more managers become accustomed to this way of working and more of them are able to use the Internet for a wide variety of functions, they may begin to see how telecommuting benefits employers or at least become more willing to give it a try.

Uncertainty works against telecommuting

Ever notice that during times of economic growth, car commercials tell how snazzy and desirable the product is, but during turbulent times, the focus shifts to safety instead? Figuring out that during times of economic uncertainty people are less willing to take risks than they are when everything is booming isn't hard.

But that kind of attitude has an adverse effect on telecommuting, because it requires taking some risk for employee and manager. Telecommuting employees risk being forgotten about while away from the office, missing out on vital information or opportunities, and even having their jobs phased out altogether if their absence makes them appear expendable. If they're working independently for the first time, they also risk finding out the hard way that they aren't cut out for it, don't have the discipline or drive to work effectively from home, or don't like the feeling of isolation.

Managers must take a risk that may be even more daunting. They must trust employees to do their jobs well even without supervision, to be responsible for valuable company equipment and perhaps sensitive company information off site, to complete projects on deadline, and to remain accessible and in touch while they're not working in the office. In most workplaces, managers are responsible for the performance of the departments they supervise, so telecommuting employees who fall down on the job make their managers look bad, too.

Of course, in a properly managed telecommuting situation, with clear goals, guidelines, and objectives, full discussion of potential issues beforehand, a written telecommuting agreement, and ideally, training for telecommuter and manager alike, risks are minimized, and the telecommuting experiment is likely to be a success for both. Still, in an atmosphere of poor corporate performance, downsizing, and company failures, neither may be willing to give it a try.

Even if they are willing, further obstacles in the form of top management or corporate policy may get in the way. In economic hard times, people who run companies can become even more risk-averse than the people who work in them. They're more likely to want to control every aspect of their employees' work in greater detail than they otherwise would have. So they'll be less likely to allow a telecommuting arrangement.

Overcrowding is less of a problem

An economic slowdown also alleviates two problems that helped spur telecommuting's growth: urban traffic congestion and workplace overcrowding. With businesses closing down and some people losing their jobs, fewer people will be on the road going to work, heading out to make deliveries or meet business associates, or going out for recreation or shopping. I'm not suggesting that a slowing economy will solve our nations traffic problems. On the contrary, traffic in many areas still will be severe enough to require drastic measures. But a slower economy means fewer vehicles on the road, and that at least eases the problem for a while.

However, an economic slowdown will have a much bigger effect on the shortage of office space, another factor that has encouraged telecommuting's growth. During boom times, companies tend to add staff but then must find places for all the new employees to sit. When many businesses grow at the same time, the finite amount of office space creates a real problem. Building more is costly, difficult to do in crowded urban areas, and takes a long time. So, for some companies faced with a choice between prohibitively expensive office expansion or asking employees to sit on each other's laps, telecommuting offers a welcome alternative.

In a time of layoffs and company closures, finding office space is less of a problem. Officers of companies that bite the dust may find themselves personally liable for workplace rent and may be eager to have someone else take over the lease. In that case, employers will lose one of their incentives for encouraging telecommuting.

Q&A: Sid Heaton, Extreme Telecommuter

Sid Heaton first coined the term *extreme telecommuter* in the summer of 1997. He and his fiancée (she's now his wife) wanted to travel before she started a master's degree program in the fall. They spent three months on the road in their Volkswagen camper, visiting 36 states and two Canadian provinces. Meantime, he telecommuted to his job as a technical writer for a software company in California.

The experiment was such a success that the Heatons decided to try it again, and in the spring of 1999, headed to Europe for an entire year of wandering. They lived in five countries and visited seven more, while Sid continued to hold down his job. In fact, he says, he has earned production bonuses and raises despite being on the road. How does he make it work? I decided to ask.

Q: Is it hard to stay disciplined enough to get your work done when you're someplace new that you want to explore?

A: Yes, it can be difficult. How are you supposed to concentrate on writing technical manuals when the Coliseum is just down the street, Prague is right outside your door, or there's a restaurant with an all-you-can-eat special on haggis down in the Grassmarket?

Having a job with clear-cut deadlines can really help. I can fudge some hours on a few days to get out and see the sights of a new place. Then, as a deadline approaches, I can buckle down and do 12-hour days to get everything done. It's sort of like college, only with 20 extra pounds and less hair.

Q: Any advice to others who want to try this?

A: Trust is definitely the most important thing. I take my deadlines seriously and never miss them. Once your manager has faith in your ability to do quality work on time, the amount of hours you spend working matters less.

At least, that's the ideal. Unfortunately, there are many pinhead micromanagers more interested in the accuracy of a timesheet than whether what you're doing is actually any good. If you find yourself with one of them, you may want to try your telecommuting experiment someplace else.

Finally, it really helps to be good at what you do. As a telecommuter, I feel it's important I do work that's at least 20 percent better than that of those on site. The powers that be are less likely to say boo if they know you're a quality contributor.

Telecommuting may grow: A differing view

On the other hand, telecommuting expert Jack Nilles believes telecommuting will grow even during an economic downturn. Nilles has more than 20 years of experience tracking telecommuting trends, enough to have seen several different economic cycles.

"My take on it is that economic pressures on companies are likely to spur the rate of adoption of telecommuting," he says. His reasoning? "It's a clear way to reduce operating costs without reducing the means of production; in other words, what's in employees' heads."

At the same time, he notes, "This may be moderated by such factors as real estate delays — you can't reduce office space if you're tied up in a long-term lease — and the usual managerial fear of change, possibly exacerbated by economic uncertainties."

Will Technology Change Telecommuting?

The continued growth and growing availability of new technologies will have a profound effect on telecommuting during the next several years. In general, staying in better touch while away from the office will become easier and easier. Specifically, the following sections discuss some technologies that I believe will make a real difference.

High-speed Internet access

The haves and have-nots of the Internet today are those with high-speed connections and those stuck using dial-up. High-speed connections are becoming more available and more affordable in more and more areas, so the number of telecommuters with access to this technology is growing. For networking functions, videoconferencing, Web conferencing, and working jointly on projects, having more bandwidth available makes a big difference.

Videoconferencing

One of the bigger benefits of high-speed access is that it enables more telecommuters and their colleagues at the office to use videoconferencing to communicate. Videoconferencing may not be the same as face-to-face communication, but it comes awfully close. It certainly can help telecommuters feel less isolated from their employers. It likely will help managers feel more in touch with employees as well.

Wireless

Handheld wireless devices can do more and more all the time, and the technology for reaching them (digital, PCS, satellite, and so on) is growing in clarity and reliability. As employees become accustomed to reliably connecting via wireless devices, where they are may make less of a difference, and the line between telecommuters and nontelecommuters may become blurred. Mobile phones and PDAs already have made huge changes in how telecommuters do their jobs. Expect more such changes in the coming years.

Changing attitudes

This isn't a new technology, but the effect of changing attitudes will be the same as that of a technological change. I believe many business executives don't know about, don't understand, or refuse to use at least one piece of technology that can help them work more effectively. But attitudes are changing as technology proves its own usefulness again and again. Software and Web designers are helping by making ever more user-friendly devices that even the most technophobic people can handle. As people become less afraid of technology, its power to transform the way telecommuters — and the rest of the workforce — do their jobs will dramatically grow.

Sue Boettcher: Life in a virtual company

When I began this book, Sue Boettcher had never met her boss. About a month ago, she met him for the first time. She'd been working for him for more than a year. "I had never actually met anyone from the company face-to-face when they hired me," she says.

Boettcher is director of community development for Web Crossing (www.webcrossing.com), a company that makes and markets chat and message board software for use on Internet sites. In other words, when you go to a Web site and click on a button to either post to a message board or enter a chat room, you may be activating Web Crossing software.

The company's mission is to help people communicate effectively in the virtual world of the Internet. So it's fitting that Web Crossing itself is a virtual company with no headquarters office. Officially based in California, the company has one sales office in San Francisco, and a technical support office near Sacramento — but together these offices house fewer than five of the more than 30 Web Crossing employees.

The rest work in home offices spread around the country, and use — what else? — Web Crossing software to communicate throughout the workday. "Most of the people, at least the higher management, have a background in online conferencing and Web community, so they're comfortable with the medium," Boettcher says. By the way, she works from her home in St. Louis. "We use the telephone surprisingly little," Boettcher says. "We talk to clients more than we do to each other."

The fact that everyone is a telecommuter helps them all stay in touch, she adds. At a nonvirtual office, passing information back and forth when they run into each other through the day is too easy for those working on-site. "Unless the people in the office make an extraordinary effort to remember that there are other people out there, the telecommuters can miss getting information, and wind up feeling left out," she says.

Part V
The Part of Tens

The 5th Wave   By Rich Tennant

Dorsey Family
SPITBALL Co.

"A large part of our success is based on our ability
to resolve conflicts before we get to work."

In this part . . .

*F*inding a telecommuting job can be tough. Actually working at home can be tougher. Use these short lists to help you find a telecommuting job and become a more effective and happier telecommuter.

Chapter 17

Ten Useful Items for Working at Home

In This Chapter

▶ Using equipment that will make your home office work better

▶ Finding technology to help you stay in touch

▶ Adding items that make working at home more enjoyable

*I*f you're like most people, all you really need to do your job is a computer, a telephone, a desk, a chair, and possibly Internet access. But just because you could get your job done with a minimum of home-office equipment doesn't mean that you should. There are pieces of equipment, pieces of furniture, and other items that can make working at home more efficient, more trouble-free, or more enjoyable. This chapter gives you a look at a few of them.

Second Computer

Trying to do your job with only one computer available is a bad idea. Computers do malfunction, and you can't just call downstairs to the technology department and ask them to bring you up a new one. If you wind up twiddling your thumbs because the only machine you can work on is out of commission, you'll be confirming every bad thought your manager ever had about telecommuters.

A desktop and laptop are an ideal combination. Using this arrangement, you can take your work anywhere, including back and forth to the office, yet you can maintain a more ergonomic workstation when you're at home. But any two computers will do, as long as each is current enough to run the software you're using. You can use home networking (or simply a cable) to keep your work up to date on both.

CDRW (Read/Write) Drive

If you deal with large amounts of information, databases, lengthy correspondence, large graphic files, or anything else that takes up a lot of computer memory, a drive that enables you to burn material onto CDs can come in handy. Instead of lugging a laptop, PDA, or external drive back and forth to the office, all you need to bring with you is a single CD. You can fit a whopping 650 megabytes of information on the typical writable CD. You don't have to spend time and effort uploading and downloading to a company Web site. And, if you need to share large amounts of work materials with others, handing them a CD is by far an easier way.

Scanner

Even if you don't work with graphics, being able to digitize images can come in handy. Having a scanner means you never really have to have a fax machine because you can always scan and then send the image of a page over your fax modem. You can scan an image of your signature so that documents created and then sent out through your fax modem still look like they were signed by hand.

Cordless Phone

A cordless phone is a wonderful asset in any combination home and office because if you pick up the phone and you're not at your desk, you can get there without having to put your caller on hold. A cordless phone with a headset is great, especially if you need to talk on the phone and type on the computer at the same time.

However, make sure a cordless phone is not the only one you have available for your office. In case of a power outage, a regular phone will still work, but a cordless one will not.

A speakerphone is another handy item. I find that the sound isn't good enough to use during an actual conversation (and I'm always secretly annoyed when someone I have to talk to uses a speakerphone for our conversation). But it's a wonderful way to keep your hands free while on hold, or while navigating through voice mail.

Wireless Phone

Many people with wireless phones wonder how they ever survived before they had one. They're especially handy for people who work outside an office because they give you the freedom to be out of the house, but still be accessible if your boss or co-workers need to reach you.

What kind of phone and service do you need to get? Here are some features to consider:

- ✔ **Free long distance:** This can be especially handy if your company is reluctant to pay for long-distance calls from a phone in your home.

- ✔ **Coverage in your area:** For many people, this is a nonissue, but if you live in a rural, low-coverage area like I do, you'll want your phone to work in as many places as possible.

- ✔ **Size:** A wireless phone that fits neatly in your pants pocket is a lot handier than one that won't.

- ✔ **Voice-activated dialing:** This is especially important if you plan to use your wireless phone while driving a car. A headset for your phone is also a good idea.

- ✔ **Ringer adjustment:** Some wireless phones come with a whole symphony of possible sounds that can let you know your phone is ringing. I like phones that vibrate instead when you have an in-coming call. You may find yourself in a setting (such as a conference) where having your phone ring is inappropriate.

- ✔ **Extra services:** The wireless revolution is coming, and your phone will be capable of bringing you e-mail, stock quotations, news of the day, text pages, and any number of other extras. Pick the ones that make the most sense for you.

PDA

You can use a PDA (personal digital assistant) to keep track of your calendar, contact information, documents, e-mails, and any number of other things. PDAs are also useful for carrying information or files between the office and home. Some have little keyboards you can plug in, while others work by handwriting recognition. If you're not absolutely dedicated to typing (I am, but I'm in the minority), the handwriting recognition serves another useful purpose by turning your notes into text files as you take them during a meeting.

If your main concern is staying in touch, instead of organizing information, tracking your calendar, or keeping notes, consider a text-based pager. These devices are only the size of a traditional pager but enable you to receive and send e-mail (they have tiny keyboards) and instant messages. You can also receive stock quotes, weather reports, headlines, traditional pages, and voice mail with these devices.

Wireless Modem

With a wireless modem and a laptop, you can work pretty much anywhere. That can be a big benefit if working in your home office makes you claustro-phobic. I know that when I'm feeling stale on a project, taking my laptop to a café for a while can be a big help.

A wireless modem is also a godsend if you travel — and will quickly pay for itself by saving you the high fees many hotels charge even for local or toll-free calls.

Rolling File Cabinet

A small file cabinet on rollers can be pushed out of sight when it isn't in use. In addition, storage bins, wicker baskets, trunks, and other such items can help you hide your work-related clutter, start the day with a clean desk, and use your living space for living. Being able to store your work stuff away neatly and attractively is especially important if you don't have a separate office to work in. Having to see your work clutter all the time makes you feel like you're never really off duty. Your spouse may not like it either.

High-Quality Sound System

Several telecommuters I know recommend having a stereo with a radio in your office. If you like music (and who doesn't?), you may find that listening to it while you work is particularly enjoyable. Investing in a stereo with a remote control is worthwhile, so you can turn the music off quickly when the phone rings.

An alternative may be to purchase high-quality speakers or headphones for your computer. After all, a computer's CD-ROM drive can also function as a CD player. That way you can pop in your favorite music while you work. Most radio stations are also available on the Internet, as are special Internet-only music sites that offer a wider variety of musical styles than the airwaves do. These last two options work best if you have a high-speed connection.

Coffeemaker with Automatic Timer

This suggestion comes from Miriam Carey, a telecommuter profiled in Chapter 1. Her comment: "The smell of coffee brewing in the morning will get you out of bed when nothing else will."

Chapter 18

Ten Services to Help You Work at Home

In This Chapter

▶ Making sure you never miss a message

▶ Dealing with software upgrades and additions

▶ Delegating home tasks to make your workday easier

*W*ant to work more dependably, with more freedom and less intrusion from household obligations? A wide array of services can help you do just that. The sections that follow are a list — by no means exhaustive — that will give you a taste of some services you may find helpful. (I find that each telecommuter has a different set.)

You may think some of these are luxuries, and perhaps they are. On the other hand, by telecommuting, you're probably saving significant sums on travel, dry cleaning, lunches out, coffee, snacks, and so on. If these savings mean that you can afford delegating some of your household chores so that they won't be a distraction during the day, it may be money well spent.

Telephone Services

Your phone service can help you work more efficiently in so many ways that I'm lumping them all into one group:

✔ **Voice mail:** Voice mail is absolutely essential in every place of business, regardless of whether it's at your workplace or in your home. An answering machine is fine when you're not at your desk, but people trying to reach you always need to have the opportunity to leave a message. These days, a caller who encounters a busy signal tends to think that your phone system is out of order. *Call waiting* is not an acceptable alternative: You have to either rudely interrupt a call you're on to take another, or make the caller listen to endless ringing, which is unprofessional.

✔ **Call forwarding:** Call forwarding is almost as useful as voice mail. Call forwarding from your company phone to your home office enables callers to reach you immediately, perhaps never even knowing that you're working at home. Call forwarding from your home office to your cell phone means you're always in touch, even if you're out taking a walk or shopping for groceries.

Call forwarding also can be a lifesaver if you're in an area where voice mail isn't available. You can replace voice mail by forwarding your calls either to your company office or to your cell phone, if you have one. Most cell phone accounts come with voice mail, so if you're on the phone or can't answer, the caller still can leave you a message. (This is how I coped with the lack of available voice mail when I lived in Massachusetts.)

✔ **Caller ID:** This line of defense, enabling you to screen your calls, may come in handier than you expect. Back at the office, the operator or receptionist probably fields a large number of sales calls, survey calls, *courtesy* calls, requests for donations, and wrong numbers every day. Working at home, I find these intrusions are proliferating and that they invariably occur when I'm trying to concentrate on my work.

Caller ID also can save you from that chatty friend or relative whom you love dearly but who is physically incapable of getting off the phone in under 40 minutes. You can always call back when you do have time to talk.

✔ **Conference calling or three-way calling:** I remember one week when my husband Bill found himself sandwiched between two software providers for the Web company where he was working. Both software providers contributed some of the technology for Bill's area. That part of the company's Web site wasn't working right, and each provider assured Bill that the other was responsible for the specific code that was causing the problem. The problem was the kind that could be solved only by talking to both providers at the same time.

This is only one of many situations in which you may need to talk to two or more parties at one time. And although someone at the office can probably set up a conference call for you, being able to do it yourself is easier and quicker. It's also handy when you realize during the course of talking to someone that someone else ought to be in on the conversation.

✔ **Call accounting:** This is a specialized service that can be incredibly useful if you need to bill your long-distance calls to more than one party. Let's say, for example, that you have only one phone line (although you should have more) and you want to be able to differentiate between your personal calls, which you pay for, and company business calls, which go on your expense report. Or you may need to bill different calls to different departments or company clients.

With call accounting, after you dial a number, you hear a tone and then enter a numerical code. When you receive your phone bill, charges are broken down according to code, so that you can tell at a glance who pays for what.

Backup Internet Service

If you're like many people, doing your job without using the Internet is next to impossible, and your colleagues at the office expect to be able to reach you as easily by e-mail as they can by phone. Unfortunately, your Internet service provider — whichever one it is — is less reliable than your phone service. So, just like your computer, your ISP requires a backup.

If you have a high-speed connection (lucky you!), I advise backing it up with a traditional dial-up service for cost and reliability reasons. If you have one dial-up service, back it up with another. Then, the only way you can be cut off from the Internet is if the power goes out or your phone service itself is disrupted. If you have a laptop and wireless modem, even that won't stop you.

Extra E-Mail Account

Having more than one e-mail account also is important, especially if your usual e-mail address goes through your company's system. For one thing, the system can malfunction, leaving people no way to e-mail you. An even bigger consideration is privacy. Sooner or later you'll want to apply for a job at another company, get the details of your co-worker's illicit affair, request drug treatment information for your black-sheep nephew, or any of a thousand other secrets that you'd like to ensure that your employer doesn't find out about.

Getting an extra e-mail account is quick, easy, and costs nothing on many services. There's no good reason not to do it.

Internet-Based Fax Service

Internet-based fax services like eFax and Jfax (`www.efax.com` or `www.jfax.com`) enable users to send and receive faxes over the Internet. You can sign up to receive faxes only for free, but you can pay for extras such as sending faxes, having some choice in your fax number's area code, and being able to transform faxes into text files. Of course, you probably don't need the fax-sending service. If your computer has a fax modem, you can send a fax directly.

For telecommuters who frequently are on the road, or work some days each week at home and other days in the office, one huge advantage of Internet faxing is that you can receive a fax regardless of where you are. Once again, there's no reason not to sign up, at least for the free service. (For more on Internet-based faxing, see Chapter 7.)

Travel Agent

Making travel arrangements over the Internet can be fun (it's a little like a treasure hunt), but also costly, especially if you spend a lot of time going to different places and you're unfamiliar with the airlines and other travel companies that service a particular area.

That's why many traveling telecommuters prefer using a travel agent to book their travel. Ideally, if you use a company travel agent (or if there's someone in your company who books travel), expenses such as your airfare can be billed directly to the company so that you don't have to lay out cash for them.

If that isn't an option, find a travel agent you trust and with whom you can develop a regular relationship. You'll be glad you did when an urgent matter arises and you have to book a trip in a hurry.

P.O. Box or Other Delivery Address

I've used a post office box for years for several reasons. The biggest is that payments to me always arrive by mail, and the area that I live in is quite rural. It may be paranoia, but the thought of my pay sitting out by the side of the road in a mailbox makes me a little uneasy. Another convenience is that I don't have to warn the post office when I'm going on a trip, as my mail is collected automatically. And because I work at home, a trip to the post office is a good excuse for getting out of the house. (When we lived in Massachusetts, I used to go to the post office on foot — a one-mile roundtrip that included a lot of uphill and downhill — thus getting my mail and my exercise at the same time.)

Although I'm personally devoted to Uncle Sam, good arguments can be made for using private services such as Mailboxes Etc. to collect your mail. You may have access to your mailbox outside of post office hours, and, unlike the post office, private services can receive UPS, Federal Express, and other non-mail deliveries.

Housecleaning

When I started this book, I expected to hear that watching TV, sleeping in, reading magazines, and snacking are big distractions during the day for people working at home. One I wasn't expecting: Housecleaning.

But it can be a problem. If you're the kind of person who can't relax in a messy house, chances are you also find it hard to concentrate on your work if dust bunnies frolic in the corners and muddy footprints march across the floor. Some telecommuters confide that they find themselves worrying about when they'll do the dishes rather than work and other deadlines they're supposed to be worrying about.

Getting help with housecleaning can take some of the burden off your shoulders. My husband Bill and I find it makes a big difference to have someone come in for just a few hours every other week to do the heavy-duty scrubbing and mopping, leaving us the day-to-day light cleaning. Another solution is to have the house cleaned on a one-time basis, whenever you feel it really needs it. The point is that housecleaning help can be an occasional thing, and it doesn't need to be an enormous expense. If it helps you relax and concentrate better while you're working at home, the investment may be worthwhile. (Incidentally, the same goes for yardwork, lawn mowing, and so forth, if applicable.)

Personal Chef

I'm the kind of person who cooks to relax, and I love making occasional trips downstairs from my office to, say, check on a pot roast. But not everyone likes cooking, and living off takeout and frozen dinners gets old quickly.

That's why the new profession of personal chef has grown to help busy people have home-cooked meals at home. You may think that only millionaires can afford to have their own chefs. And while this service is definitely more expensive than, say, a TV dinner or a trip to a local salad bar, it may cost less than you may think. According to the United States Personal Chef Association, prices can range from $7 a person to $18 a person, depending on how gourmet you want your meal to be.

In a typical arrangement, the chef comes to your house for an initial consultation and discusses your dietary requirements and food preferences. You agree on some menus. You then schedule a day for the chef to come to your home and spend the day cooking. At the end of the day, the chef leaves you with a clean kitchen, and an assortment of prepared meals, stored in containers in the freezer or refrigerator, along with reheating instructions and a meal for reheating that evening. You can find personal chefs in your area through the association's Web site www.hireachef.com (which also suggests some questions to ask), or at www.pchefnet.com.

At-Home Babysitting

As noted several times throughout this book, telecommuting is not a replacement for childcare. But it can be an opportunity to spend more time with your children. One way to do this is to opt for at-home babysitting rather than day care. Because you're in the house, you can take occasional breaks to check on your children and see how their day is going. You're also immediately available to deal with any emergencies.

Of course, this works only if the children and the baby sitter understand that you have a firm rule against interrupting your workday, except if an emergency arises. So there's a tradeoff between having your children nearby and having the discipline to keep them at bay when necessary.

Dog Care

As my husband once said to me, "Having a cat is like having a neighbor. Having a dog is like having a kid." At the time we were discussing whether to get a dog. I'm still hoping we eventually will. If you already have one, and he or she demands more attention from you than you can provide during an at-home workday, you may want to consider having someone else give you a hand.

That's what TManage's Scott Decker does. Decker has a large, active dog, and a couple of times per week, he sends his dog to "doggy day care," where he runs and plays with other dogs all day long. Decker can watch his dog whenever he wants, over the Internet, and likes to check on him every now and then. Doggie day care gets the dog's excess energy out of his system, and he's always peaceful the following day, Decker reports.

Canine day care is still a rarity and may not be available, or appropriate, for your best friend. If it isn't, you can also consider hiring someone local — perhaps even a kid — to take the dog for a walk or a romp in the park.

Chapter 19

Almost Ten Tips for Staying Motivated

*W*orking from home, or alone in a telework center, requires more motivation than working in an office. If you're in an office, surrounded by other team members, your work becomes almost a social activity. When you're at home alone, work is more like work. Staying motivated when you're alone in your home office can be a challenge, but it's also important if you're going to succeed as a telecommuter. The following sections provide some strategies that can help:

Set Specific Goals Each Day

Do not set unreachable goals for yourself. Plan to do a manageable amount of work, not as much work as you wish that you could do. Setting unrealistic goals is setting yourself up to fail and leads only to frustration. (I've learned this the hard way.) You need to be able to meet your daily goals most of the time. If you can't, it may be a clue that you're setting the bar too high.

When you meet your daily goal, and whenever you finish an important project or complete a difficult task, take a moment to acknowledge to yourself what you've accomplished. I know that sounds silly, and I'd never do it if anyone was watching, but when I've finished something that I'm proud of, I sometimes literally pat myself on the back as a reward. Self-acknowledgement is an important tool for staying enthusiastic about your work.

Reward Yourself

At the end of each workday, give yourself a small reward for all your hard work. Your reward may be a walk in the park, a cappuccino at your favorite café, or an hour spent watching that soap opera you taped. Whatever it is, it needs to be something that you enjoy, not something you think that you must do.

As a telecommuter, you become your own supervisor in some ways. Remember to use the carrot as well as the stick when supervising yourself.

Make Time for Exercise

Regular exercise helps keep you healthy, of course. But did you also know that it can completely change your mood? That is why I believe exercising several times during your workweek can help you stay motivated at your job. Your workout doesn't need to be a major workout, just enough to get your heart pumping and get you away from your desk for a while.

The form of exercise I frequently use is a brisk walk, usually for half an hour or so. I find myself working out work problems, figuring out how to word things I'm writing, and sorting through personal issues as well on these walks. Whatever you choose to do, make sure it's something you really enjoy; otherwise, you may end up getting the health benefits but not the mood-altering ones. If you work at home, something that gets you out of the house may be a good idea. But whatever you do, make sure it's something that you can stick with and have fun doing.

Fight Isolation

To battle the isolation, look for ways to stay in touch with your peers at your company and elsewhere. This is important for networking reasons, of course, but it also can help you stay motivated at your profession. Look for groups of people who do what you do so you can socialize with them and share problems and solutions, too.

Writers are extraordinarily good at this sort of thing. I belong to a small group that meets for dinner every month (we're all writers, but sometimes we talk about the movies), and I may be about to join another. I also belong to an online discussion group (some people I know belong to three or more) where I can post questions, complain about difficult editors, or generally lament the writer's lot. Or I can pick up the phone and call any of several good friends who are writers, too.

So, even though my work itself is extremely solitary, I never really feel isolated because of all this contact and support. You don't need to go that far. But finding some means of regular interaction with others who do what you do can be a big step toward keeping you interested and motivated.

Brag About What You Do

Okay, I don't really mean you should brag, but I do find that talking to people about my work helps remind me that I have an unusual and pretty special job. As a telecommuter, so do you. Most people you meet will be amazed, envious, curious, or all of the above, when they find out you get to work at home. Use these sentiments to give yourself a mental energy boost when working alone has gotten you down.

Spend Some Evenings Out

If you work at home all day, it's a good idea to make sure you get out of the house in the evening, at least some of the time. Plan to meet a friend for cocktails, take a continuing education class, or take yourself on a date to the movies. Staying in all day and all night can get you feeling stale pretty quickly.

This is especially important if you have a spouse or live-in partner who works in a traditional setting. Chances are, he or she comes home at the end of the day feeling tapped out on social activity and conversation, while you've been alone all day and need someone to interact with. One way to accommodate these incompatible moods is to not stay cooped up together. So getting out may not be good just for your own motivation, it may be good for your relationship as well.

Look for New Challenges . . .

Staying upbeat and enthusiastic about your job can be hard if your work is always the same, day in and day out. So if your boss isn't offering you new challenges or new tasks to learn, ask for them. Offer to take on a new project or learn a skill you may be able to use to advance your career.

If it's something you've never done before, great. If it's something you're not sure you can do, even better. Stepping outside your own comfort zone to stretch the boundaries of what you can do is a great way to keep feeling fresh and motivated about your job.

. . . Or Find Them Elsewhere

Sometimes, in spite of your best efforts, you simply can't find new challenges at work. Either what you do is so specialized that you can't take on other projects, or what your company does is so unchanging that it has no new projects to take on. Or else your boss doesn't want you stepping outside your traditional role. Whatever the reason, you find yourself plateaued in your job.

If you absolutely can't take on new projects at work, then consider taking them on in other parts of your life. Coach a children's athletic team, get involved with a local volunteer project, learn a new craft, or study a new language. The good feeling that you get from trying something new may keep you from feeling stale when you're working, even if the job itself offers little excitement.

Know When to Go

If you've tried your best and you still feel unmotivated by your work, consider the possibility that the job isn't right for you. Staying in a job that doesn't excite you is not a great idea for anyone. But for a telecommuter, it can pack a double whammy because staying motivated is hard to do if you hate your job, and working productively at home is hard to do if you aren't motivated. Sooner or later, your performance will suffer.

So do something about it now. Network within your industry, post your résumé on online job sites, or send out feelers for other opportunities inside and outside your company. The time to start looking is now.

Chapter 20

Ten Useful Web Sites for Telecommuters

In This Chapter

▶ Learning more about telecommuting

▶ Finding a telecommuting job

*O*ne of the better ways to keep pace with the evolution of telecommuting is by visiting the various Web sites that cover telecommuting. Many of the experts in this industry generously share what they know about telecommuting on continually updated Web sites that are an education in themselves. Other Web sites are designed to help you find a work-at-home job.

www.telecommute.org

This is the home site for ITAC, the International Telework Association & Council. It's full of statistics about telecommuting, including detailed information on surveys the group has conducted to track this trend. "Ask ITAC" is filled with questions from telecommuters and managers that are answered by an impressive array of telecommuting experts. The site also provides links to similar organizations in other countries.

www.gilgordon.com

Gil Gordon is a telecommuting consultant and author with many years of experience. His Web site serves as host to an impressive amount of information that can help you understand the many facets of telecommuting. Articles and information of all kinds and a large FAQ (frequently asked questions) area may tell you everything you ever wanted to know about telecommuting.

www.langhoff.com

This site belongs to telecommuting expert and author June Langhoff. Another information-packed site, this one is specifically directed at telecommuters rather than employers. This site also includes an FAQ area, as well as links to telecommuting organizations and other useful Web sites.

www.jala.com

JALA International is a consultancy started by Jack Nilles, who invented the terms *telecommuting* and *telework*. It's a great place to find an overview of the industry, check out Nilles's projections for the future, and discover what the telecommuting outlook is around the globe.

telecommuting.about.com

About.com's telecommuting area, moderated by Catherine Roseberry, includes telecommuting job listings, plenty of information about how to find a telecommuting job, and information on how to telecommute successfully. The site also features places to connect with other telecommuters.

www.youcanworkfromanywhere.com

This is an incredibly comprehensive and award-winning site. You can join YCWFA and receive a free newsletter, search job listings, learn about telecommuting, and even download a free e-book.

www.hoc.smalloffice.com

The Web site of *Home Office Computing* magazine offers a wide range of information geared for people who work at home, the self-employed as well as telecommuters. The site also is a good place to share experiences and ideas with other home-office workers. You may find this site especially useful if you're planning to buy technology for your home office, because it offers many product reviews.

www.2work-at-home.com

This is an at-home job-hunting Web site with a wide variety of listings, and a good supply of general information for telecommuters, too. You also can post your resume and search job listings by keyword.

www.hartmanresearch.com/telecommute

This helpful research firm has compiled a list of the most telecommuting-friendly companies among large U.S. corporations. The site posts a disclaimer that a listing does not mean a company is necessarily hiring. But contacting a company you want to work for, rather than being one of many to respond to a job listing, is a great way to look for work. (It worked for me in 1982 — a time of high unemployment!) The companies on the list are arranged alphabetically and include links so you can go directly to the various company sites.

www.telecommute-now.org

Go to this Web site to sign up for *Telecommuting Today,* a free online newsletter listing telecommuting jobs and opportunities.

Index

● *T* ●

FOR DUMMIES
BOOK REGISTRATION

We want to hear from you!

Visit **dummies.com** to register this book and tell us how you liked it!

✔ Get entered in our monthly prize giveaway.

✔ Give us feedback about this book — tell us what you like best, what you like least, or maybe what you'd like to ask the author and us to change!

✔ Let us know any other *For Dummies* topics that interest you.

Your feedback helps us determine what books to publish, tells us what coverage to add as we revise our books, and lets us know whether we're meeting your needs as a *For Dummies* reader. You're our most valuable resource, and what you have to say is important to us!

Not on the Web yet? It's easy to get started with *Dummies 101: The Internet For Windows 98* or *The Internet For Dummies* at local retailers everywhere.

Or let us know what you think by sending us a letter at the following address:

For Dummies Book Registration
Dummies Press
10475 Crosspoint Blvd.
Indianapolis, IN 46256

™
FOR DUMMIES

BESTSELLING BOOK SERIES